D0855226

Early Childhood Activities for a Greener Earth

Early Childhood ACTIVITIES FOR a GREENER EARTH

PATTY BORN SELLY

LIBRARY
RANKLIN PIERCE UNIVERSITY
RINDGE. NH 03461

 **Redleaf Press®**
www.redleafpress.org
800-423-8309

Published by Redleaf Press
10 Yorkton Court
St. Paul, MN 55117
www.redleafpress.org

© 2012 by Patty Born Selly

All rights reserved. Unless otherwise noted on a specific page, no portion of this publication may be reproduced or transmitted in any form or by any means, electronic or mechanical, including photocopying, recording, or capturing on any information storage and retrieval system, without permission in writing from the publisher, except by a reviewer, who may quote brief passages in a critical article or review to be printed in a magazine or newspaper, or electronically transmitted on radio, television, or the Internet.

First edition 2012
Cover design by Jim Handrigan
Cover photograph © Collage Photography/Veer
Interior design by Percolator
Typeset in Adobe Chaparral Pro
Printed in the United States of America
19 18 17 16 15 14 13 12   1 2 3 4 5 6 7 8

National Science Education Standards referenced throughout the book were originally published in *The National Science Education Standards* by the National Research Council (Washington, DC: National Academies Press, 1996). Reprinted with permission.

"Make a Recycling Monster" and "Absorb or Run Off?" activities were adapted from *Environmental Education Toolkit for Early Childhood and Family Education*, edited by Erin Bowley, Erin Bowley and Associates, and Patty Born Selly (Minneapolis, MN: Hennepin County Environmental Services, 2011). Adapted with permission.

The list of characteristic words on page 188 was adapted from "How to Identify Hazardous Products—Read the Label" by Hennepin County Environmental Services (Minneapolis, MN: Hennepin County Environmental Services, 2009). Adapted with permission.

"Water Cycle" graphic on page 105, © 2010 by the Minnesota Department of Natural Resources, is reprinted with permission.

Library of Congress Cataloging-in-Publication Data
Selly, Patty Born.
    Early childhood activities for a greener earth / Patty Born Selly.
       p. cm.
    Summary: "This book presents environmental lessons and activities in a manner that is appropriate for early childhood, and naturally fosters a sense of stewardship and love for our planet. It highlights a number of green topics including waste reduction, recycling, and water quality."— Provided by publisher.
    Includes bibliographical references and index.
    ISBN 978-1-60554-119-8 (pbk.)
    1. Environmental education—Activity programs. 2. Early childhood education—Activity programs.   I. Title.
    GE77.B67 2012
    372.35'7—dc23
                            2012007938

Printed on 100 percent postconsumer waste paper

MIX
Paper from
responsible sources
FSC® C011935

For Lucy and Julian

Contents

Acknowledgments

As with any book, this has been a collaborative effort, supported and enriched by the contributions of many. My deep gratitude to all the generous people who helped me along the way:

First, to the early childhood educators who love, respect, and honor children, and who know that a "greener Earth" is possible through play and shared love for nature—I couldn't agree more. Thank you for the work that you do. It is honorable work.

Thanks to Kyra Ostendorf and the team at Redleaf Press for all the hand-holding and patient support as I fumbled through this process. To Heidi Hogg, thanks for your diligent fact-checking and researching. And to Emily Green, the editor and literary alchemist who turned this book from a disorganized heap into something much, much better: your help was invaluable and I learned so much working with you.

To the amazing women who make up my writing group, this never would have happened without your encouragement and support over these years. Thank you for reading, and re-reading, sharing your photos, ideas, and stories, and offering so many helpful suggestions along the way. Thank you to my many friends and colleagues who shared inspiring pictures and activity ideas, especially Amy Blaubach of Curious Minds and my dear friend Tiffany Teske. Thanks to Anders Noren for help with the glossary.

Thanks to the Children and Nature Network for suggestions, support, and cheerleading. Thanks to the Hennepin County Library System for always being there. Of course, many thanks to Richard Louv, David Sobel, and so many others who work tirelessly to build bonds between children and nature. Your work is a gift to future generations.

To Mom and Dad, thanks for believing in me and always being willing to babysit your grandkids or look up random citation questions for me. Your support has meant the world to me.

To Dominic, my love, thank you for supporting me in innumerable ways—from keeping my water glass full to cheerfully managing the household and entertaining our children while I wrote. Thank you, thank you, thank you.

Most of all, boundless love and gratitude to my two greatest teachers: Lucy and Julian. I am constantly inspired and awed by you. It is my life's great honor to be your mom. Thank you for being so patient while I worked on this book—I'm finally finished! Let's go outside and play.

CHAPTER 1

Creating a **Greener Earth**

One doesn't have to search to find news about environmental problems affecting our world today. Most of us have become at least somewhat aware of issues such as air and water pollution, species extinctions, climate change, and health threats posed by chemicals in the environment. As early childhood professionals, many of you may have encountered parents and even young children raising questions and wanting to understand these and other environmental issues. Many parents now expressly seek child care programs that emphasize environmental awareness and experiences with children. More and more even look for child care that embraces environmentally friendly operating procedures, such as recycling and use of nontoxic cleaning products.

Some of you reading this book may be relatively new to these environmental issues and feel perplexed as you make sense of them, sorting out facts from rumors and politics. Others may already be deeply aware of the issues. You may have made changes in your lifestyle and possibly have even begun teaching environmental topics to the children in your care. Many of you are likely somewhere in between. Regardless of where you are on this spectrum, you're probably somewhat aware that we all share in the responsibility of taking care of our planet, and you understand that learning more about our impact on the environment is an important step. But it can be overwhelming to sort through the tidal wave of environmental information and recommendations and to decide how specifically to handle these matters at your program and with the children in your care.

I hope this book can serve as a resource for you. It is intended to provide a foundation for educating young children on the environment through experience and play. Each chapter focuses on a common and important environmental topic in our world today. You'll find a basic introduction to each topic followed by a set of activities for children. Although the chapter introductions cover the "problem" dimension of the environmental topic, the activities for children explicitly do not. The activities are designed *to help children simply explore the environment and develop a sense of wonder, curiosity, and joy in nature*. Though I agree that ultimately we all need to learn about Earth's problems to be prepared to address them—as I explain more fully in the section that follows—early childhood is not a good time for this emphasis. It is my deeply held philosophy—and research agrees—that the pure exploration and experience of nature in early childhood will lay the foundation for later development of stewardship: the feeling of ownership, connectedness, and desire to care for our planet. The activities in this book reflect this philosophy. The introductory information in each chapter is provided as a framework for the topic. You can use it to review or develop your core understanding of the topic and to answer your own basic questions or those of children that may arise as you do the activities.

What Is Environmental Education?

You may have heard the term *environmental education* used to describe nature-based programs led by naturalists or scientists, such as those at parks, museums, nature centers, zoos, and aquariums. Sometimes the term is used for any classroom content about nature, animals, and plants. Other times it may describe nature exploration or lessons conducted in the outdoors. Confused? Don't be. All of these examples are valid, in that they describe education focused on the natural environment.

If you think about it, education focused on the natural environment has likely been happening in an informal way throughout human history. However, the growing recognition of serious environmental problems in the 1960s sparked the formal establishment of the field of environmental education. As leaders, scientists, and everyday citizens began attending to the fact that caring for our environment is vital for our future, they also began explicitly acknowledging that education about our environment is vital for informing decisions about the care of the environment. In an important milestone, world leaders convened by the United Nations Educational, Scientific, and

Cultural Organization (UNESCO) in 1975 published *The Belgrade Charter: A Global Framework for Environmental Education*, establishing the goal "to develop a world population that is aware of, and concerned about, the environment and its associated problems, and which has the knowledge, skills, attitudes, motivations and commitment to work individually and collectively toward solutions to current problems and the prevention of new ones" (1975, 3). This declaration specified that the audience for environmental education should include all people and all levels, from preschool to adult.

This formative early declaration, and others like it that followed, clearly emphasize teaching about the problems facing our environment and taking actions to address them. And though the importance of environmental education for all ages is stressed, this declaration is truly tailored toward adults and youth. Many early childhood educators—myself among them—recognize that a different and special approach is essential when it comes to young children. The approach for early childhood environmental education acknowledges that a commitment to care for the Earth cannot be taught to or coaxed out of people; rather, it springs forth naturally from an attitude of love and care for the Earth. Moreover, this approach recognizes that it is our human nature to care for what we know, enjoy, and value. Therefore, the goal of early childhood environmental education is *not* to study explicitly about environmental problems; rather, it is to create opportunities for the experience of wonder, comfort, and love in the natural world.

This philosophy of early childhood environmental education has been spelled out in great detail in *Early Childhood Environmental Education Programs: Guidelines for Excellence*. That document states, among other things, that the goal of early childhood environmental education is to "chart an appropriate and positive process whereby educators can start young children on their journey toward becoming environmentally responsive youth and adults" (NAAEE 2010, 3). This philosophy also builds upon an understanding of the unique development and learning stages of young children. Though the topic and scope of early childhood development is quite broad and is not the core of this book, I think it is helpful to review key points about development because they are central to my philosophy of early childhood environmental education.

About Early Learners

Much of today's understanding of early childhood development is based on the work of a few well-known psychologists and scientists, including Jean Piaget, John Dewey, Lev Vygotsky, and Maria Montessori. Although the specifics of their theories and contributions differ, their ideas coincide in their emphasis on the importance of experience, or interaction with the real world around them, in young children's development of knowledge. In the early years, a child's experience provides the basis and the frame of reference for all knowledge. The approaches of these thinkers recognize that children go through distinct cognitive and emotional stages of development and that those stages shape how children understand and assimilate new information. For example, from infancy until about age two, children's understanding of the world is limited to what they take in through their senses and their immediate surroundings. As they grow through this stage, they gradually develop awareness of the world that exists beyond their immediate surroundings. Between approximately ages three and six, children still hold a strongly self-centered point of view on the world but are developing the ability to comprehend other points of view and to engage in abstract thought. They are putting together ideas and building on their own experiences. Children develop at different rates; however, these early years are a time when they tend to be fully immersed in their immediate surroundings and happenings. Therefore, it's often difficult for young children to think in abstract terms or to conceptualize things that do not connect to their experiences (Copple and Bredekamp 2009).

This general approach to children's development formed the basis of constructivism or constructivist learning, one of the most widely used educational theories in modern times. *Constructivism* essentially means that all children construct knowledge through experience and interaction with their environment. Children gather their own real data from the world around them, and that real-world data forms the basis for their developing knowledge. Their knowledge is constructed from their experience, interactions with other people, and the environment. They constantly try to make sense of their experiences and observations, sometimes in ways that make little sense to adults. For example, a young child may believe that the cloud she sees in the afternoon sky follows her wherever she goes. This idea may seem strange or even silly to an adult, but to a four-year-old it may make perfect sense. Wherever she goes, the cloud is there. Her experience leads her to form a conclusion.

An adult who understands constructivist learning will recognize that a scientific explanation is not necessarily what the child needs or wants. For an adult to give a correct or scientific explanation *without connecting to the child's real life experience* would be abstract and virtually meaningless. The explanation might also alienate the child, if the adult is unable to relate to or share the child's observation and worldview. Instead, it would be more meaningful for the adult to ask the child questions to further clarify her observations, add information to her experience, and help her refine her conclusion. For example, the adult could ask, "How do you know the cloud is following you?" or "Where does it go when you are inside?" Such thought-provoking questions will help the child make more observations, reflect more fully on what she knows, and identify more details about her experience. These questions also empower the child, letting her know that her ideas are important and that she can trust herself as a learner. When an adult simply corrects a child's "faulty" or naïve thinking by explaining or offering the "right answer," it sends a subtle message to the child that he or she cannot trust his or her experience or observations. An adult may certainly provide accurate information—and should certainly not introduce false information—about a phenomenon but should also be careful to validate the child's observations and experiences. As educators, our role is to support children's development, to listen to them, to honor them, and to help them find their meaning in the world.

BABIES NEED NATURE TOO

Babies are typically included in the "early childhood" category, but for this book I focus on children ages three through eight. In focusing on that age range, I do not mean to suggest that babies, toddlers, and two-year-olds don't belong outdoors. They most certainly do! The best way to introduce children to nature and the environment is simple: take them outside early (as babies) and often. Babies love being outdoors: there is so much stimulation, and the rhythmic waving of tree branches in the breeze, as well as the many sounds and textures, can soothe like nothing else. Don't be afraid to take babies outside. Dress them properly for the weather, and you'll find they enjoy being outdoors just as much as older children. Allow them to lie in the shade, crawl through the grass, and explore the world.

Toddlers and two-year-olds also enjoy time outside. Insatiably curious, they can roam and explore nature's infinite variety in textures, sounds, colors, and patterns. Some never stop exploring, while others will be instantly mesmerized by one phenomenon, such as the leaves rustling in the breeze. You can support their safe explorations by providing plenty of time outdoors and dressing them properly for comfort. Natural phenomena, such as breezes, clouds, flowers, and even blades of grass, are exciting and new. Move everyday activities outdoors so you can enjoy a snack or story in the afternoon shade. Take the time to introduce children to this rich source of inspiration by simply making it a part of their everyday experience.

If we think about children from this child development perspective, it is clear that an overabundance of scientifically accurate information about the environment, particularly about its problems, can be scary or lead to feelings of helplessness in young children. For example, when people think about educational lessons on the environment for children, many might jump to such common ideas as the "rainforest corner," or a unit on endangered polar bears and melting glaciers. These activities might be perfectly appropriate in some contexts and with some children; however, for many younger children, they may be overly abstract and removed from their immediate life experience. Faced with problems bigger than they can truly comprehend, children often feel guilty and confused. They may disconnect emotionally from the issues rather than stay engaged.

In addition, young children can become overwhelmed by the emphasis on taking action that is part of many issue-focused environmental education curricula. The reality is that most of the consumer decisions and behaviors that are legitimately important for environmental stewardship—such as changing household purchasing habits, reducing the use of personal vehicles, or reducing a family's electricity usage—are ones over which young children have no control. Burdening them with the responsibility to educate their parents or remind them to make different choices is ineffective and unfair. It can lead to feelings of guilt in the young child. A child sees her parents engaging in so-called negative environmental behavior and knows this isn't what they are supposed to do, yet can't change it. Then she doesn't understand why she feels guilty and sad, and perhaps even angry with her parents. On the flip side, when children see adults engaged in behaviors that are positive and helpful for the environment—such as composting, reducing fossil fuel consumption, and recycling—it normalizes these behaviors and sends the message that actions do count.

Instead of expecting children to change others, we can ask children—and inspire them—to develop a love for the Earth. We, as educators who provide children with rich, authentic opportunities to know the natural world and the environment, can accomplish this through intentional effort, dedication, and commitment. Children's interest in and commitment to environmental issues will ultimately be more solid when they have an abundance of authentic, joyful experiences in the environment. The future of our planet does indeed rest in the hands of our children, but those hands can't be asked to save the Earth before they're given a chance to get dirty: to love the Earth and to explore the environment through play and experience as only children know how. As educator David Sobel so eloquently put it, "What's important is that children have an opportunity to bond with the natural world, to learn to love it, before being asked to heal its wounds" (1996, 9).

By offering the children in your program opportunities to simply experience nature—in addition to other benefits—you will be cultivating their love for nature and their comfort in it. In the same way that caring deeply about our homes and our families leads us to want to take care of them, caring deeply about the Earth leads us to want to take good care of it. As we all know, children are our future leaders, and laying a solid foundation for their future commitment to Earth stewardship is vital. Even if you don't have acres of wilderness at your site (and few programs do) it's important to spend time outside. If you can get away from the post-and-platform play structures, by all means do so. Play and exploration are the first and foremost ways in which children form meaningful relationships and construct an understanding of the world around them. And play in nature is by far the best way for them to develop a sense of love for nature and the environment. No amount of environmental education will make a difference for the future of our planet if children do not first love it deeply.

About This Book

In addition to supporting hands-on nature exploration, this book is designed to be a resource for educators and administrators interested in lessening the environmental impact of their facilities and operations. If you are an administrator, you may have already adopted an overall environmentally friendly vision for your program, and if you supervise staff, you may be trying to engage them in changing day-to-day behaviors. Chapter 9 is specifically written to help you in that journey. In that chapter, I offer suggestions for engaging members of your staff and your community in environmentally friendly efforts. You'll find ideas for program-wide activities and family events, suggestions for effective outreach and communication with parents, and resources to guide your overall planning.

I developed this book to accompany the *Go Green Rating Scale for Early Childhood Settings* by Phil Boise (2010a). The rating scale is a valuable tool to help programs evaluate the environmental impact of their facilities and operations. Users rate specific components of their programs, such as office supply purchasing practices and water usage habits, according to well-researched environmental impact criteria. In particular, the individual rating scales address *safety* (do programs, actions, or materials minimize human exposure to toxins?), *sustainability* (do they minimize potential harm to and/or limitations on well-being and natural resource availability for future generations), and *functionality* (do they work and serve their intended purpose?). In addition to evaluating your practices, the *Go Green Rating Scale* lists steps—some small, others large—that you may take to improve your scores. Similar to this book, the *Go Green Rating Scale* is organized according to specific environmental topics. That structure allows you to choose which aspects of your program you wish to evaluate. Alternately, you may choose to work through it methodically, evaluating all areas in succession.

There are many ways to go green, and only you can be the judge of what is best for your program, staff, facility, or community. Whether you're doing a complete greening of all operations, or just incorporating a few new measures, it makes sense to coordinate your efforts in the administrative realm with your efforts with children. The children in your care may very well notice your administrative greening efforts, make the connection with your sincere care and concern for the Earth, and become even more excited than they would otherwise be to undertake learning and exploration on the same environmental topics. Furthermore, the parents involved with your program may appreciate your consistent approach to dealing with environmental topics. They may see that you're making changes to your program or operations to be more environmentally sustainable and understand that including environmental activities for children makes sense. Finally, your coworkers and staff may appreciate the connection between system-wide improvements and new activities for children. That's where this book comes in.

About the Activities

As I've said, the activities are the heart of this book. They offer ways for children to explore nature, find their own meaning from their experience, and make connections to their own lives. They are designed to promote enjoyment with the natural world simply for its own sake. Often, children engaged in nature exploration may seem to be playing, and—as you know—valuable learning does happen through play. Play can be filled with rich, rewarding, and meaningful experiences, especially if you support children in asking questions, making observations, and pursuing their curiosity. The activities in this book are designed to be playful and enjoyable for children and, at the same time, offer rich learning and stimulation. These learning opportunities develop children's scientific- and critical-thinking skills, which are vital building blocks for academic success. Although the approach and philosophy I outline in this book are not outcome-based or heavily academic in focus, the reality is that most educational settings—even in early childhood—are expected to address academic growth. With that in mind, careful review was made of the National Science Education Standards in developing these activities (National Research Council 1996). Although these standards target kindergarten through fourth grade, they are relevant and helpful guidelines for learners even at the preschool levels. I've tried to encompass as many standards as possible and have noted correlations to specific standards in the individual activities. Seeing the correlation between the activities and the National Science Education Standards can help you see that even these playful, fun activities promote very real learning and thinking skills that will benefit children throughout their school years. You'll also find suggestions for making connections across disciplines, thereby further enriching educational opportunities. For example, an activity on recycling might also have applications with art, literacy, or math.

HOW THE ACTIVITIES ARE STRUCTURED

Each activity follows the same basic format. Please note that while I urge you to get outside with children as much and as often as possible, some of the activities are specifically designed and well-suited for the outdoors. These are designated with the sunshine symbol.

In the interest of brevity, and to avoid the awkward "he/she" constructions, I've elected to use the pronouns "he" and "she" interchangeably throughout this book to refer to children.

Some Tips for Using This Book

First, remember to be positive. When doing an activity that promotes reuse, for example, be positive and upbeat. Mention how happy you are to have found a use for materials instead of throwing them away. Resist the temptation to preach or lecture. The value of a positive, joyful experience cannot be understated when it comes to environmental education!

Read through all the activities in a section. Choose activities that work well in conjunction with other topics of interest to your class and projects you may currently be doing. Look for activities you can connect to the interests of the children. For example, if you've been studying bugs and butterflies, it might be a great idea to plant a butterfly garden, or it could be a perfect jumping-off point to discover the insects that pollinate fruits and vegetables (see the Playing with Pollen activity on page 162).

Activity Title: The titles are short descriptions of the activity. A complete list of activities can be found in the table of contents.

Background: This information tells you about the content and direction of the activity and relates it to the particular environmental topic.

Activity Goals: This is a short list of goals for the activity. They are not specific assessment measures (for example, "student can describe the water cycle") but instead are statements containing words like *explore*, *discover*, and *experiment*. While these goals may seem less academic than you are accustomed to, bear in mind that a very important part of early childhood education is developing certain core habits of mind, such as exploring, discovering, questioning, and trying new things. The activity goals are designed to support the development of these habits.

National Science Education Standards: The specific National Science Education Standards that are potentially addressed by each activity are named here. If your goal is to address standards with these activities, be sure to read through the standard as well as the entire activity and think about how you will bring in the standard that is listed. A summary of the standards is provided in appendix A at the end of this book. You may need to make an intentional effort to ensure that the children make the required connection for each standard. For example, to address the standard "properties of earth materials" the children need to observe and describe earth materials, such as mud, rocks, or water.

Outdoor Activity: Many activities include this symbol so you can quickly see that the activity is best conducted outside. Most indoor activities can be adapted for the outdoors with minimal effort.

Age Range: The activities in this book are designed for children ages three through eight. Some activities target a specific age range within that spectrum. Some also include Extra Challenge connections, which can help you expand the activity for older children. The extension can be found at the end of an activity, under Connections.

Safety Note: This symbol is used at various points in the activities to highlight safety considerations.

Tips: This includes general information to help make the activity run more smoothly. It may include things to watch out for, suggestions for how to obtain materials, or steps to prepare ahead of time. It also may include tips for adapting the activity for children with special needs.

Connections: These are ideas for connecting the activity to other disciplines: Science, Literacy, Creative Art, and Extra Challenge (shown in order from left to right below).

Not all activities have all connections. This does not mean the activity doesn't connect to other disciplines. Use your creativity and experience to draw connections between subjects.

Materials and Supplies: This is a list of all necessary materials and supplies. Obvious things (tables, chairs, smocks, and so on), however, are left out, as it is assumed that you will automatically include these items when appropriate.

Procedure: This is a detailed, step-by-step list of the process for introducing and proceeding through each activity. This section also may contain suggested questions to ask to support learning.

Color Connections

Dark colors absorb heat and light, whereas light colors reflect heat and light. In this activity, children will use thermometers to measure temperature differences for different colors. Understanding the effect that color can have on temperature can help children later understand why some parts of the Earth are warmer than others. This activity will also help children understand that dressing in darker colors will keep them warmer and lighter colors will keep them cooler.

Activity Goals
- To use thermometers and compare how dark and light colors effect the temperature of water
- To experience the effect of an object's color on its temperature

National Science Education Standards
Physical science: light, heat, electricity, and magnetism

Materials and Supplies
- Three clear containers filled two-thirds full with water
- Black paper
- White paper
- A thermometer
- Tape
- Chart paper and a marker

Procedure
1. With the children, use the thermometer to measure the temperature of each container of water and record the temperature on the chart paper.
2. Tape white paper to the side of one container, tape black paper to the side of another container, and leave the third container as is.
3. Place each container in a sunny spot, arranging the wrapped containers so that the sun shines directly on the uncovered side and easily passes through to the water.
4. After thirty to sixty minutes, return to the containers and measure the temperature in each container.
5. Record and compare the results.

TIPS
 *Empty glasses will work well, but use caution with glass.*
- Provide pictures of different types of homes and buildings. For example, homes on some islands in Greece (where it is hot and very sunny) are all white to better reflect the sun's heat. Many homes in North America have black or dark gray shingles on the rooftops. Explore how the color of one's roof or home can affect its temperature.
- Have children fill the containers with water ahead of time to help prepare for this activity.

CONNECTIONS
 Ask the children what they noticed about the temperature differences and why they think the temperatures were different for each container. Have them explain what this activity can teach them about dressing for warm or cool weather.

Weather, Climate, and Energy 175

Be prepared. Read through the entire description of the activity before you begin, to ensure that you are prepared. I cannot emphasize this point enough. Pay close attention to the materials list, procedure, and tips before beginning. This will ensure that you have what you need and have a sense of how the activity is going to work before you proceed.

Use your best judgment about when to step in and provide guidance. Almost every step of every activity can be done by children. However, adult guidance is required for some steps, such as using hot glue guns. Read through the activity thoroughly, and take the precautions necessary to protect the children with whom you work. Something that seems risky to one teacher or student might not be so for another. For example, some children are extremely careful with scissors whereas others are not and need to be supervised. Use your best judgment for your individual situation.

Take necessary precautions. For activities that require painting, gluing, or other messy work, take necessary precautions to protect children's safety, clothing, and workspace. Basic items such as smocks, floor and table coverings, and wet paper towels are not listed in the materials/supplies section of each activity. Obviously different children and educators have different tolerance levels for mess and kinesthetic sensory input (messy hands!). I am assuming that you will address your own needs and those of the children in your care as you typically would.

Many of the activities involve small objects. Supervise children closely when small objects are involved to prevent accidental ingestion or "hiding" beads, buttons, and so on in ears and noses!

Certain activities also involve food items, some of which may provoke reactions in children with allergies. Please be aware of all allergies or other health concerns of children in your care, and adapt activities or otherwise take precautions to ensure children's safety when dealing with any activity that includes potentially allergenic foods or substances.

Practice sensitivity. Respect children's cultural heritage, especially with regard to food and animals.

While most cultures share the same overall values behind environmental education, cultures differ when it comes to some views about food and animals. For example, some ethnic groups fear certain animals whereas others revere them. Others may hold certain foods in very high regard, and using those foods as art materials may be seen as disrespectful and make the children uncomfortable. Learn as much as you can about the children and families in your program and their religious and cultural beliefs around food, animals, and nature before you begin, and then be sensitive to any differences. Of course, avoid singling out any child or family by calling undue attention to those differences. If an activity includes materials, actions, or images that might make a child or family uncomfortable, use alternate materials with everyone or choose a different activity. Be as inclusive as possible.

Reuse materials whenever possible. Many activities include suggestions for reusing specific items that work particularly well for the purposes of the activity (for example, empty milk cartons work great for small plant pots). But don't stop there. Look around your room. What can be reused? As an educator, you're probably already well-versed at stretching those budget dollars by reusing everyday materials. Chapter 9 provides specific ideas for identifying other useful disposable items and ways to reuse them.

Allow plenty of time. Introducing a topic, doing a quick activity, and moving on to a completely different activity the next day can squelch burgeoning interest in young scientists and stewards. Allow time for the children to really immerse themselves in their experience of creating art, exploring water and weather, and enjoying quiet (or loud!) time making discoveries. Repeat an activity day after day, if it's what the group wants to do. You may make new discoveries each time! Learning happens when information is synthesized through reflection. Reflection happens only when there is time allowed for it.

Prioritize experience over information. There is so much information to share, particularly in environmental education, and educators often have a strong desire to impart as much information as possible. However, when it comes to young children and the environment, often the less technical information you offer the better. If you're providing opportunities for rich, authentic experiences of the natural world and guiding children's exploration of the specific environmental topics in this book, you're doing enough! As I discussed earlier, children find their own meaning and construct their own knowledge through their experiences. You serve as their guide in doing this. You don't need to provide all the details behind environmental topics. You don't need to know all the answers. Ask questions together with the children!

Make connections. Build on previous learning from other activities as much as you can. There are some activities that complement each other particularly well, and I've noted those in the Tips. Consider how you can connect these activities to other disciplines or use your work in other areas to springboard into these activities. For example, if you've just read a book on life in a pond, introduce one of the many activities from chapter 5 to build on the group's interest in water.

Don't be afraid to veer off track. Some of the most important discoveries are unplanned and unscripted. Be open to changing course during an activity if that's what the children need to do. The activities will be much more meaningful if you are responsive to the interests and needs of the children. If you have an indoor activity planned but the gorgeous spring day calls you outside, find an outdoor activity in this book or follow the children's lead. Be spontaneous and go with the flow. Above all, be flexible.

Think first about your local environment. Often, when people think about nature experiences in school settings, they think first of field trips or outings to faraway established nature areas. These outings can present cost and logistical challenges. Remember that sometimes the learning experiences with the most impact are the ones that happen close to home (and school). Children typically connect best with their immediate environment. Learning about water? Instead of taking a field trip to a faraway public aquarium or other place, see what you can discover in the nearby green space. Children are familiar and comfortable with their immediate surroundings, and this familiarity and comfort can lead to deeper learning.

Remind *yourself* to be curious, be vocal, and be positive. See a new flower that you've never noticed before? Curious about the shape of the clouds? Wondering why all the ants are marching in a straight line? Talk about it! Let yourself be delighted! The positive effects of nature are not limited to children—nature is good for adults too! And children will be inspired when they see you expressing curiosity and excitement about the natural world. The more you share the positive feelings and questions you have about the natural world, the better! Your curiosity will inspire children to notice things and ask questions too. Conversely, if you hate bugs or think it's too cold outside, keep it to yourself. Try to let the children have their own experiences. Remember how important it is to be outside, despite the small challenges or annoyances you may feel. If you gripe about bugs or complain about the weather, you can be sure the children will do the same.

Set open-ended goals. Set teaching goals for *yourself* to support learning and playful outdoor exploration, as opposed to setting goals for the children based on tangible, knowledge-based, content-driven results. This may be challenging if you work in a very academic setting or are used to justifying your activities to parents hungry to know "What did my daughter learn today?" The most effective teaching goals at the early childhood level are not focused on the end result and do not require children to repeat content or memorize facts. For example, an effective early childhood teaching objective might be "To plan outdoor activities at least three times this week" or "To find three new ways to explore water with children" as opposed to "Teach children three properties of water." This third teaching objective is not wrong in itself, it is just more content-focused and places more value on the end result than on the experience of learning and discovery. This objective would be more appropriate for children at the upper end of the early childhood years than for a very young child.

Broadcast your success. Make sure your colleagues, administrators, and the parents of the children involved know what you are doing and why. Share pictures or other documentation of the children making discoveries and exploring the environment. Point out the learning and groundwork for stewardship that you're fostering through this work. Interview children about what they are feeling, what they are learning, and what they like best about certain activities. Share this information through newsletters, bulletin boards, or presentations at conferences or workshops. Sharing your success is the best way to gain and maintain a supportive community of parents and coworkers.

Get outside as much and as often as you can. Whenever possible, take these activities outside. Some of the activities lend themselves especially well to outdoor play and fun. Even for the activities that don't require being outside, consider taking the necessary materials and supplies out onto the sidewalk or to a nearby park or grassy area. There is no substitute for fresh air, sunshine, and exposure to the elements when learning about the natural world. Dress for the weather, and be sure to apply a nontoxic sunscreen and mosquito repellent if needed, to ensure that all children can enjoy the experience.

Getting Outside

Most educators, even those already strongly committed to the environment, may find themselves daunted at times by the challenge of expanding the curriculum or changing daily routines to incorporate more time outdoors. You already have very busy days and extremely full plates. Over the years, I've had many teachers and administrators share with me some of the challenges and barriers they face when it comes to getting children outside. Following is a list of some of the most common challenges and some suggestions for overcoming them.

"I can't add another thing to my day!" This very real concern might be alleviated when you consider simply moving the activities you already do inside to a comfortable place outdoors. If you have a science station in your classroom already, why not move it outside? The simple act of reading a story can be made more special when done on a blanket under the shade of a tree. Or, take the easel and paints outside and enjoy some outdoor art-making! Make a commitment to getting your class outside at least once per day, and start with just 15 minutes if that feels more within your reach. If you already go outdoors once a day, challenge yourself to go outside one more time. Bring one of your regular daily activities outside, or designate a special nature time outdoors, away from the playground. For more about taking the indoors outside, read *Cultivating Outdoor Classrooms: Designing and Implementing Child-Centered Learning Environments* by Eric Nelson.

"The children don't have appropriate outerwear." Consider starting a scholarship fund to buy extra gear for children. Ask families to donate usable rain or winter gear their children have outgrown. Hit the clearance racks after the winter season to find great deals on gear. Start a large "lending closet" of winter and rain gear so that there will always be enough clothing to ensure all children are comfortable outside. (While you're at it, you may decide to bring in a few extra things for staff too!) Chapter 9 has some creative tips for building a supply of outerwear for children that won't cost you a fortune.

"This is a logistical nightmare!" Yes, it takes a while and often feels like herding cats when it comes to getting a bunch of three-year-olds ready to go out and play in the snow. Just remember to plan well. Make getting dressed a part of the process. Sing songs, have races, or play games as everyone puts on their outerwear. It takes time, but it's worth it. As you develop the habit of regular outdoor time, you'll find that the labor-intensive process of helping everyone with their coats and boots becomes less of a challenge. And yes, when they've had time playing in the mud, they will track it in—which will be messy. First, remind

"The children are just too wild when we go outside!" This is a common fear related to taking children outdoors. The first few times you move an activity outside or have "recess" twice in one day, the children will naturally be very excited and active. This is normal! As they get used to being outside more often, and having more freedom when they do, you'll find that they can handle the freedom quite well. In fact, many educators find that after repeated, consistent time outside, children are better able to manage their energy indoors, when they need to be settled and concentrate.

"What if someone picks up a rock or a stick?" You can be sure that as long as there are rocks and sticks, there will always be children who want to play with them. (In fact, the stick itself is so popular among children it was inducted into the 2008 National Toy Hall of Fame.) Set clear parameters with the children. If you aren't comfortable with them holding sticks or rocks, make that a rule for outdoor time. Try also to

yourself that the benefits of being outdoors far outweigh the inconveniences of cleaning the muddy floor. Work with your custodial staff to remind them of the important "work" you are doing by playing outdoors in all kinds of weather. Engage the children in cleaning up the floor after messy outdoor play. Be willing to help clean up. Ask families to provide a change of clothes, and remind them that getting dirty is good for children's development!

"I am concerned someone will get hurt, stung, or sunburned." Safety considerations are as important outdoors as they are inside. To ensure the safety of the children in your care, take the same precautions outside as you take indoors: pay attention to your surroundings and minimize risk where needed. Be aware of any allergies that children may have, such as to bee stings, and have first aid equipment on hand. Remember, practice makes perfect: the more you go outside, the more familiar and comfortable you (and the children) will be with the surroundings and their inherent risks. Apply sunscreen or bug repellent if your policies allow it, or remind parents to apply it to their children before drop-off. Educate yourself about insects, such as ticks, as well as plants and animals considered to be hazardous in your area. Your local Department of Natural Resources (DNR) is a good place to find this information.

be open-minded. Allow children to satisfy their natural curiosity about these objects, and you'll find most will play quite harmlessly with them. Some teachers find that establishing a few rules, such as "You may hold a stick that is no longer than your arm," or "You may not touch another person with a stick," works well. Try asking the children how your group can play safely with sticks or rocks and engaging them in developing the class rules.

"I don't know what to do outside!" That's where this book comes in. You'll find a lot of ideas, suggestions, and specific activities to offer to the children when you go outdoors. It might also be helpful to remember that nature often provides its own inspiration. Teachable moments abound in the outdoors. Let the exploration and discovery be open-ended and unstructured when possible. Let the children's curiosity be your guide.

"We don't have a nature area, just a play structure." A school forest, garden, or natural area can be richly rewarding and extremely positive for children's development. More and more early childhood programs and elementary schools are adding nature areas to their sites, but most still have only the "traditional" play structures, with few trees or natural areas. That's okay! Take advantage of what you have. Regardless of how much nature may be available to you, you always have access to air, sun, shade, shadows, and weather! Most of the activities in this book do not require designated nature areas; rather, they are meant to be done anywhere you can—even on your sidewalk!

"Parents do not recognize the value of time outside." When parents are provided with information and evidence to support your choices, they will likely support the increased amount of time their children are spending outside. Remember to take advantage of parent education nights, program newsletters, and field trips as opportunities to educate parents about the value of outdoor time for children. The resource list in this book includes numerous helpful research-based books and articles that support the need for children to spend time outdoors. If your site has a resource library for parents, consider adding some of these titles. Many early care and education programs have book clubs or topic nights for parents where these titles could be shared and discussed.

Building on Your Experience

As you work through this book, you will likely come up with many wonderful ideas and activities of your own for the children in your program to learn about the environment. Here are some questions to ask yourself when planning science and environmental activities:

- Have the children shown an interest in this topic or some element of this topic?

- Where will this experience take us, in terms of knowledge and skills? (Not, "What is the answer here?" but, "What skills and learning could we practice in exploring this topic?")

- How can we connect this topic to our current curriculum?

- Does this activity offer opportunities for deeper learning? Is this something we can return to again and again, with opportunities for new discoveries each time?

- Will this experience promote the development of fundamental skills and concepts to increase the children's scientific ideas?

- Does this activity offer children an opportunity to experience the natural world firsthand?

Again, the principal aim of this book is to provide activities, ideas, and resources for offering meaningful environmental experiences to children ages three through eight. The ultimate goal of such experiences is to promote

- A growing awareness of the natural world and its cycles

- A developing understanding of the child's role in the environment

- Safe, joyful, and affirming experiences with nature, all of which leads to later stewardship

But even more than doing activities, I want to return to the single most important recommendation I can make when it comes to environmental education: Get outside! Do it often, no matter the weather. The more frequently and consistently you bring the children outside, the stronger their comfort level with the natural world will be. Look at your curriculum or planned activities for the month or year. How can you integrate nature into what you're already planning? Does your program focus on holidays? Consider learning together about nature-based celebrations too. Do you operate year-round or just during the school year? Make the seasons a big part of your year's rhythm. Use nature as a tool to teach other disciplines. For example, count stones or trees outside to build math skills. Invest in a set of beautiful, nature-based storybooks for the classroom. Use the changing colors of the seasons to explore color and light. Think of the outdoors as your classroom!

Finally, remember that you're likely already doing a lot to promote children's awareness and interest in the natural world. Whether you're using nature stories in the classroom, encouraging children to recycle, or exploring the outdoors together, great! Every step, no matter how small, makes a big difference toward creating a greener Earth.

CHAPTER 2

Exploring **Nature**

When some people hear the word *nature* they imagine large tracts of wilderness, untouched by humans. Others may think of well-managed gardens or forests. Still others think of unexpected flowers sprouting up through the cracks of a sidewalk in the middle of a bustling city. These are all real experiences of nature. The fact is that nature is all around us and, in whatever form or context you find it, can spark fascination, inspiration, and learning for everyone—from the youngest children to the senior citizens in your community. The more people recognize that nature really is everywhere, the more they will invest in its care. There has never been a time in our collective history when knowing and caring about nature has been more important. With the challenges facing our planet, it is imperative that we—its inhabitants—understand the ecological system and act in ways that benefit the planet. This is the foundation of *environmental literacy*, and it's just as important as any other kind of literacy. These are also the goals at the heart of most environmental education programs today.

For some educators, especially those who have a strong commitment to taking action and making a difference, prioritizing nature experiences over teaching environmental issues may take a leap of faith. How will making kites help kids care about air quality? Or how will splashing in puddles help children learn about and take responsibility for water pollution? The good news is, it works! There is a substantial body of

evidence that supports the link between time spent outside and the development of feelings of stewardship and environmentally conscious behavior (Chawla 2006; Faber Taylor and Kuo 2006). Research indicates that when children are offered frequent direct experiences with nature and the outdoors—ideally with a caring adult—and engage fully and freely with their environment, they are more likely to express feelings of love for nature and a desire to care for it. In fact, research also shows that simply knowing about or understanding environmental issues is not a strong motivator for acting on behalf of the environment. In other words, strong, positive feelings are needed to create this motivation (Wells and Lekies 2006).

Nature exploration offers other benefits to children, too. In addition to helping lay the foundation for later feelings of stewardship, time in nature has been shown to improve attention, reduce classroom aggression and behavioral challenges, improve health and physical abilities, and provide physical challenges unlike those offered by traditional play structures. When playing in nature, children tend to engage in more creative and complex play. They are also free to engage in activities that support their natural learning styles and to move at their own pace: skills that help them learn how to learn. Nature experiences also help foster children's cognitive development. Natural settings offer children opportunities to think critically, to make observations, to synthesize information, and to solve problems—skills important for intellectual development (Kellert 2005). For this reason, one of the best and most important things you can offer children is ample time for unstructured outdoor play and exploration. As fun and useful as structured activities can be, children need the opportunity to script their own play, to discover and follow their own interests outside, and to direct their own experience. Nature provides the perfect setting for these opportunities. In nature, children are free to use their gross-motor or fine-motor skills, to move quickly or slowly, and to play quietly alone under a tree or join others in stomping through puddles. Allow children the freedom and time to enjoy some unstructured playtime in natural settings as often as you can.

Nature Exploration and Scientific-Thinking Skills

Nature also offers a host of opportunities for children to develop general science skills as well as academic and scientific-thinking skills, such as inquiry and observation. It's true, scientific learning is not something that happens only in the science corner of the early childhood classroom. Opportunities for scientific learning are all around us from the structures we build, to the food we eat, to the air we breathe, and the list goes on and on. The great outdoors, whether a large tract of forestland or a few scattered trees along the edge of your parking lot, can be rich with material and opportunities for scientific exploration.

Exploring nature can be an avenue for developing the very same skills that are essential for and used daily by scientists, researchers, and engineers throughout the world. Those fundamental skills include making observations and describing those observations, classifying objects, investigating phenomena, asking questions, predicting outcomes, drawing conclusions, and explaining outcomes. Most early childhood educators will intuitively recognize that these are habits young children naturally have and already use in the world around them, simply in the course of their free play and exploration. Thus, the early childhood environment is a perfect setting for practicing science. Educators can also cultivate intentional support to develop these ways of thinking. Use the following practices in your classroom on a regular basis to help children strengthen their own scientific-thinking skills.

LEARNING THROUGH THE FIVE SENSES

Encourage the use of all senses during learning and throughout the day. Challenge children to notice ten new things on their walk to the lunchroom or to tell you five things they can hear when they are outside. Bringing awareness to the senses can really help children (and adults!) be more skilled at noticing details and subtle changes in the environment.

You can also support the development of this skill in young children by modeling it yourself. Talk about what you see, hear, feel, and smell. Mention little details throughout the day, such as "I hear a bird chirping," or "This smells a bit like blueberries," or "I can feel the rain on my face." When you tune in to your own senses in the presence of children, you remind them to use their senses as well.

OBSERVING AND DESCRIBING

Children are natural observers and love the chance to talk about what they observe. Encourage them to share their observations. You can help by offering words to the child, which is different from putting words in the child's mouth or telling a child what to observe. For example, you might list a number of qualities about something that you've observed. You could mention that a pinecone is bumpy, prickly, stiff, scratchy, and dry. Offering your own descriptive words can help inspire a child's creative mind. It can also help build literacy and vocabulary.

Another way to support children's interests in observation and description is to document what they say. You can ask them to describe what they see or what they are doing, or you can keep a list of the observations they make while outdoors or engaged in some other activity. Post this list somewhere visible so that the children can see it and know that their words have value. Refer back to the children's actual words when talking about experiences. Help the children make connections by referring to the list for words to describe other objects or experiences in nature.

When asking children for their observations, gently urge them to describe the experience, rather than simply naming it and moving on. For example, if you put a rock in a feely box, encourage the children to refrain from shouting out the name of the object and instead tell you something about how the object feels. Is it large or small? Prickly or bumpy? Smooth or rounded? Warm or cool? Generate as many words as possible to describe the object before trying to name it. This is the power of observation. It can help us notice details, shapes, sizes, colors, and behavior.

CLASSIFYING

Classifying helps children make sense of things. This in turn helps them make predictions about the world. Young children love to classify objects, experiences, and ideas. It's part of how they organize and arrange their world. They group things into sizes, shapes, colors, and familiar objects. How do children classify objects when outdoors, engaged in free play? There are many ways. Pay attention to the materials children play with and how they use them. Do the sticks and flowers become the puppets in a puppet show? How are the children using shells or stones? Ask children to find common characteristics of plants or flowers. Some children will notice colors, others will point out leaf shapes, while others might notice the scents.

Often the most obvious classifications will jump out at children—and at adults—but it can be a valuable exercise to challenge ourselves to think beyond the obvious. What are some less obvious, but potentially significant, ways that objects can be classified?

Challenge yourself on this. Think about how you organize and classify objects in the classroom. Do you have your classroom carefully organized according to different activities (for example, "dramatic play," "building," "art," and "science") with every object belonging specifically in a certain place? Challenge the children in your program to develop new ways to organize and classify. Try taking away the imaginary boundaries of those classroom areas. What happens if you put art supplies in the science corner? Building materials in dramatic play? Ask the children how they would arrange the space and let them have an active role in creating new areas based on their choices.

INVESTIGATING AND ASKING QUESTIONS

Investigation is such a fundamental and instinctive act for young children. They see things that are new, interesting, or different and they want to investigate further. For the young child, investigating involves questioning: "How does the world work?" "How am I a part of it?" and "What can I do?" These are fundamental questions that invite learning and growth at so many levels! You can support investigation by simply noticing children's interests and curiosities and encouraging them to go further. Investigation also involves making time in your day or shifting your schedule to allow the children to explore a topic further, facilitating activities to help support the investigation, and thinking about tools to facilitate exploration. You can also carefully observe the children's investigations, and when appropriate, ask questions to encourage deeper thinking. Keep a list of children's questions while they explore in nature. This list will be a rich source of inspiration for future investigations.

PREDICTING

What is predicting? Predicting is guessing based on reasoning and past experience. You might call it making an educated guess, and it's a fundamental skill of childhood! How is this helpful in science? Prediction challenges children—and adults—to think critically about what they know, what they've experienced in the past, and what they've observed. Predicting involves analyzing experiences, then synthesizing that information and imagining what to expect—or not. Predictions can take us to the next level of learning by constructing knowledge based on past experience. You can help children make predictions by asking thought-provoking questions, such as "What do you think could be making that noise? Have you ever heard something like that before?" or "What do you think will happen next? Why do you think so?"

DRAWING CONCLUSIONS AND GIVING EXPLANATIONS

When children have the opportunity to make observations and describe their observations—and are able to repeat an experience or connect it to their own lives—they can draw conclusions based on that experience. When their investigations and curiosity are supported, they form conclusions and synthesize information about what has happened and what is likely to happen. For example, the child who drops pinecone after pinecone into a stream from a bridge and quickly turns to see the pinecones traveling downstream has drawn a conclusion that the pinecones will come out on the other side of the bridge as they travel downstream. He has also concluded that they float. Through trial and error, he's tested his observations and has come to expect a certain outcome. As an educator, you can support a child's growing skill in drawing conclusions by asking him to give you an explanation. In science, evidence is key. Ask a child to explain to you what he did, how he knows the pinecones will travel under the bridge, how they actually traveled, and how he learned that would happen. Asking children to explain their investigations—their questions, what they did, and what they discovered—will strengthen their skills in thinking scientifically. When you ask questions, provide adequate time for reflection, discussion, and explanation.

Intentional support for developing scientific-thinking skills is an enormous contribution that educators can make to young children. You help create a foundation—a scaffold—upon which they can continue to build critical learning skills. Use the following activities as a starting point for your nature exploration. Some activities require significant outdoor space or access to natural areas, while most may be done in limited outdoor settings or even indoors. Try a few, and find out what works best for you. The idea of free, unstructured time for exploration might be challenging for some educators, whereas for others it's already a part of the day's routine. Many of these activities may seem structured at first, but I encourage you to allow the children to take them in their own direction. Often things happen outdoors that can't be predicted or planned for: a beautiful rainbow peeking out from behind a cloud; a busy squirrel rummaging on the edge of the playground; the parade of ants coming down the sidewalk. Be open to nature's own program. You will soon find that opportunities for discovery and learning present themselves.

Stop, Look, and Listen

There is tremendous value in the skill of observation. Children are naturally observant, noticing and pointing out details that adult eyes and ears often miss. Yet there are ways you can encourage children to develop and hone observation skills. Observing something new can be very exciting and empowering for children. Putting words to those observations is a great exercise in building language skills, as children are challenged to develop clear and accurate descriptions. This activity offers children a chance to find something new in their everyday surroundings. It is great to do during seasonal change, as well as during days of "interesting weather" such as snow or rain.

Activity Goals

→ To enjoy the experience of nature

→ To practice using observation skills

→ To make new discoveries about the natural world

National Science Education Standards

Life science: characteristics of organisms, life cycles of organisms, organisms and environments

Earth and space science: properties of earth materials, objects in the sky, changes in earth and sky

Science in personal and social perspectives: characteristics and changes in populations, changes in environments

Materials and Supplies

None

Procedure

1. Take the children outside and have everyone find a place to stand still. Use your best judgment; you may have the children stand in a circle or somewhere within your sight, or you may be comfortable letting them explore at a safe distance.

2. Ask the children to stand still, feet firmly on the ground, and look around, only moving their eyes and heads. Encourage them to find something new that they've never noticed before. While they do this, encourage them to listen. With no one making a sound, just let the children take in the noises that they hear.

3. After a short time, gather the group together and talk about what the children saw or heard. Some things the children might notice are sounds of traffic, the sound of children moving, snow covering the sidewalk, a puddle forming, and so on.

TIPS

- Use this activity to help children tune in to the world around them and manage their attention. It can also be very calming for a wild group of children, or a nice way to end outdoor time.

- Assign a certain number of observations, especially for younger children, if so desired. A good starting point is one observation for every year of the child's age.

- Allow children time to wander away from the group a bit (safely, of course). The powers of observation are often enhanced when there are no distractions from other children.

CONNECTIONS

Provide materials so the children can sketch or paint images of the sounds they hear, or ask them to each choose one thing and draw it. Encourage them to really observe every detail.

Count Ten Things

In this activity, you'll encourage the children to find ten things that they can experience with their senses. This is another great tuning-in activity that helps children practice shifting their attention to different areas of awareness.

Activity Goals

→ To explore the five senses

→ To practice using all of one's senses

→ To enjoy making discoveries in nature

National Science Education Standards

Science as inquiry: abilities necessary to do scientific inquiry

Physical science: properties of objects and materials; position and motion of objects; light, heat, electricity, and magnetism

Life science: characteristics of organisms, life cycles of organisms, organisms and environments

Earth and space science: properties of earth materials, objects in the sky, changes in earth and sky

Science in personal and social perspectives: characteristics and changes in populations, changes in environments

History and nature of science: science as a human endeavor

Materials and Supplies

☐ Safe walking path

Procedure

1. Venture out on a nature walk through a natural area or the neighborhood, or choose a natural area and let the children explore on their own.

2. Encourage the children to notice their surroundings.

3. Encourage them to find ten things they can see, ten things they can hear, and ten things they can feel. If you're on a walk in the neighborhood, try for ten things they can smell too!

4. Repeat this activity often, challenging the children to find new things each time.

TIPS

- For older children, set a target number much higher than ten.

- For younger children, set a lower number, or make ten a group goal.

- For children who find it difficult to make observations with many senses at once, have them focus on just one sense during each outing, such as hearing.

CONNECTIONS

Keep an ongoing list of the children's observations. Refer to this list often when you need writing prompts. Encourage the children to write about the observations they made or to speculate about one observation; for example, ask children how a pinecone lands so far from any tree or why there was a pile of feathers near a rock.

Sound Walk

Sound is one of many ways we can observe and learn more about our world. Most of us live with a constant level of noise throughout the day—and in some urban areas, even at night. This is a great opportunity for children to tune in to their sense of hearing and to discuss the difference between natural noises and human-made noises.

Activity Goals

To enjoy using one's sense of hearing to discover new things in nature

National Science Education Standards

History and nature of science: science as a human endeavor

Materials and Supplies

☐ A walking path or sidewalk at any safe outdoor location

Procedure

1. Go on a walk, and invite the children to identify different sounds they hear. Remind them to stay as quiet as possible, because they will be "collecting" sounds as they go.

2. Periodically, stop the group and ask the children what they've heard and record their answers.

3. Ask the children if each sound is from nature or is human made.

4. Make a chart with the children listing all of the sounds. Observe which category had the longest list.

TIPS

- Repeat this activity once per week at different times of the day.

- Keep a tally of the results in your classroom to observe how sounds change as the seasons change.

- Ask children if they hear different sounds depending on the time of year or if there are things they hear all year round.

CONNECTIONS

Do some research and determine if there is a particular time of year in which songbirds migrate through your area. If there is, make sure to conduct a sound walk during that window of time. Morning is a great time for hearing birdsong. Invite the children to try to hear an individual bird song.

Ask children if human-made sounds can be considered "natural." Have them explain why or why not.

Look Up!

Aside from naptime, children spend very little time lying down. This experience offers children an opportunity for quiet reflection and an appreciation for nature's beauty.

Activity Goals

→ To enjoy the feeling of relaxing and letting one's body be held by the Earth

→ To enjoy quiet time in nature

National Science Education Standards

Life science: characteristics of organisms, organisms and environments

Earth and space science: objects in the sky, changes in earth and sky

Materials and Supplies

None

Procedure

1. Take the children outside and have everyone find a place to lie on their backs. Ask them what they see.

2. On a relatively cloudy day, have children look at the clouds. Otherwise, have children lie under the spreading branches of a tree and look at the patterns made by the leaves.

3. Allow plenty of time for the children to relax and enjoy the stillness.

4. Ask the children how this made them feel, what they saw, and whether anything surprised them.

TIPS

- If children aren't comfortable lying directly on the ground, spread out a special blanket reserved just for this purpose. Over time, they will come to cherish the blanket and the shared experience of lying down together to enjoy nature.

- If this experience is too challenging for some children, bring a nice nature story outdoors and read to the children while they lie down.

 Remind children never to look directly into the sun.

CONNECTIONS

Read stories about the weather, animals, or other science topics, and use them as jumping-off points for scientific explorations outdoors.

Look Down!

Just as it is important for children to lie on their backs and take it all in, children need an opportunity to look down and study the small stuff too. This experience offers children the chance to get up close and personal with the ground, and they'll discover tiny treasures such as bugs, small stones, shells, and more.

Activity Goals

→ To creep and crawl along the ground in search of tiny details

→ To make new discoveries in nature

National Science Education Standards

Science as inquiry: abilities necessary to do scientific inquiry, understandings about scientific inquiry

Physical science: properties of objects and materials; light, heat, electricity, and magnetism

Life science: characteristics of organisms, life cycles of organisms, organisms and environments

Earth and space science: properties of earth materials, changes in earth and sky

Science in personal and social perspectives: changes in environments

Materials and Supplies

☐ Several hula hoops or loops of rope, one for every three to four children

☐ Magnifying lenses

Procedure

1. Toss the hula hoops or loops of rope into a grassy spot or other natural area.

2. Encourage the children to lie on their tummies and explore what they see within the designated space.

3. Provide magnifying lenses for the children to more closely examine the ground.

4. Give the children a challenge. For example, invite them to find ten different colors or to count the number of ants they can find.

TIPS

- Use this activity as an opportunity to practice counting and listing.

CONNECTIONS

Use this activity as an opportunity to sort and classify objects that children find. Encourage them to create categories for objects, such as round things, things an ant could or could not carry, and wet or dry things.

Invite each child to choose one thing from inside their hoops that they'd like to learn more about.

Provide each child with a journal. Then have them write or dictate a story about an ant's journey within the hoop they explored. Ask the children to describe what happened to the ant, where the ant went, and what the ant saw.

Ask children to sketch the entire circle and everything inside it in a very short time. This gets them thinking about the main things they remember and want to include. Alternately, invite them to draw "an ant's eye view" of life within the hoop.

Soil Search

This is a great experience for children who love dirt. They have a chance to sort and sift the dirt, exploring it and examining it to their hearts' content. Also, as I mention in chapter 4, soil is the most biologically diverse *ecosystem* on the planet (USDA NRCS 1998b). In one teaspoon of soil, there are more organisms than people on the entire Earth (USDA NRCS 2010)! The healthier the soil is, the more organisms there will be—many of those organisms are microscopic and cannot be detected without sophisticated microscopes.

Activity Goals

→ To enjoy getting one's hands dirty and exploring soil

National Science Education Standards

Science as inquiry: understandings about scientific inquiry

Life science: organisms and environments

Earth and space science: properties of earth materials

Materials and Supplies

☐ A shovel

☐ Sieves or strainers

☐ Buckets

☐ An old, light-colored sheet or access to a table or sidewalk

☐ Magnifying lenses

Procedure

1. Use the shovel to scoop a few buckets of soil from different areas around your building.

2. Pour the soil onto the sheet and invite the children to work in small groups using the sieves to see what they find. Ask the children if they can find chunks of soil, sand, or small rocks. Ask them if they see any critters, such as worms, ants, or beetles.

3. Encourage the children to use magnifying lenses to study different objects.

4. Ask the children if all the soil samples contain the same kinds of things or if the samples are different.

5. At the end of the activity, return the soil samples and living creatures to the area where they were collected.

TIPS

• Be prepared for the various reactions children might have to finding insects, worms, and other organisms in the soil. Some children might scream or becoming very excited at the discovery of tiny critters. Respond to children's reactions with care and resist shushing them. Remind children that being gentle and careful is especially important when dealing with tiny creatures.

• If a child is afraid of the live critters in the soil, allow him to observe the activity from a safe distance. Encourage him to move closer to the soil as he begins to feel more comfortable.

CONNECTIONS

Have children identify any critters they find in the soil. Help them make a graph or diagram indicating the approximate number of species found, where they found them, and other information they find. If you have a compost pile at your site, compare soil to compost.

Use the soil to paint pictures! Simply moisten very dry soil, or use the naturally moist soil that you find. Provide the children with blank paper and invite them to paint with dirt.

Encourage children to write in their journals about the soil. Ask them to write about what they know about soil, what they are still wondering about, and what they learned. Also ask them to write about how they felt about dirt when they started the activity and how they felt about it after.

Color Search

If you ask children to name the colors of nature, you'll likely hear, "brown, green, and blue," but there are so many more colors to be found. This simple activity allows children to go on a treasure hunt of sorts to seek out colors on cards they've chosen. It is great fun year-round.

Activity Goals

→ To build an awareness of the amazing array of colors found in the natural world

National Science Education Standards

Physical science: properties of objects and materials

Life science: characteristics of organisms

Earth and space science: properties of earth materials

Materials and Supplies

☐ A wide variety of paint color sample cards from a home improvement or paint store, at least one per child

Procedure

1. Gather outside, then provide a color sample to each child. Ask the children to find something that matches their color as closely as possible.

2. If possible, collect the materials and make a color collage.

3. Repeat this activity during different times of the year.

TIPS

- Cut cards with multiple colors into separate color cards.

CONNECTIONS

Ask the children which colors were the easiest to find, which were the most difficult, and why they think so. Have the children list the most common colors in nature in your area.

Obtain a color wheel and let children arrange their cards in a similar pattern. Provide watercolors and encourage them to mix and match colors.

Conduct this activity in the winter months, when finding color matches will be more of a challenge.

Set parameters for the children; for example, ask them to match only plants.

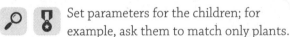

Leaf Match

AGES 3+

This activity deepens a connection with nature by encouraging children to look closely and notice details. Using leaves as the focus, children play a simple recognition game. This activity can easily be taken outside, if the weather permits.

Activity Goals

→ To make observations about subtle details

National Science Education Standards

Life science: characteristics of organisms

History and nature of science: science as a human endeavor (if a dichotomous key is used)

Materials and Supplies

☐ A variety of leaves, at least one per child

Procedure

1. Distribute a leaf to each child, or let each child choose one.

2. Gather the group together and ask them to show their leaves and tell the other children what makes their leaf special.

3. Ask them about the colors, the shapes, and any small details (such as a tear or a fold in the leaf) that they notice.

4. Invite each child to toss the leaf into a pile after she finishes describing it.

5. When all the leaves have been shared, the children can search in the pile to find their leaves.

TIPS

• Use real leaves if at all possible.

• Have the children gather the leaves during a walk just before you do this activity.

CONNECTIONS

Help the children learn the names of trees by providing a chart with the outline of several common leaves. They can take their own leaves and find the outline that most closely matches their leaf.

Allow time for children to paint or sketch their leaves with colored pencils, pastels, or watercolors, or invite the children to work together to create a picture out of the leaves.

Gather the children and develop a *dichotomous key* together. A dichotomous key asks a set of questions about the characteristics of an organism, and then follows with two additional questions based on the response, and so on and so on, limiting the choices each time. The final choice reveals the name or species of the organism. Here is an example of a dichotomous key for leaves:

1. Broad leaves or needle leaves? If broad leaves, go to question 2. If needle leaves, go to question 3.

2. Are leaves smooth along edges or jagged along edges? If smooth, go to question 4. If jagged, go to question 5.

3. Are needles longer than one inch, or shorter than one inch?

Continue the key until the final choice reveals the name or species of the tree. You can adjust the level of detail for each question. There are many good dichotomous keys online, and many common field guides also have them.

Keep a Calendar

In this activity, children will create their own nature calendar by observing and recording seasonal changes over time. You can repeat this activity year after year, creating an informal record of weather patterns in your area.

Activity Goals

→ To connect to the natural world through observation and recording of information

→ To notice patterns and trends in the natural world over time

National Science Education Standards

Science as inquiry: abilities necessary to do scientific inquiry

Physical science: properties of objects and materials; position and motion of objects; light, heat, electricity, and magnetism

Life science: characteristics of organisms, life cycles of organisms, organisms and environments

Earth and space science: properties of earth materials, objects in the sky, changes in earth and sky

Science in personal and social perspectives: characteristics and changes in populations, changes in environments, science and technology in local challenges

History and nature of science: science as a human endeavor

Materials and Supplies

☐ A large, wall-type yearlong calendar or one calendar per child

Procedure

1. Using your natural area or school grounds, make and record nature observations every day as a group.

2. Record the temperature as well as other things the children notice; for example, leaves changing, windiness, and behavior of the nearby animals (pigeons, squirrels, and so on).

3. If you are in an area with pronounced seasonal changes, encourage the children to use the data they collect to make predictions about seasonal events, such as the first frost, first snowfall, and the first appearance of ice on the pond.

TIPS

• Explain to the children that the word *phenology* describes the process of observing seasonal changes and other phenomena in nature. This practice not only helps us learn about and appreciate nature but also helps children hone their observation skills, improve their ability to make predictions, and inspire further questions.

• Keep in mind that this activity is particularly enjoyable for children during the transition of seasons, when more dramatic weather changes often happen (sometimes on a daily basis)!

• Encourage very young children to record their observations by drawing pictures.

CONNECTIONS

Use this activity to have children practice reading a thermometer and understanding the significance of temperature. For example, ask the children what the difference is between 10 degrees and 80 degrees Fahrenheit.

Have the children act out the way they feel when the temperature is very cold and when it is very warm.

If you've made rain gauges from the Rain Gauges activity in chapter 5, use them to measure rainfall. With practice and some help making connections, children will become familiar with how nature looks and feels after a heavy rain, a light drizzle, and dry weather. For example, one morning you might notice your rain gauge is full. The tree trunks are black and wet, the plants have lots of raindrops left on them, and the grass feels wet and soggy.

Have the children write detailed descriptions of how nature looks, feels, and smells in different seasons and during different weather, then have them share their descriptions while the group tries to guess what weather they are writing about.

Plant a Sensory Garden

Gardening is a great way to stimulate children's senses. You can select herbs and flowers specifically for their sensory qualities, which will entertain and delight children year-round. Choosing plants with a variety of textures will also enhance delight. Children can explore the feeling of soft new buds or fuzzy leaves. In the winter months, you can use the seedpods or dry leaves from plants for art supplies, to explore texture and sound, and as inspiration for drawing simple shapes. Plants with a distinctive smell need little justification—who doesn't love the scent of lilacs on a bright spring day? Many of the plants listed here may be eaten raw, added to soups or sauces, or brewed into teas. Most are easy to grow and require sunny locations. Consider some of the suggestions below for their sensory appeal.

Scent: lemon balm, geranium, petunia, lavender, sage, basil, rosemary, dill, mint, lilac, yarrow, and thyme all provide pleasant aromas.

Feel/Touch: lamb's ears, lady's mantle, fern, dill, yarrow, milkweed (for the "milk" that oozes when a leaf is broken off), goldenrod, witch hazel, bedstraw, and money plant have interesting textures in all seasons.

Sight: cosmos, crape myrtle, lavender, and yarrow are brightly colored; hosta, sedum, and fern can help begin a garden with many shades of green.

Sound: moonflower, wisteria, hollyhock, and many others create interesting sounds when they go to seed and have lovely textures in the winter months.

Activity Goals

→ To delight in gardening and working with plants

→ To work together as a class to grow something

→ To contribute to a long-term project

National Science Education Standards

Life science: characteristics of organisms, life cycles of organisms, organisms and environments

Materials and Supplies

☐ Gardening gloves, shovels, rakes, and trowels

☐ Potting soil

☐ Compost (see appendix F for information on starting your own compost pile)

☐ Other materials will vary, depending on your plant selections

Procedure

1. Prepare containers for planting or dig your garden with the children. Turn over shovelfuls of soil to soften the dirt, break up any chunks, and aerate the soil.

2. Plant according to instructions on the labels.

3. Water the garden well.

TIP

• Investigate which plants grow well in your region.

 Before eating the plants or using them for tea, make sure they are safe to consume.

CONNECTIONS

Explain to children that a sensory garden stimulates our sense of smell, and that the sense of smell in humans varies widely from person to person. When we smell something, we are actually inhaling tiny molecules of that object! Also mention that the sense of smell is highly connected to the sense of taste, which is why when you have a cold or are congested, you often can't taste anything.

Observe the garden over time and note the insects that visit.

Use the plants or their leaves to apply paint to paper.

If plants go dormant in your area during the winter months, sketch the dry leaves and stems. Enjoy the textures of the dried plants too.

My Nature Name

AGES 4+

This activity builds on early literacy and nature awareness by encouraging children to find (or identify) natural objects that share the same first letter as each letter in the child's name. The children will be creating *acrostic poems*, in which the first letter of each line is one letter of a child's name. For example, Lucy's poem might be

Leaf

Upside-down flower

Chickadee

Yellow sun

Activity Goals

→ To personalize nature treasures

→ To enjoy the fun of a treasure hunt

National Science Education Standards

Earth and space science: properties of earth materials

Life science: organisms and environments

Materials and Supplies

☐ Paper bags or other containers

☐ Large pieces of paper

☐ Glue

☐ Art supplies, such as paint and colored pencils

☐ Clipboards or other hard surfaces to write on

Procedure

1. Take the children outside and give them each a piece of paper and a clipboard. Have each child write his name on the paper—help those who need it.

2. Ask the children to collect and place in their bags small objects from nature that begin with each letter of their name. If they can't collect something for a letter in their name, encourage them to write down the name of something big that they see or remember from another time outside.

3. Back inside, provide paper and glue and invite the children to arrange and glue their items onto the paper.

4. If children saw larger objects, or remember items that can't be collected, provide art supplies so the children can draw or paint those items.

5. Help the children find or draw at least one object that corresponds with each of the letters in their names.

TIPS

• Allow a few days to complete this project. Children who finish early can make additional name pictures for family members or friends. Challenge the children to find as many natural objects as possible that begin with the same letters as their names.

• Allow children enough time to consider and organize their thoughts for this activity.

• Before beginning this activity, review the names of some common natural objects to help the children in their search.

• Do this activity in different seasons to find different materials and get new ideas.

CONNECTIONS

Set parameters and choose a theme; for example, all objects selected must relate to water or to winter.

Nature Is Art!

This activity offers children the chance to do a variety of artistic things using natural materials. You may wish to repeat this activity often, sometimes letting the children work in groups, other times encouraging them to work individually. This activity can easily be done outside if the weather permits.

Activity Goals

→ To use natural materials in a creative manner

National Science Education Standards

Physical science: properties of objects and materials

Life science: characteristics of organisms

Earth and space science: properties of earth materials

Science and technology: abilities to distinguish between natural objects and objects made by humans (if bridge and structure-building extension is done), abilities of technological design

Materials and Supplies

☐ A variety of natural materials, such as pinecones, leaves, sand, rocks and pebbles, and soil

☐ Glue or hot glue gun (for adult use only)

☐ Paint and paintbrushes

☐ Large pieces of paper, tagboard, or cardboard

Procedure

1. Discuss with the children how many different ways there are to make nature art. Elicit their suggestions.

2. Decide which ideas to implement, and work with the children to set up the activity. Consider the following ideas:

- Collect leaves, grasses, and other materials and invite the children to make a collage on the ground or glue the items onto a piece of paper or cardboard.

- Crumble leaves or sand into tempera paint and experiment with the effects.

- Use rainwater or mud to paint pictures on sturdy paper or cardboard.

- Use pine needles, grasses, or other objects from nature in place of paintbrushes.

TIP

- Make the search part of the process! Go outside and collect natural materials for this activity.

CONNECTIONS

Choose a science theme and collect only items related to that theme. For example, the children may decide to paint with rocks or dried leaves and compare the different textures and shapes that result.

Try using natural objects to make structures and bridges. Challenge the children to make a structure or bridge strong enough to support a particular object, such as a stick or a rock.

Invite children to use natural materials to spell their names. Sticks make great materials for shaping capital letters, or you can find grasses or thin twigs to bend into the shapes of lowercase letters. Ask children to find other natural materials they can use to make their names.

Nature Scavenger Hunt

Scavenger hunts are always fun, and nature scavenger hunts are even better because there is always so much to discover. In this activity, the children search for objects based on clues you provide.

Activity Goals

→ To experience the joy of discovery in nature

National Science Education Standards

Earth and space science: properties of earth materials

Physical science: properties of objects and materials

Materials and Supplies

☐ Strips of paper with clues, such as "something soft," "something bumpy," "something blue," and so on, at least one per child

Procedure

1. Have each child choose a piece of paper and invite them to read their clues, or read the clues to the children.

2. Head outside and allow time for the children to choose objects that match their clues.

3. Afterward, have time for sharing and invite the children to reveal their clues and the objects they found.

4. Allow children to trade clues and play again, if time allows.

TIPS

- Have children come up with clues for each other (or for you!).

- Allow plenty of time for this activity.

- Invite the children to show their objects and have the other children guess what the clue was for each object.

CONNECTIONS

🔍 Using the clues, work together as a group to generate a list of all the things in nature you can think of that might match that clue. For example, if the clue is "Things that are blue," the group should generate a list of all the things they can think of in nature that are blue. (You can also limit this to all the things they've seen on your school grounds that are blue.)

🔍 Write the clues so that the objects will be small and easy for the children to collect. Then work together as a group to sort and organize the objects and then classify them according to categories.

Treasure Hunt

It is important for children to have authentic experiences in nature with objects they are allowed to see, touch, and even collect. "Look but don't touch" is something children hear often, but sometimes they need to hold something in their hands, smell it, and carry it around for a while in order to really connect with it. Within reason, children should be allowed to collect some items from nature, bearing in mind safety and conservation concerns. This treasure hunt is different from the scavenger hunt in the previous activity primarily in that it encourages children to find their own treasures, as opposed to the scavenger hunt, where they are finding something suggested by a clue.

Activity Goals

→ To reflect on what makes something special

→ To hold and explore objects from nature

National Science Education Standards

Physical science: properties of objects and materials; light, heat, electricity, and magnetism (if sunprints are made)

Life science: characteristics of organisms, life cycles of organisms, organisms and environments

Earth and space science: properties of earth materials

Materials and Supplies

☐ Small notebooks, one for each child, optional

☐ Colored pencils, optional

☐ Digital camera, optional

Procedure

1. On a nature walk, allow the children to explore the area and pick up objects.

2. Invite them to choose one thing from nature that feels particularly special to them. It might be a stone, a piece of bark—from the ground, *not* pulled from a tree, or a flower.

3. If you prefer that they do not take the items back to the classroom, provide small notebooks and colored pencils, and give the children time to sketch or trace their objects.

4. Photograph the objects, then print the pictures for children to use as decorations for their cubbies, for their nature journals, or to bring home.

TIPS

- If you are in a park or nature preserve, ensure you are following the site's rules with regard to object collection.

- Familiarize yourself with your state's or region's endangered and threatened species. Don't collect any live animals or insects. Do not collect endangered plants.

- Use "the rule of ten"—if there are ten of something, a child may take one.

CONNECTIONS

Purchase photosensitive paper—also called *sunprint paper*—and invite children to make silhouette pages of the objects they find. Discuss how photosensitive paper is coated with special chemicals that react to light. When you place objects on such paper, the paper remains blue, while the objects block the light, leaving a silhouette. Rinse the paper in water and the image is fixed. Photosensitive paper may be purchased online or at most larger art supply stores.

Create a classroom rock collection. When geologists collect rocks, they label them with the rock type as well as where it was collected.

(continues on next page)

Ask children to identify the types of rocks and minerals they collect. You can also have the children identify tree species (from pinecones or leaves collected) or flowers. Create a log book to document the many different objects and species found.

Invite the children to paint or sketch their objects using charcoal pencils. If desired, dip rocks and other hard treasures in paint and make pictures by pressing the painted objects onto paper.

Spend some time sharing. Ask the children where they found their stones or what makes the stone special to them. Invite the children to write stories or poems about their treasures.

Tale of a Tree

One way to connect with nature is to find a tree and imagine its life story. What has it seen? How long has it been there? Children love imagining the life of a tree and considering all the animals that might make their homes there. This activity also builds empathy and compassion, as the children are encouraged to consider the perspective of another living thing.

Activity Goals

→ To sensitively care for another living thing that is very different from ourselves

National Science Education Standards

Science as inquiry: abilities necessary to do scientific inquiry, understandings about scientific inquiry

Physical science: properties of objects and materials, position and motion of objects

Life science: characteristics of organisms, life cycles of organisms, organisms and environments

Materials and Supplies

☐ Access to trees

Procedure

1. Choose a special tree together. Discuss what the group likes about the tree. It might be the shape, the shade it provides, or the color of the leaves.

2. Tell a "shared story" under the tree, where the group works together to tell the story of the tree's life. Use a leaf or branch (picked up from the ground, not pulled from the tree) as the "sharing stick." One person begins and then passes the sharing stick to another person, who adds to the story.

3. Continue this process until each child has had a chance to contribute to the story. Encourage children to include such details as how the tree was planted, what animals make their homes there, and how it feels when the children sit beneath it.

4. Visit the tree in all seasons.

TIPS

- Provide opportunities for children to read, have a snack, and engage in other everyday routines near the tree. The special tree might become their favorite place or a place where children find sanctuary.

CONNECTIONS

Invite the children to measure the tree. Use a variety of measuring tools, such as rope, tape measures, and even arm spans. Find out how many children can hold hands around the tree's trunk, how tall the tree is, or how many children—if they were standing on each other's shoulders—it would take to get to the top of the tree. Also find out what type of tree it is and its *life cycle* (the stages of its life). Collect leaves and twigs from the tree in all seasons.

Ask children what they'd like to know about the tree, and develop a research project to answer their questions.

Have the children lay some paper on the ground under the tree so the leaves make shadows on the paper. Then have them trace around the shadow images with watercolor paints. Visit the tree during all kinds of weather and sketch it in all seasons. Make bark rubbings. Paint a picture of the tree using crazy colors, like purple. Draw an outline of the tree and then apply fabric scraps with glue for texture.

Invite the children to write down their favorite things about the tree and then share them with the group.

Wishing Tree

AGES 3+

It is fun to imagine the wind carrying wishes and good thoughts into the world. In many cultures, prayer flags are hung from trees so that when breezes blow, the prayers will be carried out into the world. This experience gives children a fun way to make a wish as they lovingly decorate a tree or shrub with their "wish ribbons."

Activity Goals

→ To play with the wind and imagine wonderful things

National Science Education Standards

Physical science: position and motion of objects

Earth and space science: properties of earth materials

Materials and Supplies

☐ Strips of paper or colorful ribbons, at least one per child

☐ Permanent markers

☐ Access to a tree or shrub

Procedure

1. Provide the children with strips of paper or colorful ribbons. Invite them to write their wish on the paper or to tell you their wish for you to write.

2. Attach the ribbons to the branches of trees or anyplace they will flutter in the wind.

3. Invite the children to imagine that as the breezes blow, their wishes are on their way to coming true!

TIPS

- Plan this activity around a civil rights holiday or other well-known observation of peace and harmony to inspire children to think about peace.

- Be flexible about how long the ribbons stay on the tree. Some children may find it reassuring to visit their ribbon from time to time, believing that as it degrades, it is making their wish come true. Other children may want to save their ribbon as a keepsake.

CONNECTIONS

Have the children draw a picture of the wishing tree. Ask them to choose a color family to represent the tree in the current season; for example, a child might choose shades of whites and blues for winter, shades of green for summer, and so on. Repeat this activity seasonally.

Animal Watch

What animals do you observe on a regular basis? In urban areas in North America, children can see squirrels, pigeons, and crows without too much difficulty. In other areas, less common wildlife may be easily observed.

Activity Goals

→ To explore feelings about animals

→ To delight in watching, learning about, and making connections to animals through observation

National Science Education Standards

Science as inquiry: abilities necessary to do scientific inquiry, understandings about scientific inquiry

Life science: characteristics of organisms, life cycles of organisms, organisms and environments

History and nature of science: science as a human endeavor

Materials and Supplies

☐ Bird feeders and/or birdbaths, optional

☐ Children's binoculars, if available

Procedure

1. If possible, set up bird-feeding stations and watering areas outside your classroom or in a nature area and observe the animals as they visit the area.

2. If feeding stations aren't an option, find another way for the children to monitor animals, such as with binoculars or simply by sitting quietly off to the edge of an outdoor area.

3. Observe every day. A perfect reason to get outside every day is to check on the squirrel and see what she's up to! Children will enjoy getting to know the animals by watching them every day.

4. Work together to make a chart or write observations about the animals' behaviors.

TIPS

- Plant a butterfly garden to attract, observe, and enjoy wildlife.

CONNECTIONS

Track the animals' activities over time. Each day, at roughly the same time, take notes about what the animals are doing. Ask the children if they detect any patterns in behavior.

Encourage the children to write or tell a story from the animal's point of view.

Ask children what other questions they have about these animals, and invite them to research the answer together or independently.

Animal Friends

AGES 3+

Connecting with animals is important for all children; it is something they are naturally inclined to do. Children are curious about animals and fascinated by them. This experience lets them learn about animals in many creative ways and share their enthusiasm for the animals with their class. This activity can easily be done outside.

Activity Goals

→ To experience a fun and playful way to learn about animals

→ To have ideas for connecting with animals

National Science Education Standards

Science as inquiry: abilities necessary to do scientific inquiry, understandings about scientific inquiry

Life science: characteristics of organisms, life cycles of organisms, organisms and environments

History and nature of science: science as a human endeavor

Materials and Supplies

☐ Photographs of a variety of animals—from books or magazines—that are native to your area

☐ Books about the animals' habitats, food sources, and behavior

☐ Age-appropriate storybooks about those animals, if possible

☐ Access to the Internet, if possible

Procedure

1. Provide the children with photographs of the animals and allow time for them to look at and compare the photographs.

2. Talk about how the animals are alike and different. Elicit from the children what they know about those animals and any questions they have.

3. Lead a class discussion about the animals. Ask the children how they can find out more about them. Use the Internet, school library, storybooks, and tales from the children.

4. Choose from below a connection idea to implement with the group, or be creative and think up your own fun extension.

TIPS

• Learn which animals are *native*, or naturally make their homes in your area, region, and country. Include mammals, amphibians, birds, insects, and reptiles. You can use field guides or contact your local Department of Natural Resources (DNR) to learn more.

• Take a field trip to a local university, extension agency, or nature center. They often have collections of animal artifacts—such as pelts (furs), bones, and skulls, as well as track-making kits—and provide these collections as resources to educators at no or low cost.

CONNECTIONS

Invite each child to choose a favorite animal and draw a picture of the animal and its natural habitat or sculpt the animal out of clay or playdough, or have them draw the animal on a large piece of cardboard and paint it. Another idea is to create costumes and allow the children to dress up as an animal or use the large cardboard animals as puppets and have a parade.

Research the tracks that the animals make or other signs of their presence, such as chewed tree stumps, nests, feathers, or scat (animal droppings). There are numerous easy-to-use books on animal tracks and signs.

Invite children to develop a project of their own design about an animal. For example, they could paint or sculpt a habitat.

Have the children write stories or make up plays depicting the life of an animal.

Barefoot Explorations

Walking around outside without shoes is a special treat. In this activity, children are invited to explore different outdoor surfaces simply by walking around and noticing the texture and terrain beneath their feet.

Activity Goals

→ To playfully explore nature—barefoot!

National Science Education Standards

Earth and space science: properties of earth materials

Materials and Supplies

None

Procedure

1. While outside, invite the children to walk barefoot and notice different surfaces with their feet.

2. Ask the children what the ground feels like or if it feels bumpy or smooth.

3. Compare different areas in the schoolyard, such as the lawn, the sandbox, and the sidewalk.

TIPS

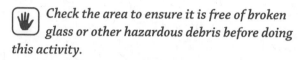 *Check the area to ensure it is free of broken glass or other hazardous debris before doing this activity.*

- Try going barefoot after a rainfall or through fallen leaves in autumn.

CONNECTIONS

Have children step in mud and make a picture or mural with muddy footprints. Alternately, have children step into a dishpan of water and leave watery footprints behind.

Gratitude

In this fast-paced world, children often don't have time to sit down and reflect on or talk about what they're grateful for. This activity offers them a chance to reflect on their favorite things about nature.

Activity Goals

 To reflect on feelings of gratitude for the natural world

National Science Education Standards

Life science: characteristics of organisms, organisms and environments

Earth and space science: properties of earth materials

Materials and Supplies

☐ A safe outdoor space

Procedure

1. While outside, invite the children to spend time on their own, directing their own play and exploration.

2. After the group has had some time to do that, gather together in a circle.

3. Allow time for everyone to share their favorite thing about nature and why they like it.

TIPS

- If not everyone wants to share, don't force the issue. Children will be thinking about their feelings during this activity whether they share or not.

- Ask the children to focus on one specific element of nature, such as a prominent tree or a nearby pond you frequently visit.

- Repeat this activity often.

CONNECTIONS

 Have the children paint or draw something they are grateful for.

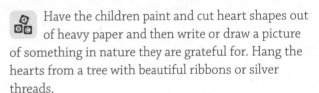 Use lengths of string and objects you've collected from nature to hang the objects to create a "gratitude tree."

Have the children paint and cut heart shapes out of heavy paper and then write or draw a picture of something in nature they are grateful for. Hang the hearts from a tree with beautiful ribbons or silver threads.

CHAPTER 3

The Three Rs:
Reduce, Reuse, Recycle

In the developed world, we enjoy many luxuries, one of which is easy access to products of all kinds, at all times. So many products—from electronics, to clothing, to sports equipment, to books, to household goods, and more—are created to make our lives easier and more fun. And they are abundantly available to anyone with the means to purchase them. In addition, we are inundated with advertising messages about the "need" to purchase more and more goods to enrich our lives. We are told in ways both subtle and obvious that buying "new and improved" products, the latest and greatest version of things, will make our lives better. Children in particular are huge targets for advertisers, who entice them into wanting and demanding new things all the time. The end result of all of this product availability and enticement is that many of us are swimming in stuff.

It's easy to go about our days and not think about the flow of goods in and out of our lives, much less the impact of those goods on the planet's health. But the truth is the impact can be substantial. Virtually everything we buy was produced or transformed somewhere, somehow, and out of some raw material. Regardless of the product, the production process requires energy—energy to obtain raw materials, energy to power the manufacturing machines that transform raw materials into something new, energy to transform more raw materials into packaging, energy to transport products to market, and so on.

Consider a very common item found in many early childhood settings: plastic building blocks. The plastic in those blocks is made from petroleum that was extracted from the Earth. The factory likely used energy derived from fossil fuels and other resources to manufacture the blocks. Once produced, the blocks were packaged in containers made from cardboard or from more plastic. Then the packages were shipped via fossil-fuel burning planes, ships, or trucks, or a combination of those. And that's just the front end of the product's "life cycle," before it gets into our hands.

All That Trash

Then there's the issue of the trash that results from our consumption of stuff. The vast majority of goods come wrapped in packaging, and once purchased, the packaging is generally discarded. About 30 percent of waste (what we throw away or recycle) in the United States is packaging: wrappers, boxes, bags, and plastic coverings (US EPA 2009). During the holiday season, this number increases.

Unfortunately, many of the actual goods we buy also become trash. Recall those plastic building blocks; if they break or wear out, they will undoubtedly be thrown away. Much of the stuff we buy these days is not intended—or simply is not suitable—for long-term use. A variety of factors, including the efficiency of large-scale manufacturing practices and the inexpensive cost of certain manufacturing materials, make it easy for companies to produce huge quantities of cheap goods that are not intended to last. Cheap goods mean more waste. If an electronic toy can be manufactured cheaply, then it is usually easier for us to throw it away and buy a replacement rather than repair it. Most trash is carried away from our homes, schools, and workplaces by a waste hauler, a process that also requires fossil fuels.

TRASH IN LANDFILLS

Much of our household waste is taken to *landfills*, huge areas where trash literally piles up. While some materials in landfills do break down over time, many do not. Some materials, such as the plastic in those building blocks, may break down into smaller bits but do not decompose easily or quickly. That plastic will take up space in the landfill for a very long time. How long? Some scientists say hundreds of years or longer, but no one really knows for certain because plastics have only been in use since the middle of the last century. Even normally decomposable materials such as newspapers might take an extremely long time to decompose in landfills because they wind up compacted under many layers of trash where sunlight, water, and oxygen—the essential ingredients of decomposition—cannot easily reach them. Most landfills have heavy-duty membranes underneath the waste that are necessary to contain waste and prevent chemical *leaching* or soil contamination.

Landfills pose other environmental challenges. In rare cases, the membranes may leak or break, allowing *contaminants* into the soil below. Chemicals or heavy metals may leach into the groundwater, contaminating the water supply in neighboring towns or cities. Landfills also generate air pollution. In particular they generate *methane*, one of the most potent

of the gases—called greenhouse gases—linked to global warming. According to the United States Environmental Protection Agency (US EPA) landfills are presently the third-largest human-made source of methane in the United States (US EPA 2011d).

Chapter 7 contains more information about methane and other greenhouse gases; however, it pays to consider the impact those piles of trash have on our air quality.

Once full, a landfill has to be expanded or a new one must be created. Landfills cost money to build and maintain, and they occupy space that can be very valuable. While some parts of the world still have space for new landfills, other places, especially heavily populated areas like the East Coast of the United States, are hard-pressed to find new landfill space. Some states actually pay to ship their trash to other states to avoid creation of additional landfills.

TRASH TO INCINERATORS

Incinerators are another destination for our trash. These burn trash, which generates both gaseous *emissions* (something given off into the air) and tiny solid particles of *pollutants* (materials that cause pollution) that are carried in the air. Depending on what is burned, the emissions can contain such pollutants as mercury and carbon monoxide, both hazardous to human health and the environment. Waste incineration can also generate carbon dioxide, another major greenhouse gas that I discuss more in chapter 7 (Environment Canada 2010).

TRASH AS LITTER

Many of our cast-off scraps also wind up as litter scattered throughout our environment. We see litter along the roads, in our city streets, in parks, on beaches, everywhere. Would you believe there are concentrated areas of litter in the Pacific Ocean? These areas are known as *garbage patches*, and they are made up of hundreds of thousands of tiny pieces of trash. The litter in it comes from many sources: some litter has been discarded from oceangoing vessels, some has washed out to sea from beaches, some has even come from far inland and traveled down rivers into the ocean. Currents and winds cause the trash to cluster together in these areas. When exposed to weather and sunlight, many plastics break down into small pieces, but they don't decompose. Most of the scraps in the garbage patches are tiny bits of plastic, so small they would be extremely difficult to remove from the ocean even if someone were making a concerted effort to do so (NOAA 2011b).

Many children are naturally deeply concerned when they see litter. And they are experts at spotting it! A simple walk down the street can turn up dozens, if not more, carelessly discarded scraps. Some children point them out sadly and demand that you pick up the trash. They have heard that litter can harm wildlife and nature. Even the youngest children know that litter doesn't belong in the environment, in their classrooms, or in other spaces. It can be upsetting and difficult for children to try to make sense of why anyone would litter. This is also a hard question for adults to answer. Engaging children in a community cleanup, in a school beautification project, and in thoughtful discussions about choices and responsibility will help alleviate their concerns. Discussing the harm that litter can cause to wildlife and nature can be counterproductive. Why? Burdening children with sad stories of animals who suffer as a result of someone's carelessly thrown trash can spark fear and anxiety in them. Instead be matter-of-fact, agree with the children that it doesn't belong, and pick it up for later disposal. A comment as simple as "Oh, that doesn't belong there!" while you carefully put the litter into a reusable bag (that you've packed just for this purpose!) normalizes the act of removing the litter without making a big deal out of it.

All this discussion of stuff, waste, and litter can be eye opening and somewhat depressing. On the upside, many people—including many early childhood educators—are becoming aware that it is possible to take positive, small, and often easy steps toward taking better care of the Earth. Simply becoming more aware of our participation in this cycle of buying and throwing away *stuff* can be a great start.

Environmental Footprint

The term *environmental footprint* refers to the amount of natural resources required to support an individual's buying, living, and waste habits. An environmental footprint includes all dimensions of one's lifestyle: from the land used to grow the food one eats, to the energy used to produce, transport, and sell the products one consumes, to the energy needed to haul away and store, burn, or transform one's waste. (You may have also heard the similar term *carbon footprint*, which refers *specifically to the amount of carbon emissions* produced by one's consumption and lifestyle habits—this is discussed in chapter 7.) More people are becoming increasingly aware of their individual environmental footprints and are looking for opportunities to lessen their impact. Every step that we take as individuals to reduce our own environmental footprint is important. Small steps also help on a bigger scale. What could be more important than that? According to the nonprofit Global Footprint Network, our world population now uses "the equivalent of 1.5 planets to provide the resources we use and absorb our waste. This means it now takes the Earth one year and six months to regenerate [the resources] we use in a year." Moreover, "Moderate UN [United Nations] scenarios suggest that if current population and consumption trends continue, by the 2030s, we will need the equivalent of two Earths to support us" (Global Footprint Network 2011).

By now the phrase "reduce, reuse, recycle" has become commonplace, and most people are familiar with the steps recommended for the care of the Earth. It can be helpful to think carefully about each one of these steps, as each has its own unique importance and its own significance in the early childhood classroom.

REDUCE: SHRINKING YOUR ENVIRONMENTAL FOOTPRINT

"Reduce" in this context means reducing both the amount of natural resources and stuff we consume and the amount of stuff that we throw away. Reducing is one of the most important steps we can take on behalf of our planet and one of the simplest. Reducing has another huge benefit—it can save us money.

Reducing starts with buying less stuff. As simple as it sounds, this step can really challenge many of us. If we are to adopt new habits around buying, we must first consider whether we really need something before we buy it. We are all susceptible to confusing our *needs* with our *wants*. In the developed world, these words are often used interchangeably, but in fact, there is a big difference. If we truly have a need, we should first try to purchase a used item. This practice helps cut down on manufacturing and on landfill accumulation. It is also a great practice to choose the highest quality product that we can afford when buying something new. This might seem counterintuitive, but considering the relatively short life span of products made cheaply to sell cheaply, it makes financial sense to purchase products built to last, rather than replacing items over and over again.

Children are especially vulnerable to feelings of wanting many things. They are a target market for advertisers, and many children's events—such as birthday celebrations—may involve a large amount of goods and presents. This tide of goods can actually obscure the deeper meaning of celebrations. The feelings brought on by so many presents and goods, though exciting, can also be overwhelming. It's hard to sort out these feelings, but we can help children understand them. Talk with children about needs versus wants. Help them understand that they don't "have to have" everything they want. It can be helpful to point out advertisements that you see and explain that an advertisement is designed to make you want something. Elicit their opinions about why certain toys are so popular. When you find the children (or yourself) feeling like you "just can't live without" a particular product, ask yourself if the purchase can wait a few days. Maybe there is a substitute you already have or could make. That sense of urgent "need" for a new toy or product will often fade if given a few days. Modeling the behaviors of reusing and reducing our own consumption will help too. The truth is that having fewer items often leads children to treasure and care for those things they do have, whereas having a huge sea of things can lead them to be more

careless and neglectful of what they have. As child development researcher and author David Elkind observes, "To be sure, many children still become attached to their toys and build a fantasy life around them. But it is much more difficult for children to do so when they are receiving new playthings all year long" (Elkind 2005, 11).

There are many opportunities to reduce. As I discuss in the next section, thinking creatively and intentionally about *reuse*, especially in terms of supplies, toys, and activities, is a fantastic way to *reduce* what we need or want to buy for our programs. We can also reduce the amount of fossil fuels we consume by keeping thermostats just a bit lower in winter and wearing a sweater or opening the curtains to warm the room with natural sunlight. Keep the thermostat a bit higher in the summer and open windows (if possible) to let breezes and circulating air naturally cool the rooms in your home or center.

One of the best opportunities for reducing waste comes through altering practices around snacks and lunches. It's true! Although it may seem as if a simple snack doesn't generate much garbage, over the course of a school year, the average elementary student generates a huge amount of food-related waste, including packaging and uneaten food scraps. It's estimated that the average public elementary school in Minnesota generates about 195,000 pounds of waste per *day* (Cioci and Farnan 2010). This number may be even higher in an early childhood setting, since children have snacks more frequently and, due to health, safety, and logistical issues, snacks are often prepackaged single servings, or are served in disposable cups or containers.

Unfortunately those single-serving snacks, while convenient and popular, generate a huge amount of waste relative to their food content. They are also hard on the budget. Consider the amount of actual food and packaging in twelve single-serving packs of graham crackers (two crackers per pack). Then compare that with the amounts of food and packaging that come in a full-size box of graham crackers. Now think about the cost comparison. The fact is that when you buy single-serving foods you're paying for the convenience, but you're also paying for all that packaging. To put it another way, you're paying for a lot of trash. Although slightly less convenient, buying food in bulk reduces waste and saves a lot of money over the long haul.

REUSE: GETTING CREATIVE

"Reuse" is the act of using a product again for the same or for a different purpose. It's a great way to *reduce* the amount of stuff you need to purchase. It is also a form of recycling, even better than a community-sponsored recycling program, because there are no rules or regulations to follow and it takes no energy or money.

Chances are you're already well versed in the art of reuse. Most educators know very well that there are many creative ways to reuse items, and they do it every day, in many ways. Such things as magazines, scrap paper, paper towel tubes, and grocery bags have so many uses in the early childhood classroom. Egg cartons, cardboard, construction paper, gift wrap, plastic food containers, fabric scraps, and many other things may already be finding new life in your program. Even using newspapers for painting projects is a great example of reuse. Take a look around your program and see how many things you use that were once something else. For everything you see, you deserve a pat on the back!

Why is it important to reuse items? First and foremost it will reduce the amount of stuff you throw away. Another reason is that it saves money and stretches your budget. Not needing to buy a new supply of paint mixing cups or paper every season can really make a difference in a small program's budget. Depending on your circumstances, you may choose to reuse a few things or many things. Depending on how you choose to reuse, you can save your program hundreds, possibly even thousands, of dollars on materials and supplies.

Of course, another important reason to reuse items is the message that it sends to children. When we flip over a piece of paper to write on the other side before recycling it, we convey the message that we recognize there is still value in that paper. When we reuse found objects—or doodads—we're teaching children

to think creatively. When we reuse materials such as magazines or old calendars, we're showing children that even though we're finished reading or using these materials, they still have plenty to offer. Reusing materials teaches children to be careful and thoughtful in how they use items. When they see adults using classroom materials with care and creatively reusing items, they will be inspired to do the same.

Of course, there are plenty of opportunities to practice reuse in your own life too! Consider investing in a reusable water bottle, coffee cup, and shopping bags. Doing so will make a positive impact on the environment, and you'll feel great about "walking the talk" when your coworkers and the families with whom you work notice your efforts!

The activities and art ideas in this chapter will help you create materials from everyday items that might otherwise be thrown away. Since most early care and education providers are already well versed in the art of reuse, it's not hard to view your "throw-away items" with an eye toward reuse. And at the end of chapter 9, you'll find ideas for reusing items in the administration and operation of your program and some suggestions for encouraging families to practice the art of reuse at home.

RECYCLE: MAKING THE EFFORT

To recycle is to turn materials otherwise destined for the trash into new products or materials. In other words, recycling helps lessen the amount of material going into landfills and incinerators. In the United States, there are highly successful recycling programs for many materials, including tires, yard waste, and steel. Probably the most well known, due to the proliferation of residential curbside collection programs, are the programs to recycle common household waste: paper (including newspaper), cardboard, aluminum, and glass.

By so many measures, recycling is a great action for our planet and our society. Most people intuitively recognize that creating something new from something old makes good sense, but recycling has many specific environmental benefits. In addition to reducing the waste flow to landfills and incinerators, making products from recycled materials results in less air and water pollution than making the same products from new, or "virgin," materials (US EPA 2011f). Making products from recycled materials obviously requires far less extraction of *new* natural resources. For example, manufacturing recycled paper means fewer trees harvested. Since trees absorb carbon dioxide and also have a cooling effect, leaving more of them standing is good for our planet's health. Forested areas also provide important habitats for wildlife and protect wetlands and other water resources. Recycling saves water too. Another example from the paper industry, recycling one ton of paper saves seven thousand gallons of water in comparison to producing the equivalent amount of paper from virgin materials (US EPA 2011e).

Making products from recycled materials generally uses less fossil fuels, and this can make a difference in slowing global climate change. In chapter 7, I discuss in much more depth the connection between fossil fuel usage and global warming. For this context, I will simply give some examples. For instance, recycling one ton of aluminum cans conserves the equivalent of thirty-six barrels of oil or 1,655 gallons of gasoline (US EPA 2008b). Recycling one ton of paper saves enough energy to run a typical home in the United States for six months (US EPA 2011e). The US EPA has stated that the combined total of all forms of waste recycled and reused in 2009 (in comparison to estimates of the equivalent amount of products produced from virgin materials) resulted in a reduction in greenhouse gas emissions that is comparable to removing the emissions from nearly 33 million passenger vehicles (US EPA 2010a). Importantly, recycling teaches children that we value the Earth and the materials we get from its resources. It teaches children that we are mindful of what we use and careful about how we use and dispose of things.

A substantial variety of products are made from recycled materials. Recycled paper is readily available in most areas and often cannot be distinguished from paper made out of virgin materials. Glass jars may be recycled into new glass containers and aluminum cans can become new cans. In addition, recycled materials can be turned into some pretty fun things!

For example, did you know that plastic bottles can be turned into weather-resistant materials for decks, outdoor furniture, and even toys? They may also be turned into soft fleece for jackets and blankets or fibers for carpeting

Despite widespread familiarity with recycling, recycling rules can vary from place to place, even in some cases from neighborhood to neighborhood within a single city. Rules can also change over time as different recycling programs adapt to new markets and new pressures. It is important that you know exactly what is accepted in your recycling program and whether or how recyclables must be sorted. There are a number of ways to get this information. Start by checking with your custodial staff, if you have one. Many municipalities have recycling hotlines, publish flyers, or maintain websites with the specific details. If necessary, make a phone call to your waste hauler to get the specifics. In some cases, plastics that are not accepted by your hauler may be accepted for recycling at other locations, such as grocery stores or hardware stores. Ask around your local community and you may find that you can recycle items from your program by bringing them to a collection station.

Making Recycling Work for You

If you're using this book as a companion to the *Go Green Rating Scale* by Phil Boise, you've probably already begun to consider your program's waste and recycling practices. Perhaps you're just beginning to evaluate your program, or maybe you're looking to expand what you're already doing. Regardless, keep in mind that the easier you make it the more successful your recycling efforts will be. Work with your coworkers to ensure that there are clearly labeled recycling bins in convenient locations throughout your facility. If sorting of recyclables is required in your area, be as specific as you can in your labels; for example, "glass," "plastics #1 and #2," and "office paper." Explicit labels can help educate guests about what can be recycled. Do you need more bins? Contact your waste hauler. Often if there is a curbside collection program at your site, your hauler will provide bins at

MAKING SENSE OF SYMBOLS

Many recognize this as the universal recycling symbol. Because this symbol is not patented or owned by any one corporation or entity, its use is not regulated. Unfortunately, that can sometimes lead to confusion. In some cases this symbol indicates that a product contains or is made of recycled materials. In some cases it indicates that a product can be recycled after use. In the case of plastics, it typically surrounds the number code indicating the type of plastic resin material used for that container. It does *not* automatically mean that type of plastic is accepted by the local recycling contractor.

no cost upon request. In other cases, you may need to allocate some funds to purchase them—or reuse large cardboard boxes or paper bags. For fun ideas on creating and decorating bins, see the Create a Recycling Station activity on page 61.

If your program has custodial staff, be sure to engage them in your recycling efforts. The value of support from your custodial or operations staff cannot be understated. Be sure to communicate your plan and desire to improve recycling at your site, and enlist their help. Be enthusiastic and positive. Make sure you are willing to share the responsibility of obtaining bins and educating staff. If you need to help empty the recycling bins, do so. It will send a strong message that you are committed and willing to pitch in. Finally, be prepared to revisit your system after a time and evaluate how it's working. Are staff members recycling in the classrooms? Do you see recyclable items being discarded in the trash, despite your best efforts? Ask your staff for feedback. What do they see that is working? Where could improvements be made? Jot down some notes, and be sure to revisit them a few months after you implement these suggested changes.

Remember that many things beyond those accepted in curbside collection can be recycled. We can recycle our food waste by putting it into a compost pile, where it can decompose into a rich soil that is good for gardens. You'll find a lot more about composting in chapter 5. In addition, though you may have to look for them, specific collection programs exist for everyday items such as corks, yogurt containers, juice packs, electronics, cell phones, toothbrushes, holiday lights, and even candy wrappers and plastic bags. Examples of collection sites include grocery stores, hardware stores, sometimes even museums or zoos. For more information on finding collection sites for specific items, visit www.earth911.com and type the name of the item into the search box. Since you're reading this book, it's a good bet you have plans to engage children and families in your efforts.

Recycling can be a constructive, positive way to engage young children in caring for the environment. By making a conscious effort to recycle in your classrooms and programs, you send the message that recycling is important. You can talk about what items you are recycling and why. Remember to keep it positive. Instead of saying, "I'm recycling this because too many forests are being cut down to make paper," you might try, "I'm recycling this paper so that it can be turned into something new, like wrapping paper or stickers!" Showing children examples of products made from recycled materials can help make it more real for them. You might even consider creating a display of common household items made from recycled materials. Many parents will be surprised to learn about all the neat recycled products, and the children will love to "teach" them! People love the idea of recycling because it is tangible, is easy to do, and lets them feel like they are making a difference. And, of course, they are. Ultimately, though, keep in mind that there is a reason why recycling is the third action listed in the three Rs. As important as recycling is for the Earth, public recycling collection programs still require fossil fuel energy, so the benefit of this "R" for the Earth is less significant than reducing and reusing.

The early childhood environment is a perfect setting in which to engage children with the behaviors of reducing, reusing, and recycling. The activities included here, like the others in this book, are intended to be a jumping-off point for you, the educator. Chances are you will be inspired to come up with many other activities on your own. Have fun!

What's It Made Of?

AGES
5+

Most people don't give much thought to the variety of materials used to create everyday objects, such as tables, desks, and craft supplies. For example, many of our favorite everyday items are made of paper, wood, plastic, metal, or glass. Some of these materials, like paper, come from natural resources that must be extracted or harvested and then processed to turn them into the objects we use. Other materials, such as plastics, are generated in factories. Whether or not we know about the origins and processing of common materials, becoming more attuned to what things are made of can be a first step toward not taking the everyday materials in our lives for granted and ultimately becoming more Earth-conscious consumers. In this activity, the children will examine familiar objects and talk about what materials they are made of.

Activity Goals

→ To look at familiar objects in the classroom and consider their origins

National Science Education Standards

Physical science: properties of objects and materials

Science and technology: abilities to distinguish between natural objects and objects made by humans

Materials and Supplies

☐ Items made from paper, wood, metal, plastic, fabric, and glass—several samples of each

☐ Chart paper and markers

Procedure

1. Present the children with the items and discuss how things in your classroom are made from those materials.

2. Go on a scavenger hunt! As a group, look around the classroom and identify objects made from the different raw materials. Examine toys, books, furniture, rugs, clothing, and so forth. Some of the objects will likely be from unknown materials.

3. Create seven columns on your chart labeled "wood," "fabric," "metal," "plastic," "glass," "paper," and "unknown." Be sure to allow lots of space in each column. You may wish to use one page per material.

4. As the children explore the classroom, write the names of the objects in the categories they choose. Some items will require class discussion.

5. Gather the objects in the "unknown" category and work together to try to determine what they are made from.

6. Ask children what they think becomes of the objects in their lives when they break, are no longer wanted, or have reached the end of their useful lives. For example, clothing that is outgrown can be donated, or cut into fabric pieces for crafting or other uses.

TIPS

• Do this activity over the course of several days, choosing one area of your room to explore at a time.

CONNECTIONS

🔍 Revisit the categories with the children, and discuss which category was the biggest, which was the smallest, and possible reasons for the differences. Discuss whether the children found anything that didn't fit any category and how they might determine what the object is made from.

Create a Doodad Center

AGES
3+

Although we can recycle many things, there are some things that just aren't recyclable. Consider saving and asking families to bring in doodads—any small piece of trash that would otherwise be thrown away but that has potential for creative use later. Suggestions include loose puzzle pieces, game tokens, lids from plastic bottles and containers, and scraps of ribbon. Collect them in a large box or bin labeled "Doodad Bucket." You'll be surprised at how quickly your collection grows! When you have an ample collection, implement this activity.

Activity Goals

→ To work together to develop categories and sort and organize doodads into those categories

→ To build a supply of materials to be used in later creative work

National Science Education Standards

Physical science: properties of objects and materials

Materials and Supplies

☐ Numerous clear plastic containers for sorting (clear plastic deli containers work well)

☐ Assorted doodads

☐ Chart paper and markers

Procedure

1. Dump the doodads onto the floor or table and let the children examine them. Tell them you'd like them to identify categories and organize the doodads for use in the art center.

2. Encourage the children to use descriptive words as they think of categories. Jot down the words you hear them use. This will be a starting point for your organization. Examples of categories the children might identify are "wheels," "yellow things," "soft things," and so on. Any categories are okay as long as they make sense to you and the children!

3. When you have agreed on several categories, create name labels for the containers and sort the doodads into the containers. Remember to use them often and incorporate them into your activities!

TIPS

• Encourage the children to use doodads for a variety of purposes—as toys, game pieces, "money" or other tokens in dramatic play, or for making textures in clay, and so on. Allow the children to access the doodads whenever they want to incorporate them into their play.

• Tell families you will be using the items they bring in for collages, art projects, craft activities, and science projects. Refer to appendix D for a sample letter to parents to help you build your supply of doodads.

CONNECTIONS

🔎 Encourage the group to come up with different ways to sort and classify the doodads. You can use your supply of doodads for games involving classifying, sorting, counting, and measuring. For example, ask the children to count all the orange objects they can find, to arrange them from lightest to darkest and biggest to smallest, and to describe the different shades of orange.

🔎 Choose some doodads and make some predictions about whether they'll sink or float. Put them in the water table and discuss your observations.

🔎 Challenge children to use doodads for building. Ask them what they think they can build with doodads. Try a bridge, tower, or house. When they

(continues on next page)

stack doodads to build a structure, ask them what they notice about which sizes and shapes work best on the bottom of the stack and higher up on the stack. Have them describe how they can arrange the doodads to make something very tall. Ask about the characteristics that make some doodads better suited for building (answers will include "they are flat," "they are large," "they are wide," and so on).

Found Object Mosaic

Your doodads can be a source of artistic creativity for many projects. In this activity, your class will work together to create a beautiful mosaic.

Activity Goals

→ To explore different colors, shapes, textures, and sizes

→ To have fun using imagination to create art

→ To practice scientific-thinking skills, such as sorting, classifying, predicting, observing, and measuring

National Science Education Standards

Physical science: properties of objects and materials

Materials and Supplies

☐ Assorted doodads

☐ Large piece of plywood or sturdy cardboard

☐ Strong, nontoxic glue

☐ Markers

☐ Paint and paintbrushes, optional

Procedure

1. Choose together a theme, such as a rainbow, a picture of your school, a garden, or an animal.

2. Sketch the picture on the plywood or cardboard. Paint the background if desired.

3. Ask the children to sort the doodads into colors.

4. Before you do any gluing, arrange the pieces on the background in a way that is pleasing to the eye. Encourage the children to work together to find the right doodads for each spot.

5. The children can glue the doodads onto the mosaic using the glue.

6. Allow the mosaic to dry before mounting it on a wall.

7. Encourage the children to talk about the mural with their parents and each other. Ask what objects are their favorites and why.

TIPS

• If hard plastic objects need to be affixed to the mural with hot glue, be sure this is done by an adult.

CONNECTIONS

Introduce new words and encourage the children to use them to describe various textures and patterns found on the doodads.

Find doodads that resemble letters or numbers. See if you can create an alphabet! Make "name posters" by spelling out each child's name with doodads on cardboard.

My Recycled Journal

AGES 4+

You can help children create their own journals from materials that would otherwise be thrown away or recycled. As you create the journals together, take time to admire the variety of materials you're putting to use instead of discarding. The journals may be used by the children to write or draw pictures, or as science journals. They also make lovely handmade gifts.

Activity Goals

→ To have a fun, creative way of using products that would otherwise be discarded

National Science Education Standards

History and nature of science: science as a human endeavor (when journals are used for science journals)

Materials and Supplies

☐ Thin cardboard, such as from food boxes, cut into six-by-five-inch rectangles, with holes punched along one side

☐ Scraps of fabric, wrapping paper, construction paper, magazine pictures, and other materials for decorating the cover

☐ Art supplies, such as paint and glitter

☐ Glue

☐ Yarn, cut into five-inch pieces, one piece per journal

☐ Hole punch

☐ Used paper—such as construction paper, office paper, or used coloring pages—that is blank on one side, folded in half, and glued to make approximately an eight-by-five-inch rectangle with the used side on the inside

Procedure

1. Let each child choose two pieces of cardboard for a journal. Share that they will be decorating the side that does not have printing or images.

2. Invite the children to select the materials they wish to use for decorating their journal covers. Be sure each child writes his or her name on the journal cover.

3. Allow the children ample time to decorate the journal covers, using glue, paper, and the other materials you've provided. Encourage creative freedom. You may ask them to work within a certain theme. For example, if you plan to use the journals for a nature study, the children may choose to depict nature scenes or use images of nature.

4. Once the covers and backs are dry, add the folded insert pages and hole punch two holes along the "spine" of the book. Bind the journals by threading the yarn through the holes a few times and tying a knot. Be sure to tie it loosely enough so the journal will still open yet tightly enough so it will be easy to use.

5. Place the journals where children can easily access them for use when desired.

TIPS

• Have the children paint the printed side of the cardboard with tempera paint before assembling their journals.

• Collect decorating items ahead of time by saving paper scraps and old magazines. Cutting paper and magazine pictures is great fun for young preschoolers. Set up a "cutting station" in your classroom ahead of time to begin your collection of pictures and paper scraps. Children can spend time in the cutting station when they're ready for a quiet activity on their own.

• Treat the journals with care, which teaches children to respect their work and the materials they've used.

CONNECTIONS

If children are using the journals as science journals, have them make notes on the weather or jot down observations based on experiments you're conducting in class.

 Encourage children to cut letters and words from the paper scraps or to find letters and words in magazines. They can spell their names or spell out the title of their journals using these paper scraps.

Invite the children to use the journals as sketch pads or painting pads.

Recycled Puzzles

AGES
4+

There are so many crafts that can be done with recyclable materials. Here is a way children can make a simple puzzle of their own design from a cereal or cracker box.

Activity Goals

→ To create a puzzle of one's own design

→ To create a new product out of something that would otherwise be discarded

National Science Education Standards

Physical science: properties of objects and materials

Materials and Supplies

☐ A good supply of clean, lightweight cardboard boxes, such as cereal or cracker boxes

☐ Office paper or construction paper that is used on one side

☐ Glue sticks

☐ Crayons or markers

☐ Children's scissors

Procedure

1. Provide each child with a piece of cardboard that is roughly the same size as the paper he will be using.

2. Instruct the children to glue the paper, blank side up, onto the cardboard.

3. When the glue is dry (see Tips), invite the children to draw a picture on the paper using markers or crayons. The picture might have a theme ("My favorite thing in nature," for example).

4. After the children complete their pictures, instruct them to cut their picture into several pieces of random shape and size to make a puzzle. Younger children can cut theirs into strips or squares instead (provide help cutting as needed so children do not become discouraged).

5. Give the children a few minutes to work on their puzzles, then encourage them to temporarily trade puzzles with another child.

TIPS

• Avoid cardboard that is used for refrigerated or frozen food products. These types of cardboard are often coated with waterproofing wax, and it is difficult to get some glues to adhere on the printed side. Use cracker or cereal boxes instead.

• Allow adequate time for the glue to dry. Trying to color a picture on a soggy piece of paper while the glue is wet is frustrating! Do the gluing in the morning and finish the activity in the afternoon, or complete the activity over a couple of days. Alternately, the children can color the picture before adhering it to the cardboard (you still have to wait for the glue to dry before cutting the puzzle pieces).

CONNECTIONS

Encourage the children to make the subject of their pictures something you have been studying about, such as weather, seasons, fruits, or gardens. Invite them to describe their drawings to you and tell why they chose those particular objects.

Instead of drawing pictures on the puzzles, spell each child's name in large letters and have them decorate the images. Invite older children to write new words.

Recyclable Gift Wrap

AGES
3+

Most commercially available wrapping paper is made from virgin materials (Urban Mining 2011). Also, it is typically not recyclable because it is often laminated, may contain additives such as glitter or plastic, may be very thin, may not have the good quality fibers important for recycling, or it has tape attached to it, which makes it difficult to recycle. This means that during the holiday season a lot more waste is added to our environment. In the United States, an extra one million tons of waste is generated during the time between Thanksgiving and New Year's. We throw away about thirty-eight thousand miles of ribbon every year—that's "enough to tie a bow around the Earth" (CalRecycle 2010)! Although more and more companies are responding to consumer demands for recycled and recyclable wrapping paper, it still can be difficult to come by.

Children love painting and creating art. In this activity, they'll paint and decorate large pieces of newsprint and other materials, creating beautiful homemade gift wrap. What makes this gift wrap so special, in addition to its being beautiful and handmade, is that it is recyclable.

Activity Goals

To experience creative, artistic expression while creating something useful and beautiful

National Science Education Standards

Physical science: properties of objects and materials

Earth and space science: properties of earth materials (if painting with natural materials)

Science in personal and social perspectives: types of resources

Materials and Supplies

☐ Large pieces of newspaper—one piece per child

☐ Tempera paint and brushes

☐ Fabric scraps and used ribbons

☐ Glue

☐ Natural materials, if desired (see Tips)

Procedure

1. Invite the children to paint and decorate their pieces of newspaper.

2. After the paintings and glue have dried, send them home with the children to use as gift wrap.

TIPS

- Move the painting time outside for a special treat.

- Use the classifieds section of the newspaper. It has fewer photos.

- If you want to use blank paper, request donations of used plain newsprint paper from a moving supply or packing store.

- Invite the children to tear or cut fabric into thin strips to create beautiful ribbons for use in gift wrapping.

- Use cardboard boxes of various shapes and sizes. With paint and decoration they are instant gift boxes!

CONNECTIONS

 Consider the lovely effects leaves, thin twigs, cattails, long grasses, pine needles, and even stones can have on paper. This is a great opportunity to use natural materials for painting.

Encourage the children to experiment with repeating patterns or making large designs.

The Packaging Problem

Food packaging serves several purposes. It protects food, keeps it fresh, and also provides information about the product inside. However, food packaging is also one of the biggest sources of everyday waste. Many of our convenience foods are individually wrapped and packaged, and most of this packaging is not recyclable. In this activity, you will examine some common food packages and determine as a group whether they can be reused or recycled, or if there is any way to reduce the packaging.

Activity Goals

→ To become more aware of food packaging as a source of waste

→ To think creatively about reusing objects

National Science Education Standards

Science and technology: abilities of technological design

History and nature of science: science as a human endeavor

Materials and Supplies

☐ Clean, empty food packaging, such as juice boxes and pouches, prepared meal boxes, and single serving snack containers—at least one per child

Procedure

1. Place all the clean food packages on a table or in the center of a circle.

2. Ask the children why they think packaging is important for food.

3. Invite the children to each choose a package and describe it. Ask questions such as, "What is it made of?" "Why is that kind of package used for that kind of food?" "What can we learn about what's inside by looking at the package?"

4. Ask the children if they think their package is recyclable or if it can be used for something else.

TIPS

• Collect items for a week or so before leading this activity.

• Save packaging materials from a fast food children's meal and examine these items with the children.

• Use this activity to kick off a "no-waste" lunch (or snack) effort at your program.

CONNECTIONS

Help students compile comparative amounts of packaging for the single serving snacks and the bulk quantity of the same food. If a standard kitchen scale is available, have them weigh the packaging for each type of product. Invite children to make a poster or display depicting the comparison of packaging along with actual quantities of food contained in each. To develop math skills, have them compare the cost of each.

Create a Recycling Station

Recycling bins need to be easy to find and easy to use. Otherwise, people won't recycle! But recycling bins don't need to be fancy or expensive. Engage the children in creating a recycling station for your classroom. The children can use pictures cut from old magazines—as well as crayons, markers, and their own creativity—to show the items that are collected for recycling at your site. If sorting of recyclable materials is required at your site, children can decorate individual boxes, one for each category of material. If sorting is not required, children can show all the recyclable materials on a single box.

Choose an area of your classroom where you can place the recycling station, and keep it there consistently. Knowing exactly where to find the bins will help everyone get into the habit of recycling as much as possible. The children will be proud of their creation and happy to use it.

Activity Goals

→ To create a recycling station for the classroom that will help raise awareness about recycling and inspire participation in recycling

→ To understand what materials may and may not be recycled in the classroom

National Science Education Standards

Physical science: properties of objects and materials

Science in personal and social perspectives: types of resources

Materials and Supplies

☐ Cardboard boxes

☐ Old magazines and newspapers

☐ Children's scissors

☐ Glue sticks

Procedure

1. Engage the children in a discussion about what recycling is. For example, discuss how we recycle to make new products out of certain things.

2. Mention your desire to have a nice, beautiful space where children and adults can recycle. State that instead of buying new bins, you'd like to create a recycling station from boxes and art materials you already have on hand.

3. Discuss with the children what items can be recycled and decide what "theme" each bin will have. For example, "Paper," "Glass and Cans," and "Plastics" are common recyclable materials.

4. Distribute magazines and children's scissors. Invite the children to page through the magazines in search of images that relate to their theme.

5. Allow the children plenty of time to search for photographs. Note: Some children will finish this step quickly, but others will want to spend lots of time on it. Allow for different preferences.

6. When children are finished cutting out photographs, encourage them to affix the pictures to the bins with glue sticks.

TIPS

• Scout the magazines ahead of time and tear out pages that contain images of recyclable materials. Provide the pages for cutting to children who find looking through magazines in search of photographs distracting or difficult.

• Divide the children into groups and have one group work on paper, for example, while another works on plastics. The children can collaborate,

(continues on next page)

sharing pictures from the magazines. This also gives the children a narrower focus when looking for photographs.

- If possible, make sure the boxes you start with are the same size. This will ensure a feeling of equity among the children participating.

- If the boxes are printed with labels or ads, paint the cardboard with tempera paint ahead of time so there is a solid background, or cut brown paper bags and use them to cover the outside of the boxes. Use packaging tape to secure the paper onto the boxes.

- Bring in a few examples of what the recyclable materials are, and discuss them with the children. This will help them as they look for images of these materials in the magazines.

- Knowing which materials, as well as which numbers of plastics are recyclable at your site (for example, if you are limited to collecting plastics number 1 and 2), will be helpful for this activity. Children can identify the numbers and label the boxes accordingly. They can also find images of a few recognizable forms of those numbers, such as on plastic water bottles or plastic milk jugs.

CONNECTIONS

 Invite children to sketch or paint images instead of cutting them out.

The Great Recycle Hunt

To successfully communicate the value of recycling, you must have a consistent approach that is easy and fun. Engage the children in finding recycling bins throughout the building to ensure that recycling is as easy as possible. This might also help your coworkers remember where the recycling bins are and encourage them to recycle more!

Activity Goals

→ To have fun exploring the building

→ To see what the recycling bins in the program look like

National Science Education Standards

Unifying concepts and processes: systems, order, and organization

Materials and Supplies

☐ A digital camera, if desired

☐ Large pieces of paper

☐ A marker for each child

Procedure

1. Explain to the children that you have been wondering if there are recycling bins in each classroom for teachers and children to use, and wonder aloud how you might find out.

2. Discuss as a group the different things that are recycled at your program.

3. Invite them to suggest places where recycling bins might be found. Encourage them to consider the materials that are recycled and where those materials may be found. For example, if aluminum cans are recycled at your site, where would you likely find aluminum cans?

4. As a group, define some rules for exploring the building. Examples might be that everyone must hold hands, whisper so as not to disturb other classes, and follow the teacher at the front of the line.

5. Together, or in small groups, visit different classrooms and areas of the building and discover where the bins are located.

6. If desired, photograph the bins. Later, print the pictures and try to guess which rooms they were in.

7. Return to the classroom and make maps, together or individually, noting where the recycling bins are located.

TIPS

• If possible, present this activity as a special treat and allow the children to explore places in the building that they don't normally see, such as offices and a staff kitchen.

• Be sure that there are recycling bins located throughout the classrooms and the building.

• Know ahead of time what materials can be recycled at your site and whether or not they must be sorted.

CONNECTIONS

Ask the children to count how many rooms there are and how many bins are located in the center. Ask them if each room has a bin or how many bins you would need so that each room could have one. Invite them to experiment with how many cardboard boxes or how much paper it takes to fill one recycling bin. Discuss ways that you could get more boxes or more paper into a bin.

Make a Recycling Monster

This is another idea for involving children in creating recycling bins for your site using paper bags and discarded paper scraps. Cans, plastic bottles, and even glass can be put into recycling monsters, but if your recycling collection program requires it, be sure to sort the recycling before putting it out for collection.

Activity Goals

→ To have fun making artistic creations that promote recycling

National Science Education Standards

Science and technology: abilities of technological design

Science in personal and social perspectives: types of resources

Materials and Supplies

☐ Paper grocery bags, two per recycling monster

☐ Glue

☐ Children's scissors

☐ Bin or box of paper scraps, such as magazine pictures, construction paper scraps, and fabric scraps

☐ Art supplies, such as glitter and paints

Procedure

1. Using two paper grocery bags, cut a large oval in the bottom of one of the bags. Slide it upside down over the other bag, so the oval is on top. The oval will be the monster's mouth.

2. Decorate the bag with fabric scraps, or use crayons or paints to make the monster's eyes, teeth, hair, and so on.

3. Place the recycling monster in an area accessible to the children so they can easily place their items for recycling in it.

4. When the monster is full, pull off the decorated bag, put the recycling out for collection and replace the inner bag.

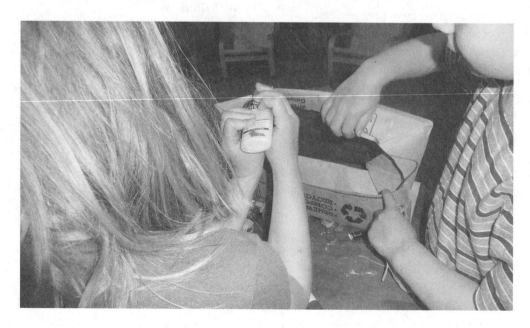

TIPS

- Encourage the children to think about how they want their recycling monster to look before they get started. Offer a few suggestions, but be sure to allow for creative freedom.

- If you have enough bags, invite each child to make a recycling monster to take home.

- Be careful! Children will be so excited to "feed" their recycling monsters that they may recycle paper before it's even been used!

- Add a pipe cleaner or other sturdy handle to make removing the top bag easier.

CONNECTIONS

Create monsters that resemble favorite characters from a book or favorite animals. Invite children to make up a "life story" for their recycling monster.

Choose a theme for the monsters, such as favorite colors or animals. Invite children to use that theme to inspire their decorations.

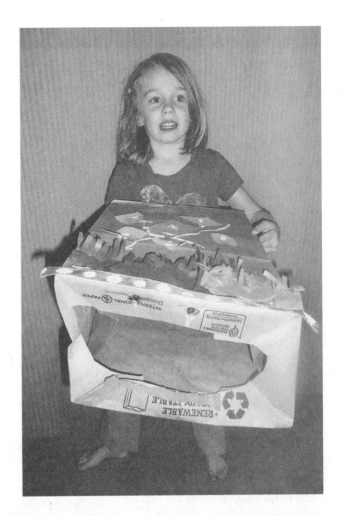

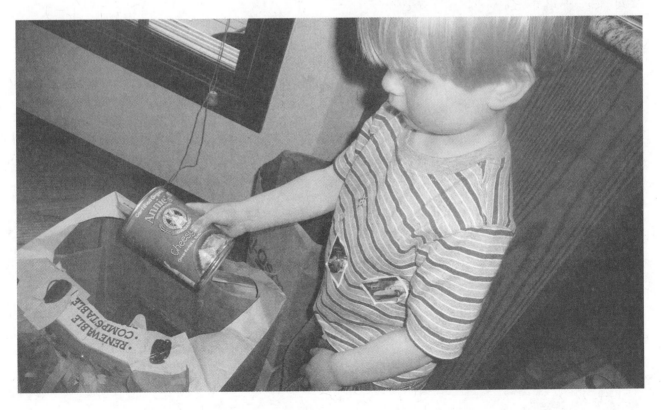

Recycle Sorting Game

This activity is designed for use in facilities that are required to sort recyclables. Involve the children in sorting recyclable materials while they have fun and develop the scientific-thinking skills of classifying and sorting.

Activity Goals

→ To create logical categories in a fun and lively way

→ To sort recyclables in the classroom

National Science Education Standards

Physical science: properties of objects and materials

Science and technology: abilities to distinguish between natural objects and objects made by humans

Materials and Supplies

☐ Assorted clean, dry items that can be recycled—at least one object per child

☐ Four large paper bags or other containers, or your recycling bins from the Create a Recycling Station activity, if you've made them

☐ Chart paper and markers

Procedure

1. Spread the recyclable items on a large rug or grassy area.

2. Ask the children what the items have in common and how they are different. Allow time for discussion. Record their observations on the chart paper.

3. Invite the children to work together to sort and organize the materials in the categories they determine. Allow adequate time for them to discuss the categories and sorting techniques.

4. Finally, invite them to deposit the objects into the bags or boxes you've brought along. Tell them that in order for the materials to be recycled they need to be sorted in a specific way.

5. Point out the labels on each recycling container and invite the children to place the objects in the appropriate container.

6. Review the children's observations and make connections.

TIPS

 Do not use items with sharp edges for this activity.

CONNECTIONS

Encourage the children to count the different ways can they can group or organize the items. Ask them what the items have in common and what is different about them.

Trash Audit

It can be surprising and eye-opening to discover how much trash is discarded at your site in any given week. Despite everyone's best intentions, many recyclable or reusable items may be thrown in the trash. This activity will let you get your hands dirty—literally!—as you go through your garbage. It can be helpful to do this activity early, as you embark on the greening of your program, because it provides baseline information about your current recycling and waste practices. Repeated again at the end of the year, it will give you good information about improvements you have made.

In this activity, you'll work with the children to actually go through the garbage generated by your program and sort it. You'll find that all of your garbage fits into one of the following categories:

Food waste includes things that can be composted, such as banana peels, apple cores, and leftover crackers or sandwich crusts. Paper napkins and used coffee filters also fit into this category, but plastic food packaging does not.

Recyclable material describes things that were inadvertently put into the trash, such as cans, bottles, plastics, and recyclable paper that could be collected at your site.

True trash is made up of things that can't be recycled, reused, or composted, such as string cheese wrappers and plastics that your site isn't capable of recycling.

Reusable is the category for things that have been thrown away too early! Construction paper scraps, plastic lids, and lost puzzle pieces are some examples. Encourage the children to think creatively about how each item could be reused.

Activity Goals

→ To examine, measure, sort, and weigh trash

→ To experience an up-close look at the program's waste management practices

National Science Education Standards

Physical science: properties of objects and materials

Science in personal and social perspectives: personal health

Materials and Supplies

☐ Gardening gloves or latex gloves, one pair for each person participating

☐ Smocks, one for each participant

☐ Large tarp

☐ Two or three bathroom scales

☐ Trash bags

☐ Chart paper and a marker

Procedure

1. Choose a location for the waste sort. Gymnasiums, parking lots, or any large open area will work well.

2. Spread a large tarp on the ground.

3. Obtain all the full trash bags you can from your site. This may require coordination with custodial staff. Ensure each trash bag is sealed before you place it on the scale.

(continues on next page)

4. Place one bag at a time on the scale and record its weight.

5. Ensure that each participant is wearing gloves and a smock.

6. Next, open each trash bag—except for those that contain human waste or bodily fluids; see safety notes—and carefully sort the items into the four categories described above.

7. Work carefully to sort the items into their appropriate piles. If there is uncertainty, discuss as a group which category the items belong in.

8. When all the bags have been emptied and items sorted, place the contents for each category into bags. You may wish to remove "reusable" items from the trash piles.

9. After the bags have been refilled, weigh them again. Record the weight for each category.

10. When you have completed this activity, discuss your findings.

TIPS

- Encourage families to provide old clothes for children to wear during this activity.

- Tell only those who need to know about the activity prior to conducting the audit. While it is tempting to share the news of this unusual experience with everyone, it will affect people's usual habits of throwing away and recycling. You want as accurate a picture as possible of waste management practices at your site. Once the audit is finished, you can tell everyone about it!

- Designate one child to record the weight of each bag. If you are working with preschool-age children, invite a few grown-ups to help weigh bags, read the scale, and write the numbers.

- To get a sense of your site's habits, do this activity on a typical day. Refrain from doing it on a day when many teachers and children may be absent or on a field trip, so very little trash will be generated, or after a large event, when excessive amounts of trash may have been generated.

- If you have custodial staff, work with them ahead of time to ensure this activity runs smoothly.

- Consider the timing: If you do this activity with your class on a Wednesday morning, for example, your program may not have generated much trash by midday. Instead, you may need to arrange for all of one day's trash to be left at the audit site.

- Ask children or adults who are squeamish about this activity to help by recording data or weighing bags.

- Prepare your data chart ahead of time. Divide the chart paper into four categories for recording data.

Do not *open bags that contain any toxic products (such as hazardous cleaning supplies, paint, and so on) or sharp objects.*

Do not *open bags or sort items that contain human waste or bodily fluids (such as soiled diapers or tissues). In most cases, those items will be contained in specific bags from the bathroom and changing room areas. Instead of opening those bags and sorting the contents, simply weigh them and record the weight.*

CONNECTIONS

Work with the children to extrapolate the number of pounds of garbage that your site produces in one week or one month. Ask children in which category the most trash belonged.

Invite children to quantify how much recyclable material is currently being thrown away and why they think this is. Ask them why it was important to keep the trash audit a secret and how the result might have been different if everyone had known about the audit. Discuss with the children how your program could reduce the amount of food waste generated, such as by composting (see appendix F), and what are some other ways to reduce waste. Have the children make graphs or pie charts representing each category of waste and the relative percentages.

What Are You Buying?

People, young and old, are subjected to a barrage of advertisements on a daily basis. We see these ads on television, in newspapers and magazines, and on billboards, posters, and even public transportation vehicles. In this activity, you'll guide the children through an examination of some advertisements for children's toys to help them identify the subtle—and often misleading—information shown in ads.

Activity Goals

→ To develop the skills of analysis and critical thinking

→ To share feelings and expectations (and disappointment) about what toys will do

National Science Education Standards

Physical science: properties of objects and materials

Science and technology: abilities of technological design, understanding about science and technology

Materials and Supplies

☐ Selection of print ads depicting children's toys

Procedure

1. Introduce the concept of advertisement—something that is designed to make you want an object or experience. Ask the children where they see advertisements.

2. Ask the children if they have ever received a toy as a present or seen one at a friend's house and found out it wasn't quite as great as they imagined or expected it would be. Part of the reason for this disappointment, which is very common, is that toys are often depicted as being better or different than they actually are. For example, on a box containing a robotic animal, the image depicts the animal as really big, but when you get the toy out of the package, it's much smaller.

3. Present the first ad, and discuss what you see. Are the images of the toy illustrations or photographs?

Do they depict or suggest the toy doing something that it can't really do? Why would a manufacturer portray this toy doing something that it can't do?

4. Are there children on the box? Are they boys or girls? Children may refer to some toys as being either for girls or boys. Explore this thinking. Why is something considered a "girl" toy or a "boy" toy? Is it really?

5. What colors are used in the packaging? Why do the children think the manufacturer chose to use these colors?

6. What other inaccuracies do the children see? Are there items on the box that are "sold separately" but they had expected to find inside?

TIPS

- If possible, bring in examples of children's toys that are depicted in the ads, so the group can compare the real thing to its appearance in an advertisement.

- With older children, consider doing this activity in small groups. With younger children, use one ad and have a group discussion.

CONNECTIONS

Have the children re-create the package with illustrations that more accurately represent the product inside.

Ask the children what they would change about the way the product is described and if the words used to describe this product are accurate or exaggerations.

Ask the children how they could make the product actually do the things that are shown on the package. Ask them if it is even possible.

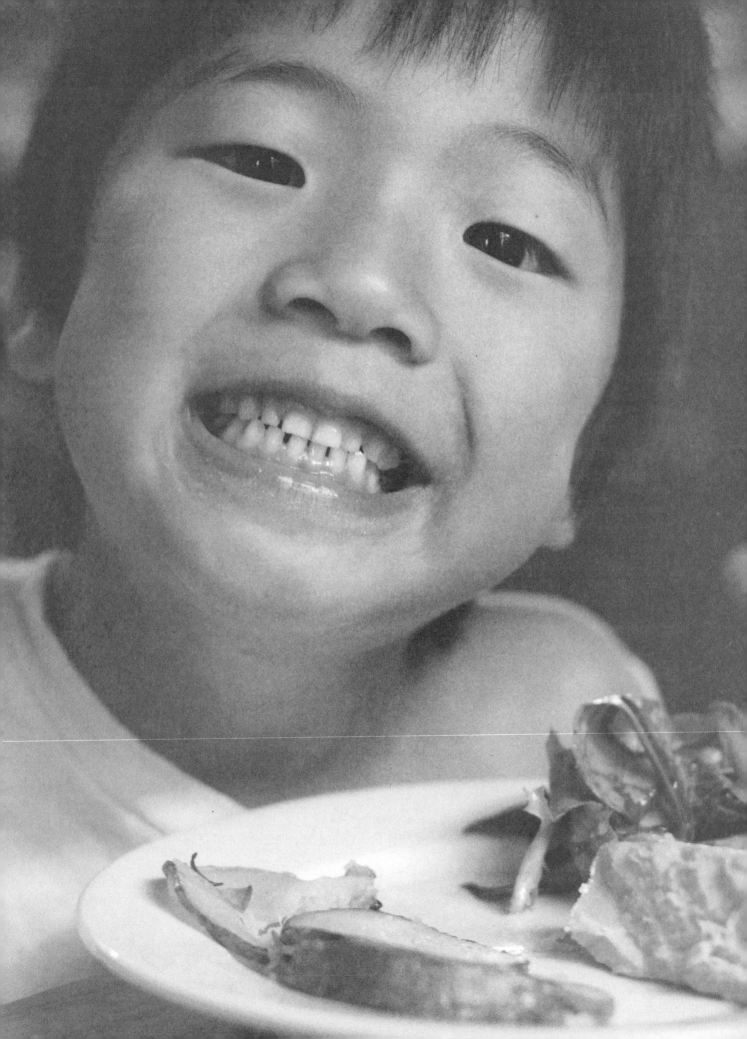

CHAPTER 4

The **Food** We Eat

Nothing brings families and communities together like food. Throughout history people have worked together to plant, harvest, and prepare food. Sharing food with others provides opportunities to forge ties and deepen relationships. Holiday celebrations and special occasions in every culture are often associated with particular foods or traditional meals. Indeed, food can be a great source of pleasure and entertainment for people.

Food is also essential for life. We need to consume a minimum number of calories each day just to keep our bodies functioning. A nutritious diet is also key to good health and wellness, whereas a poor diet is associated with health problems and diseases. For example, I'm sure you're aware of the obesity epidemic. Though genetic factors can contribute to obesity, research now clearly shows links between rising obesity rates and global food-system changes since the 1970s, specifically the rise in mass-produced, packaged foods that are high in sugar, salt, and fat. Obesity has been called the "largest preventable cause of disease burden" in many parts of the world and a "global pandemic" because of the dramatic and widespread rise in obesity in recent decades (Swinburn et al. 2011, 805). Obesity, in turn, is linked to increases in cancer, cardiovascular disease, and Type II diabetes (WHO 2011).

The incidence of food-related health challenges in children is especially concerning. Since 1980 in the United States, the rate of obesity in children has doubled (AAP 2011a)! Almost 10 percent of children between the ages of two and five are now considered obese (Ogden et al. 2010). Again, though genetic factors exist, the food-system issues described above have played a role. The occurrence of Type II diabetes in children has also been reported with increased frequency (CDC 2011b). Until recently this type of diabetes occurred primarily in adults and thus was referred to as "adult-onset diabetes." Due to increasing incidence of obesity in children, doctors have now abandoned that phrase. Obesity in childhood is also linked to many other potential problems, from bone and joint issues to high blood pressure and some cancers. Unfortunately, all these health challenges, when developed early, often continue to haunt children as they age (AAP 2011b).

Why Teach about Food?

Food is central to health and daily living, and it is enjoyable for all of us, especially children. Those characteristics make food a great topic for learning and exploration in the early childhood classroom. Learning more about food can help children—and all of us—make better choices for our own health. Learning more about food can also help us take better care of our planet. Though food may not be the first topic most people jump to when they think about "going green," the fact is that it is truly an environmental issue. From food's production, to processing, packaging, and distribution, at every stage there are environmental impacts large and small, positive and negative. Presently 37 percent of the Earth's land surface is used for agricultural production (FAO 2003). With all of that agriculture happening on the worldwide landscape, growers' decisions about how to manage their environmental impacts are extremely important. Learning more about the environmental impacts of food can help us make food choices that are good for the Earth. And the great news, as I will explain, is that often the best food choices for the Earth are also the best ones for our health, and vice versa.

So where can we start in learning more about food as an environmental issue? For me the best starting point is simply to remind you, and myself, that all food comes from plants. It's true! Even meats come from plants. Animals eat plants, converting the energy plants provide into their flesh. Stopping to reflect on this basic fact can help remind us that the act of eating gives us our most basic and most frequent connection to nature—three or possibly even more times a day for many of us.

Reflecting on food's origins as plants can help us see that agriculture—growing food—is fundamentally an environmental act. Plants grow in soil and require adequate sunlight, water, and nutrients to thrive. Food growers face multiple and constant decisions that affect the environment, including choosing what, when, and how much to plant in a given area. Growers also must manage soil, water, fertilizer, pests, waste, and energy. It is obvious that growers can impact the environment in countless ways. Just as with the overall topic of food, there are so many points of connection between agriculture and the environment, I can't possibly cover them all. Many are quite complex. I'd like to focus on a few of the most fundamental ones.

The Importance of Soil

Let's start with soil. Though easy to overlook, soil is not just a lifeless substance that holds and supports plants. Soil is a natural resource, and many farmers, biologists, and resource professionals would argue that it is just as important as air and water. Soil contains nutrients and holds them in storage for use by plants. Soil also holds water and makes it available for plants, which is essential for their success. Soil manages water flow by absorbing rainfall and filtering runoff. It is home to organisms that assist in plant decomposition. In fact, there are so many microscopic creatures living in the soil that it is the most biologically diverse community on Earth (USDA NRCS 1998b)! Just one teaspoon of soil contains more organisms than there are people on Earth (USDA NRCS 2010).

Food growers have many options to consider with regard to caring for and maintaining healthy soil. Many agricultural practices affect whether the soil even stays in place. *Erosion* is the term used to describe soil being carried away by water flow or blown off by wind. Growers' decisions about how much and how often the soil is disturbed can have a big impact, because certain practices can make soil much more vulnerable to erosion. Choices about which crops to grow and whether or not to apply fertilizer or pesticides all affect the health, fertility, and biodiversity of soil. The likelihood and extent of erosion can be lessened when the soil community is healthy and rich (USDA NRCS 2012). A nutrient-rich soil that has ample vegetation allows water to soak into, or *infiltrate*, the soil rather than run off and carry soil away with it.

The Use of Herbicides and Pesticides

Growers also face the challenge of managing weeds and pests, so their plants can succeed. There are many practices from which they can choose, and their choices can have minimal to major environmental impacts. For example, growers can rotate the crops that are planted in a given field each year, plant a variety and mixture of crops that offer a natural pest-fighting advantage, or limit how much soil is turned over before planting each spring. Growers may also use natural, plant-derived weed- or pest-fighting products. These options are more environmentally friendly than the practices that many growers implement—the use of *synthetic* chemical herbicides and pesticides. While effective at protecting crops, chemical herbicides and pesticides can pose harm to the environment. These chemicals can—and frequently do—run off with rainfall and enter nearby water supplies. Once in bodies of water, these chemicals can disrupt *aquatic*—or underwater—ecosystems and harm wildlife. Chemical residue can also persist in the soil for months, even years (USDA NCRS 1998a). Such residue can percolate deep underground, contaminating drinking water supplies.

Chemical residue can also be found in our food. No matter how much you wash that broccoli before eating it, if chemicals were applied to it, chances are that some residue remains. Chemicals in our food enter our bodies when we eat foods with chemical residue. Scientists have established "tolerance limits" for many of the agricultural chemical residues found in foods (Mintzer and Osteen 1997). However, there is general acknowledgement that the health effects of pesticide residue are largely unknown, and that children's bodies may be especially susceptible to the negative effects of chemicals such as pesticide residue (NIEHS 2012).

Food that is grown, processed, and packaged without the use of synthetic chemicals is called *organic* and is becoming more and more popular in places around the world as people become more aware of the environmental and health issues associated with the use of synthetic chemicals. In 2000, the United States Department of Agriculture (USDA) finalized a set of national standards—known as the National Organic Program—by which foods can be certified organic (USDA 2012). In the United States, foods must comply with these standards to be labeled organic. Foods that are not labeled organic are sometimes referred to as *conventionally grown*. But that phrase doesn't necessarily have any significance. There is no real way to know whether, how much, and which chemicals were used for a given item of conventionally grown food.

If you're using this book as a companion to the *Go Green Rating Scale* by Phil Boise, you'll see that sections 8 and 9 deal with the topic of food at your program, helping you to evaluate your practices around food and food waste. Section 9, in particular, addresses the concept of organic food. If your program offers a snack or lunch, buying organic is preferred. Children's bodies and brains are still developing and thus are more sensitive than adults' to potential toxic inputs to their systems (US EPA 2002a). Though we don't know the full extent of whether and how agricultural chemicals impact children, it is best to follow the *precautionary principle,* which states, "When an activity raises threats of harm to the environment or human health, precautionary measures should be taken even if some cause and effect relationships are not fully established scientifically" (SEHN 1998, 1). Thinking of the agricultural chemicals, it's possible that chemical residue isn't on the food or isn't harmful, but why take the chance if a safer, organic choice is possible? Buying organic is also a way of "voting" for the reduced use of chemicals in agriculture. The more people that buy organic or ask for organic products in their stores, the more pressure producers will have to deliver those products. However, the higher price of organic food means that it is often beyond the means of many programs. If your resources are limited (as they are for most of us), start with choosing organic for just one or a few fresh fruits and vegetables. A national nonprofit called the Environmental Working Group regularly publishes a list of the top ten fruits and vegetables most likely to contain high levels of pesticides and residue (www.ewg.org/foodnews). Check out this list and choose organic for even just one of these foods the next time you go to the store.

The Impact of Raising Animals

Another major link between food and the environment is in the area of raising animals for meat, or livestock production. Remember that earlier fact that approximately 37 percent of the world's land surface is devoted to agriculture? Considering the areas taken up by grazing animals and growing crops *just for animal feed*, livestock production accounts for about three-quarters of that worldwide total of land use (FAO 2006). It is estimated that livestock production accounts for more than 8 percent of water usage worldwide. Livestock production also typically uses a lot of energy and fossil fuels. As I discuss in chapter 7, burning fossil fuels sends greenhouse gases into the atmosphere. The greenhouse gas emissions associated with large-scale livestock production account for a whopping 18 percent of the total worldwide contribution (FAO 2011).

In addition to the ones I've mentioned thus far, there are countless other potential environmental impacts from food production. For example, growers can choose whether and how to manage their landscape to make it more hospitable for wild creatures, insects, and birds. If managed for this purpose, agricultural landscapes can provide habitat for countless species of plants, animals, insects, and other organisms.

Where Food Is Grown

Moving beyond agriculture, there are major environmental impacts in the food processing industry, as well as in food transport and distribution. In the developed world, we've come to expect any food we want, whenever we want it! There are some places where strawberries grow year-round, but not many. The idea of eating a fresh strawberry in Wisconsin in January may seem like no big deal, but when you stop to consider where it was grown and how it likely got to the store, you realize that there is a significant cost to this choice. That strawberry had to be grown either in a greenhouse or in a climate that is warm in January. Then the strawberry had to be picked and shipped. Different foods pose different challenges in the shipping stage. Some foods must be refrigerated to keep them fresh on the long journey. Some foods are sprayed with pesticides to prevent infestations during shipping. Depending on where that strawberry was grown, it perhaps will be flown to a distribution center in the United States. There it will be loaded onto a massive truck carrying thousands of pounds of refrigerated produce and then delivered to a grocery store. All of these steps require the use of fossil fuel energy and generate greenhouse gas emissions. Some studies show that processed foods travel an average of thirteen hundred miles before reaching

your plate, and that fresh foods in particular travel over fifteen hundred miles (Hill 2008).

Being aware of which foods are grown in your area as well as their growing and harvesting seasons can help you make choices about which foods to eat. If, as often as you can, you choose foods that are grown locally, say within a hundred or so miles, you'll be reducing the environmental impact of your choices. The food will not have to be shipped thousands of miles to reach your table, thereby reducing the fossil fuels involved (and greenhouse gases emitted) in its production and transit.

Food is not only better for the environment when it comes from local sources, it tastes better too! Conduct a taste test of your own to see if you agree. You can obtain locally grown foods at your co-op, farmers market, or garden stand. In areas where the growing season is short, eating locally-grown foods year-round will be more difficult. But even if you can only obtain locally grown foods for part of the year, it will be worth it. You'll reduce your impact on the environment, and you may learn more about your local climate, such as which foods grow best, and when. (See the Seasons of Food activity on page 93 for ideas that you can use in the classroom.) And you'll enjoy the taste of these foods, too.

Teaching about Food in Early Childhood

There's a lot to think about when it comes to food and the environment, and I'm not suggesting that you need to go back to school to choose what to eat for dinner or what to serve the children at your program. So what *am* I recommending? Clearly, teaching children about soil erosion or pesticide contamination is not the best approach. Instead, start with the basics: teach children, and remind yourself, that all food comes from plants and, thus, nature. And plants need sun, soil, air, and water to grow. Though this may seem overly basic, it's a great starting point for becoming more attuned to the importance of taking good care of our natural resources.

Next, teach children about the origins of common foods, and their journey to our plates. Unfortunately, many children in the developed world today have little understanding of where their food originates. When asked, many children might answer "the grocery store" or "the refrigerator"! While such comments may seem charming or cute, this disconnect between what's on their plates and where it comes from keeps children in the dark about what they're actually eating. In the fast-paced and time-pressured world in which many of us find ourselves, it is all too common for children (and their families) to eat a preponderance of processed, packaged, and convenience foods. Though these foods also contain ingredients that come from plants, those plant origins can be mighty hard to recognize in the lengthy ingredient lists on some packages. When children have no concept of where their food is grown, how it is processed, how it got to the table, or even what core plant ingredients it contains, they're missing out on some very important information that is essential for ultimately taking charge of their own food choices.

Making food's origins a part of everyday activities and conversations is a great way to help children get to know their food and prepare to be Earth-conscious consumers. Invite children to think about the core ingredients in some of their favorite foods and where those ingredients come from. For example, ask them what the core ingredient in ice cream is. Obviously, milk! But do they know where it comes from? What about the core ingredient in pasta? Wheat! What does that look like? Where and how does it grow?

Finally, help children eat "real" foods as often and to the greatest extent that you can. According to food researcher and author Anna Lappé, real foods are those that "are as close to their natural state as possible, that haven't undergone energy-intensive processing and don't contain chemically laden ingredients" (Lappé 2010, 202). Providing children with healthy, fresh choices sets them on a path of enjoying a variety of foods as they grow. In fact, the United States Department of Agriculture Dietary Guidelines recommend choosing nutrient-dense foods such as whole grains, fruits, and vegetables, and limiting sugar and refined foods (USDA and US

HHS 2010). Eating fresh, whole foods whenever possible is also a great way to avoid higher prices and excessive waste from packaging. As you read in chapter 3, food packaging—though serving an important function—is a tremendous source of waste in the United States. In particular, those ever-popular single serving snacks, though handy in a pinch, are quite wasteful and far more expensive than buying in bulk.

Before I move on, I want to acknowledge that getting children to eat fresh fruits and vegetables, and more healthy foods in general, can be a challenge. As parents and educators, we may fully embrace the value of healthy food but face the reality of children picking at their food, refusing to eat or try anything new, or even throwing tantrums at the sight of certain foods or the proximity of foods on their plates. Many parents simply want their children to eat *something* at mealtime. It's a natural tendency to provide the same things, day after day, in order to avoid conflict or power struggles at the dinner table. Packaged, processed convenience foods are extremely tempting for adults to serve due to their palatability for children, the ease of their preparation, and their perceived nutritional value. It is not my intention to judge or guilt-trip parents or educators who are already doing the best they can. I would only encourage you to not give up! Include healthy whole and fresh foods as options at every meal and snack. Engage children in conversation about food, and interest them in new information about food. You may find a food that intrigues or excites them just when you least expect it.

Busy families often don't consistently share mealtimes, much less discuss or reflect on their daily meals or foods. Educators in early childhood environments can do so much on this topic. There are many simple and easy ways to help children connect with their food. Identifying and learning about the major food groups—grains, proteins, fruits and vegetables, and dairy—is often a great first step. As most early childhood educators already know, there are so many creative ways of using games, stories, songs, and art projects to help children learn more about and appreciate food.

GARDENING WITH CHILDREN

Growing, harvesting, and preparing food are great activities for the early child care environment. Gardens offer the early childhood educator countless ways to connect children with their food and to provide learning opportunities, chances to get outside, and opportunities to reap the benefits of their own hard work. In addition, when children participate in growing and preparing their own food, they are often more excited, enthusiastic, and willing to try new flavors and textures. Try it and see. Growing your own food is also the ultimate way to eat local! Remember that freshly picked food, which hasn't traveled long distances to your plate, tastes amazing! Even children reluctant to try new foods may open their minds when faced with a juicy, sweet, bright red cherry tomato just waiting to be picked, and the sight of their peers gobbling them up.

Gardening projects can range from a full-fledged garden plot to a few containers outside your door or on your window ledge. Regardless of which way you choose, growing vegetables will do wonders in generating children's interest in them. Many programs develop an entire year's worth of curriculum around gardening and plants. You can use the winter months to plan your garden, start seeds indoors, and plan some special food-related events. In the spring and summer months, harvest your vegetables and prepare some special meals for the community to share. Although food is perhaps the most obvious reason for a schoolyard garden, there are numerous other themes that might appeal to you and your colleagues as you explore the possibilities of a schoolyard garden. Consider planting a garden to attract butterflies and moths, or a scent garden (see Plant a Sensory Garden in chapter 2).

Another way to make connections about food, and food waste in particular, is by maintaining a *compost* pile at your site. Uneaten food typically forms a huge part of a child care program's waste. It is difficult to estimate the average amount because programs and services vary so much. But where does that food waste go? If you put it in the trash, it will end up at the same destination as the rest of your trash, most likely a landfill or incinerator. In chapter 3, I addressed waste issues and some of the reasons why landfills and incinerators are problematic.

A compost pile is a great alternative to throwing food waste in the trash. Composting is a natural process whereby any material that once came from plants (that is, leftover food) is turned into a natural soil material. It's a fairly simple process: place your food scraps in the pile along with other plant materials such as grass clippings and leaves. You can also add non-food items that were made from plants, such as paper napkins, tea bags, and newspapers. These days it is even possible to find flatware and paper products made with plant-derived, and thus compostable, material. I provide more detailed instructions for starting and maintaining a compost pile in appendix F. Though you must pay attention to your compost pile to a certain degree (for example, ensuring that you have a balanced ratio of "wet" food scraps and "dry" paper and yard waste additions), generally speaking the process is pretty foolproof. Once you've collected your waste materials, your compost pile only needs water, oxygen, and the sun's heat. It works because harmless bacteria and other living organisms break down—or *decompose*—the material into a moist, dark brown, crumbly substance. This is the compost, and it is both a nutritious food for plants and a great contributor to healthy soil (see appendix F).

When properly maintained and contained, a compost pile doesn't smell or attract pests. It's a great activity if you have a school garden or even container plants, in which case you most likely would buy soil enhancement material for your plants. Generating your own compost helps you avoid that expense, and it's a great way for children to see waste turn into something beneficial. It will also reduce the size of the bags you send to the trash each week.

If outdoor space is limited at your facility, you may be interested in *vermicomposting*, a method of composting on a smaller scale indoors, using worms, newspaper scraps, and a small bin. Similar to the method described above, you simply deposit leftover food scraps into the bin. Worms eat the food scraps and create compost as they digest them. This technique of composting can be endlessly fascinating for young children, as it provides great opportunities to learn about biology, life cycles, and worms. There are numerous resources available for the educator who desires a more comprehensive description of vermicomposting and how to get started. See appendix H for resource suggestions.

There are many great ways and opportunities to help engage children with the topic of food and encourage their awareness and exploration of food's origins and its journey to their plates. Learning about food is not only fascinating and fun for young children, it also builds a foundation for becoming consumers who make Earth-conscious and Earth-friendly food choices. I also want to return to the very important point I made at the start of this chapter: often the choices best for the environment are also the best for our bodies and health. What do I mean by this? Again, the field of nutrition and health is flooded with information, and it is impossible within the scope of this book to cover specific dietary recommendations. That said, from a health perspective, recommendations abound to make fresh, whole fruits and vegetables a

bigger proportion of our daily diet. For example, the United States Department of Agriculture's most current guidelines recommend (among other things) to "increase vegetable and fruit intake" and "consume at least half of all grains as whole grains" (USDA and US HHS 2010, xi). In light of known links between diet and cancer, the World Cancer Research Fund similarly recommends eating mostly plant-based foods, stressing that some fruits and vegetables may help prevent certain cancers (WCRF and AICR 2007). And then there's the recommendation of food writer and environmentalist Michael Pollan: "Eat food. Not too much. Mostly plants" (Pollan 2008, 1).

Educating children about food lays an important foundation for helping them make healthy choices. Establishing good habits, such as a healthy, nutritious diet, plenty of exercise, and lots of time outdoors, can start at a young age, so early childhood settings are a perfect place to focus on these goals. Providing lots of exciting, fun activities and experiences around food sets a positive tone for cultivating curiosity and interest in different foods and the way they are grown and prepared. Children are naturally excited and delighted by food. Its many textures, colors, shapes, and smells provide a multisensory feast, and food offers myriad ways to expand one's horizons. Whether we stop to think about it or not, the act of eating provides us with a daily connection to nature. Our food choices have real consequences—for the shape of the food industry and the health of our planet.

Helping children learn about and appreciate food helps plant the seeds of stewardship that children will use later to act on behalf of the planet when it comes to their food choices. There are many ways you can help support the accomplishment of these goals. I hope that the exercises that follow will provide opportunities for fun and learning as well as inspire you to try new things of your own devising as you make deeper connections to food with the children in your program.

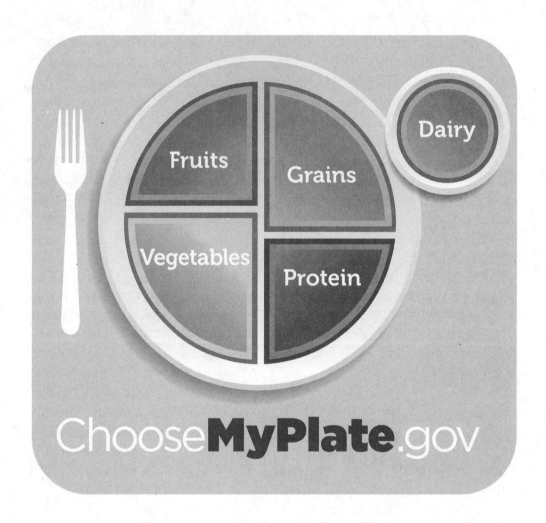

Plants on My Plate

Food comes from plants. Even sweets contain ingredients that get their start in the soil. Since many of the foods we eat are processed and packaged, it can be easy to forget about the core plant ingredients in our food in general and the importance of plants in our daily diets. Knowing how all food is connected can help children—and adults—be more conscious about what they're eating. Building an awareness of all the elements involved in something as simple as, say, a container of banana yogurt can be very eye-opening and can even help plant the seeds of gratitude. In this activity, you'll help children make connections between the foods they eat and the plants that helped make them.

Activity Goals

→ To make a connection between foods commonly eaten and their base plant ingredient

→ To examine foods closely and think about where they came from

National Science Education Standards

Physical science: properties of objects and materials

Science in personal and social perspectives: personal health

Materials and Supplies

☐ Assorted grains or photographs of grains, such as rice, wheat, and oats

☐ Assorted dried beans

☐ Assorted nuts; use photographs of nuts if there are children with nut allergies

☐ Assorted fruits and vegetables, or photographs of them

☐ Spice containers, such as pepper, cinnamon, and nutmeg

☐ Chart paper and a marker

Procedure

1. Discuss that all the food we eat comes from plants, which are grown in the soil. Even meat comes from plants, because animals eat plants and then convert that food energy into their meat. Even sweet treats contain ingredients that come from plants.

2. Ask the children to tell the group their favorite foods. List them on chart paper. Ask if they think the foods come from plants; then ask them which plant each food comes from.

3. Present the children with pictures or samples of the grains, beans, nuts, and other foods listed above. Let them explore and discuss the foods. Ask them to share some ideas about foods they eat that contain these products. Make a list of all the foods they can think of.

TIPS

• If possible, bring in actual samples of plants and grains for the children to examine, rather than just photographs. You can eat them for snacktime or have a picnic lunch after this activity.

• If there are children with food allergies, omit those substances from this activity, substituting photographs instead, or using plastic or wooden representations of the foods.

• Do this activity prior to lunchtime or snacktime, so children can examine their own food as well as the foods presented in this activity.

• Use the following chart to help identify foods and their common plant origins.

(continues on next page)

Macaroni and cheese, spaghetti	Wheat (flour) to make pasta; grasses and grains to feed cows, whose milk is produced into cheese
Chocolate	Cacao pods (trees)
Cupcakes	Wheat (flour), sugar (sugar cane or sugar beet plant), corn syrup (corn plant) Cupcakes are typically flavored with vanilla (a type of orchid) or chocolate (cocoa tree)
French fries	Potatoes
Hamburgers, chicken nuggets	Grain or corn fed to animals
Bread	Wheat or oats
Ice cream	Grains and grasses are fed to cows who produce milk, which is the primary ingredient in ice cream. Like cupcakes, ice cream can be flavored with chocolate (cocoa tree) or vanilla (orchid). Strawberries and other fruits also provide ingredients for popular flavorings, as do various nuts, such as pistachios and pecans (trees) and peanuts (vines).

- Despite the fact that plants are important contributors to the above foods, and that there are plant-derived ingredients in many popular treats, this does not necessarily mean that the treats are healthful foods. Many processed, sugary "treats" are not healthy for children, no matter what plants were involved in their production!

- Keep in mind that the diets of animals raised for meat production vary widely. Chickens and cows raised in large-scale animal operations are typically fed a diet consisting mainly of corn. Cattle and chickens can also be fed grains, such as wheat, as well as soybeans. Some cattle are raised on a diet of grasses, which is the plant species that cow's systems are naturally evolved to digest.

CONNECTIONS

Discuss with the children how many different plants are represented by the food in the room. Ask if anything surprised them.

Meal Memories

All children love to tell stories. This activity invites children to share stories of their favorite foods and meals. Each child will draw or paint a picture of her family enjoying a favorite meal, share the picture with the other children, and then—as a group—identify the basic foods that go into their favorite meals.

Activity Goals

→ To recall details of a favorite memory

→ To identify basic food groups

National Science Education Standards

Physical science: properties of objects and materials

Science in personal and social perspectives: personal health

Materials and Supplies

☐ Large pieces of paper, one for each child

☐ Art supplies, such as paint, markers, crayons, or colored pencils

☐ Chart paper and a marker

Procedure

1. Share with the children a favorite memory you have of a meal with your family. You might remember a snack on a hike or a holiday meal together. Tell the children all about it, and invite them to think of a time they too shared a special meal with family.

2. Ask the children to become quiet as they think of this memory. Encourage them to recall how the food smelled, where they were during the meal, and what it felt like to be hungry for that meal and to enjoy eating together. Invite them to recall the feeling of satisfaction they had at the end of the meal.

3. Next, invite them to draw or color a picture of this memory. Ask them to include as many details as they can remember. Allow the children to share their pictures with the group, telling about the meal and the memory.

4. As a group, identify the main foods, or ingredients from those foods, shared during the meal. You may wish to make a list or chart depicting all the ingredients.

TIPS

• Allow lots of time for this activity. Children will love sharing their memories and will want time to retell their stories. If children need prompts, ask questions such as "When was it?" "Where did it take place?" and "Who was there?"

• Let the children do what comes naturally. Some will draw a plate with food on it, others will draw a whole scene, and other drawings may be abstract. This is okay!

• Consider posting these pictures during a family potluck meal at your program.

CONNECTIONS

Discuss the patterns that emerged with the children. For example, ask them how many foods were represented. If you made a chart or list of ingredients, ask the children which ones were the most common. Discuss how many of the meals were plant-based, how many were mostly meat, and how many were mostly sweets.

Invite children to dictate or write about their favorite meal. Challenge them to describe as many details of the meal—including the texture, smell, and color of the food—as thoroughly as possible.

Spice of Life

AGES
4+

Many common spices are easily recognized by children. This activity provides an opportunity for children to identify spices using their sense of smell and then to make a simple snack using cinnamon and sugar.

Activity Goals

→ To explore a variety of spices using the sense of smell

→ To make a simple snack using common spices, such as cinnamon

National Science Education Standards

Life science: characteristics of organisms

Materials and Supplies

☐ Jars containing a number of familiar spices, such as cinnamon, cumin, black pepper, dried oregano, dried dill, cloves, and dried ginger

☐ Sugar

☐ Additional cinnamon

☐ Apples, sliced; several slices per child

☐ Small stirring sticks or spoons, one for each child

☐ Small bowls, one for each child

Procedure

1. Explain to children that part of what makes up the huge variety of tastes and flavors in our food is the addition of spices. Spices come from plants. They might be leaves (such as oregano), seeds or seed pods (such as cumin), or even berries that are dried and ground (black pepper). They even come from tree bark (cinnamon), roots (ginger), or even flower parts (cloves).

2. Tell the children that they are going to smell different spices and then try to remember where they've tasted or smelled that spice before.

3. Pass the jars around, letting the children smell and look at the spices. Encourage them to tell you what the smell is (if they know) or what food it reminds them of.

4. Share the names of the different spices, and talk about some ways they are used in cooking and baking.

5. Finally, as a special treat, pass out apple slices, bowls, and stir sticks and allow each child to mix up his own blend of cinnamon and sugar to dip the apples in.

6. Enjoy the snack together.

TIPS

- Demonstrate the wafting technique—hold a jar near your nose and wave the other hand slowly over the opening to bring the scent toward your nose—to avoid inhalation of the spice. Otherwise, some children may sneeze if they smell black pepper or other spices.

- Send a note home ahead of time telling families about the upcoming activity, listing the spices you are planning to have on hand, and inviting them to send a small sample if there is a spice not on your list that is used regularly in their home cooking. If possible, invite families to provide a description of the source of that spice.

CONNECTIONS

Keep a list of the different plant parts in your spice collection. Ask the children how many parts they counted.

Seed Hide-and-Seek

Seeds are a very important part of plants. They are the means by which many plants reproduce. Children are often delighted and surprised to get an up-close look at the seeds hidden away—or in plain site on the surface—in the fruits they know so well. In this activity, children will discover the diversity of shapes and sizes that seeds have, and they'll see firsthand in what form plants start out.

Activity Goals

→ To provide an exciting look inside plants

→ To understand that both fruits and vegetables start out as seeds

→ To understand that there are some seeds we eat, and others that we don't

National Science Education Standards

Life science: characteristics of organisms, life cycles of organisms

Materials and Supplies

☐ Assorted fruits and vegetables (for example, melon, cucumber, zucchini, green pepper, tomato, strawberry, apple, pear, kiwi, grapes [with seeds], pumpkin, and squash)

☐ Chart paper and a marker

☐ Sharp knife, for teacher use, or children's knives

☐ Magnifying lenses, one for each child

☐ Fine mesh sieve

☐ Cloth dish towel

Procedure

1. Display the fruits and vegetables you've brought in, and talk about similarities and differences. Allow time for children to react and respond.

2. Next, invite them to explore the foods. Talk about shapes, textures, colors, and smells.

3. Cut open each food item, except any with seeds on the outside, such as strawberries, and examine its seeds. If possible, scoop out the seeds and look carefully at them. Discuss and describe the seeds.

Record the children's observations about the seeds. If you have a vegetable without seeds, talk about that too. For example, potatoes, carrots, radishes, celery, and lettuce are foods we eat, but the seeds for these plants are not in the part of the plant we eat.

4. Rinse the seeds in the sieve and pat them dry with a dish towel.

5. Eat the fruits and vegetables, if desired.

6. Help the children make connections about how each food contained many seeds, or just a few. Ask the children how the seeds are protected. Examine the seeds very closely, noticing the harder outer covering and the insides.

TIPS

• Do this activity outdoors. It reduces the mess and it feels like a picnic!

• If you have children's knives, allow them to do some of the cutting.

• Have an adult cut hard-shelled squashes, melons, and pumpkins, which are very difficult to cut.

CONNECTIONS

Ask children to sort and organize the seeds, weigh and measure the seeds, and group them from smallest to largest. Ask children why the seeds are located where they are in the fruits and vegetables. Save the seeds and mix them up. Ask the children if they remember which seeds belong with which fruit or vegetable. Discuss the life cycle of the plants for the various seeds.

Use the seeds to make mosaic art, or dip them in paint and roll them around on paper in shallow trays.

Sketch the seeds and the fruits as accurately as possible.

The Great Seed Sort

AGES
3+

Seeds are wonderfully diverse. They come in all shapes, sizes, and colors. In this activity, children have the opportunity to sort their very own collection of seeds, examining them and putting them into categories that you first define; later, they will create their own categories. They will enjoy exploring the different textures and qualities of the seeds.

Activity Goals

→ To observe and identify attributes

→ To explore a collection of different kinds of seeds with all senses

→ To identify categories and practice sorting

National Science Education Standards

Life science: characteristics of organisms

Materials and Supplies

☐ Small bags of assorted seeds (for example, birdseed, dried vegetable and fruit seeds, or flower seeds), one bag for each child

☐ Small plastic containers for sorting (empty yogurt or margarine containers work perfectly), two for each child

☐ Small trays (clean microwave food containers work perfectly!), one for each child

☐ Magnifying lenses

Procedure

1. Invite the children to open their bags and sort the seeds by type. They can dump them into the trays to keep them from spilling.

2. As they sort and examine their seeds, note their reactions. What words are they using to describe the seeds? What questions are they asking? Invite them to share their observations.

3. Invite them to mix their seeds again, then call out a descriptive word, such as "round," or "bumpy," or "two-colored." Ask the children to sort the seeds again according to this feature.

4. Choose one or two of the children's own descriptive words and repeat the sorting activity.

5. Conclude by reminding children that just as seeds are diverse in shape, size, and color, so are the foods that grow from the seeds.

TIPS

Read the contents of premixed birdseed carefully. Many bags contain peanuts, which may cause an allergic reaction in some children. Be aware of any food allergies the children in your program have before beginning this activity.

• Choose birdseed mixtures that contain larger seeds, such as sunflower seeds, corn, and others. Some very small seeds, such as millet, would be difficult for young children to handle and organize—not to mention difficult to clean up!

• For extra practice with fine-motor skills, provide the children with tweezers or forceps to grasp and move the seeds as they work.

• Bring in photographs of all the foods and plants that correspond to the seed samples.

CONNECTIONS

Challenge the children to line up the seeds, smallest to largest. Ask them how many different kinds of seeds there are and how they can tell them apart. Plant some of the seeds and see what grows.

Invite the children to make pictures with their seeds, using glue sticks and markers. They may draw a scribble and fill in with seeds or create a scene of their own choosing.

Seed Eaters

Many of the foods we eat are seeds. Children are delighted to make the connection that not only do some of their favorite foods contain seeds but also many of their favorite foods are themselves seeds. This activity offers a hands-on exploration of the common seeds we eat, use to flavor our foods, and make into other foods, such as breads.

Activity Goals

→ To explore some edible seeds

National Science Education Standards

Physical science: properties of objects and materials

Life science: characteristics of organisms, life cycles of organisms

Earth and space science: properties of earth materials

Materials and Supplies

☐ Variety of ready-to-eat nuts, unless there are children with nut allergies present

☐ Whole peppercorns and a pepper grinder

☐ Variety of ready-to-eat seeds, such as sunflower seeds, pumpkin seeds, chickpeas, and peas

☐ Sunflower seeds in the shell

☐ Variety of nuts in shells, unless there are children with nut allergies present

☐ White or brown rice, uncooked

☐ Oatmeal, uncooked

☐ Loaf of oatmeal bread

☐ Popcorn, unpopped

☐ Seeds used as spices, such as fennel, coriander, cumin, poppy, and sesame seeds

☐ Additional ingredients and equipment as called for in the recipes that follow

Procedure

1. Ask the children if they ate any seeds for breakfast, snack, or lunch. Mention the huge array of nuts and seeds that are available for eating, seasoning our food, and making into other foods. Ask for ideas of what those might be. See the list above for ideas.

2. Present the various seeds that you have brought into the classroom.

3. Ask the children when they have seen these seeds before.

4. Tell them that some seeds are even better when they are prepared. They may be baked, boiled, toasted, or even ground up into a paste.

5. Use the recipes on the following page to prepare the seeds with the children and enjoy them as a snack.

6. Sniff the seasonings and ask the children if they recognize them from dishes their families have cooked.

TIPS

 Ensure that there are no allergies to any of the foods presented in this activity before proceeding.

- Ensure all necessary safety measures are taken before proceeding with the cooking and baking portion of this activity.

- Use this activity as a complement to the Seed Hide-and-Seek activity on page 83.

CONNECTIONS

Engage the group in a discussion or project related to the variety of seeds that are eaten by animals, such as livestock (grain), wild birds (pinecone seeds, acorns, and so on), and pets. Ask the children if they can identify other seed eaters and other kinds of seeds.

(continues on next page)

Invite families to share favorite family or cultural recipes involving seeds or spices that come from seeds. Invite the children to bring in a favorite seed and talk about the dishes it is used to flavor. Host a "seed eating" potluck at your site, where every family contributes something that includes seeds.

Toasted Pumpkin or Sesame Seeds

Toss seeds with a mild seasoning (try salt and paprika or cinnamon and sugar) and spread in a thin layer on a cookie sheet. Gently warm in the oven or toaster oven at 325 degrees for 20–25 minutes, or until golden brown. Chickpeas can also be toasted in this fashion. Sprinkle with spices, such as mild curry powder, chili powder, or cinnamon and cumin, and toast until golden brown.

Popcorn

Many children are familiar with popcorn but, due to the prevalence of microwave popcorn, have not seen it popped. Seeing the kernels before popping and watching them pop helps children make the connection that this is a natural, whole food. What makes popcorn pop, anyway? Within each kernel (seed!) of popcorn, there is a tiny bit of water inside a hard case of starch. As the water inside heats up, the case explodes from the pressure building inside. As it pops, the kernel actually turns inside out!

Seed Snack

Crack walnuts, almonds, and sunflower seeds and talk about how different the shells are. Mix the nuts and seeds together for a high-protein snack. Sprinkle with salt or a little cinnamon sugar.

Rice

Rice grains don't look like seeds, but they are. The tiny rice grains that we eat are the very same grains we put into the ground for planting. Rice is often eaten as-is, but it also can be made into flour. For a comforting snack on a cold day, cook a large pot of rice and serve it with butter, soy sauce, or raisins and honey.

Garbanzo Beans (Chickpeas)

This seed belongs to a family of vegetables known as "pulses," which are seeds that grow inside a pod. Other common pulses are lentils and peas. Grind or mash garbanzo beans into a thick paste, add garlic and lemon juice, and you have hummus, a delicious and nutritious snack that is great as a veggie dip or spread on crackers.

Seeds to Sprouts

AGES
3+

Children are intrigued by the idea that plants come from seeds; however, it's difficult to imagine such a transformation! In this activity, you'll sprout lemon seeds over the course of several days. This activity can easily be conducted outside, if the weather cooperates.

Activity Goals

→ To plant seeds and watch them grow

National Science Education Standards

Life science: life cycles of organisms

Materials and Supplies

☐ Lemons

☐ Paper towels

☐ Clear containers, one per child

☐ Water-filled spray bottle

Procedure

1. Work with the children to remove the seeds from the lemons.

2. Begin a discussion with the children about how plants start out as seeds. Mention that you could plant seeds in a pot or in the garden, but it would also be neat to see them growing.

3. Have the children moisten the paper towels and place one in the bottom of each container.

4. Allow children to choose one or two seeds, then gently place the seeds on the moist paper towel. Spray the paper towels every day to keep them moist; the seeds should sprout in about ten days.

TIPS

- Use empty baby food jars, which are the perfect size for this activity and can be used with care. Ask parents with babies to donate their empty jars before recycling them.

- Use avocado seeds, which are also very exciting to sprout. Simply poke a clean seed with three toothpicks. The toothpicks form a "frame" so the seed can rest on the top of an open jar. Fill the jar with enough water that the avocado seed is partially submerged. The avocado seed will sprout in approximately two weeks.

- If your climate permits, plant the seeds outdoors.

- Use small zip-close plastic bags for this activity. Simply place the moistened seed and paper towel inside. This is a great way to reuse plastic lunch bags after you clean them.

CONNECTIONS

Have the children place the seeds in various locations and compare the rate at which they sprout. Ask the children to predict or observe whether the location of the jar in the classroom will make a difference, or if having the seeds outside will make a difference.

Have the children draw their seed or sprout each day. This will help them really notice fine details. Provide magnifying lenses.

Twist and Sprout

Children are more likely to eat things that they've had a hand in growing. And sprouts are very easy to grow in the early childhood classroom. They are crisp and refreshing and fun to eat.

Activity Goals

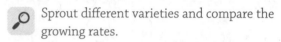 To plant seeds and eat the sprouted plant

National Science Education Standards

Life science: life cycles of organisms

Materials and Supplies

Gather these materials for each group of children:

- ☐ Quart-size jar or plastic container
- ☐ Pieces of thin cloth, such as cheesecloth or loosely woven cotton
- ☐ Rubber bands
- ☐ Seeds for sprouting, such as alfalfa, sunflower, mung bean, or wheatgrass
- ☐ Measuring spoons
- ☐ Sieve or colander
- ☐ Water

Procedure

1. Have each group of children place three tablespoons of seeds into their jar and cover the seeds with water. Allow the seeds to soak overnight.

2. Pour the seeds into a sieve and rinse them well.

3. Place the seeds back in the jar; cover the top of the jar with the cloth and secure with a rubber band.

4. Place the jar on its side so the seeds can spread out.

5. Each day, rinse the seeds again and return them to the jar.

6. When the seeds have sprouted and are about one to two inches long, rinse them one last time and enjoy them with crackers or fruit.

TIPS

- Purchase seeds for sprouting at health food stores or online.

- Keep in mind that the sprouting time will vary depending on the variety of seed used.

- Use dried beans as an alternative for this activity.

CONNECTIONS

Sprout different varieties and compare the growing rates.

Measure the temperature inside the jars. Notice that there is water condensing on the sides of the jar each morning. This is evidence of the water cycle!

Invite the children to write poems or stories about the sprouts' lives. Ask them to write about what it might be like living in the jar and if the sprouts play together at night inside the jar. You might also ask if the sprouts are scared or excited to be eaten by children to help them grow.

Plant Parts

Plants have a number of different parts, and often we can eat them all. For example, the leaves, root, and seeds are plant parts that are frequently edible. This activity helps children identify the different parts of a plant and realize just how much is edible! This activity is a great way to introduce a snack or picnic lunch. Consider taking this activity outdoors on a nice day.

Activity Goals

→ To identify all the parts of a plant

→ To understand we eat all the parts of a plant

National Science Education Standards

Life science: characteristics of organisms, life cycles of organisms

Science in personal and social perspectives: personal health, types of resources

Materials and Supplies

☐ Chart paper and markers

☐ Assorted vegetables and fruits (see Tips below)

☐ Knife and cutting board, for teacher use only

Procedure

1. Prior to the activity, cut a few fruits or vegetables open to expose the seeds.

2. Ask the children if they can name some of the different parts of plants.

3. They will call out different parts, such as "stem," "leaves," "flower," "root," and "berry."

4. As they call out the plant parts, draw a large plant on the chart paper so the children can see the different parts.

5. Ask them if they can think of any foods that come from those parts.

6. As they call out their ideas, show examples of fruits and vegetables that come from the plant parts. If the children miss any plant parts, prompt them by showing the food and asking what part of the plant it is.

TIPS

- Use the following examples of edible plant parts:

  › Roots: carrots, turnips, parsnips

  › Stems: celery, green onion, spinach

  › Bulbs: onions, shallots, garlic

  › Leaves: spinach, celery leaves, romaine and other lettuces, brussels sprouts, cabbage

  › Fruits and berries: peppers, apples, peaches, string beans, peapods, watermelon

  › Flowers: saffron threads, nasturtium flowers, violet blossoms

  › Seeds: sunflower seeds, pumpkin seeds, pinto beans, garbanzo beans

- Explain that there are also plant parts known as tubers, which are basically modified stems or roots.

CONNECTIONS

Work with the children to think of a meal that consists of plant parts in their whole or natural form. If possible, prepare the foods.

Invite each child to draw or sketch a favorite edible plant and then label all of its parts.

Slurp!

Plants need water and nutrients to grow. Most plants *absorb* these elements from the soil. Their roots take in water and nutrients, and their cells carry the water and nutrients throughout the parts of the plant. In this activity, celery is used to provide children with a firsthand look at how water travels through a plant. It serves as a great introduction to gardening, as children can see the way plants take up water.

Activity Goals

→ To have a direct experience with how food absorbs water

National Science Education Standards

Life science: characteristics of organisms, life cycles of organisms

Materials and Supplies

☐ Celery, one rib or branch per child

☐ Drinking glasses or jars, one per child, half filled with water

☐ Red or blue food coloring

☐ Magnifying lenses, one per child

Procedure

1. Explain that celery, like all plants, has long cells that absorb water. In celery, those cells are particularly easy to see.

2. Allow children some time with the celery and the magnifying lenses. Encourage them to hold the lens close to their eye and then get close to the celery in order to really magnify the celery.

3. Next, ask the children what all plants need in order to grow. One of the things they need is water. Fill each drinking glass or jar about halfway with water.

4. Before putting the celery in, discuss how plants will absorb everything that is in the water, so if there are paints in the water, the plants absorb those as well.

5. Next, put three or four drops of food coloring in each glass of water. Tell the children that food coloring is not harmful to them or the plants.

6. Place the celery stalks in the water and gently stir to distribute the food coloring.

7. Let the celery sit overnight. In the morning, the celery stalks will have absorbed the water and taken on a red or blue hue.

8. Discuss what happened. Ask the children how the color got into the celery.

TIPS

- Use food coloring with care. It will stain clothing and skin.

- Demonstrate the use of magnifying lenses before you begin. Place the lens close to your eye, and then get very close to the object you wish to view. For younger children, have them cover one eye with a hand while using the other eye to look through the lens.

- If this activity inspires some children to try celery, and even though food coloring is nontoxic, offer fresh celery sticks as a snack.

CONNECTIONS

Measure different concentrations of food coloring into the water, and observe the changes in the celery over time. Ask the children if they think the same thing would happen with other kinds of plants and why.

Growing a Pizza

Children love gardening. Digging in the soil, watering seedlings, and even pulling weeds are experiences that even the youngest children can participate in. Tending to plants and observing how they change and grow over time is an experience that can easily lead to later environmental stewardship. Knowing that they had a hand in growing and caring for the vegetables and herbs will also make children more inclined to try them. In this activity, a collection of containers or a small garden bed serves as a "pizza garden." Children will plant tomatoes, basil, oregano, rosemary, and thyme to make a savory sauce.

Activity Goals

→ To garden with a few plants that require little maintenance

National Science Education Standards

Physical science: properties of objects and materials

Earth and space science: properties of earth materials

Science in personal and social perspectives: personal health

Materials and Supplies

☐ Planting boxes or containers, enough to hold as many plants as you intend to cultivate

☐ Small herb seedlings, such as basil, thyme, oregano, and rosemary

☐ Tomato plants and tomato cages

☐ Gardening gloves, for the children who desire them

☐ Small trowels or shovels

☐ Potting soil and compost, if available

☐ Filled watering cans

Procedure

1. Ensure that every child who wants gloves has a pair to wear.

2. Work with the children to fill the containers with soil and compost, if you're using it.

3. Make a hole in the soil with a trowel or your hands. Place a seedling in the hole so that its root ball is parallel with the surface of the soil in your container.

4. Plant the remaining seedlings in the same manner, ensuring that there is at least twelve to eighteen inches of space between plants, to allow room for growth.

5. Pat the soil gently to settle the plants in, and water them thoroughly.

6. Place the containers in a sunny location and water as needed.

7. Pick the herbs as soon as they are mature. Tomatoes can be harvested when they are red and firm.

8. Harvest the ingredients and prepare a tomato sauce for the children to enjoy. A simple recipe follows. Spread sauce on ready-made pizza crust, top with cheese, bake, and enjoy!

Tomato Sauce

In large bowl, mash tomatoes to a thick paste. Drain excess liquid from bowl. Finely chop or tear basil, thyme, rosemary, and oregano. Mix into sauce. Add salt and pepper if desired.

(continues on next page)

- Keep in mind that some children really enjoy getting their hands dirty, but others do not. Provide gloves for the children who want to wear them.

- For children who are reluctant to get dirty, offer jobs such as watering plants, filling watering cans, or washing gardening tools when the project is complete.

- Check and water (if needed) container plants daily. These plants need more water than plants in the ground.

- Research the types and varieties of the plants you're using, and plan to stretch this activity over the course of several weeks to several months.

- Grow one of these other simple gardens:

  > Salsa garden: tomatoes, green peppers, red onion, and cilantro

  > Vegetable soup garden: tomatoes, green beans, potatoes, green and red peppers, and carrots

> If you want to pursue any of these, or other, specialty garden themes, research the specific plants and planting recommendations in each case. Check out one of the helpful gardening resources mentioned in appendix H at the end of this book.

CONNECTIONS

Observe the changes in the plants over time. Place the containers in locations that offer different amounts of sun and shade and note the effect on the plant's growth.

Have younger children mix watercolor paints to try to match the different shades of green visible in the plants. Have older children sketch the plants, making a new sketch each week to observe and document the changes taking place.

Seasons of Food

Different areas of the world have different climates. Different climates mean that certain fruits and vegetables grow well in some places but not in others. Different climates also mean that every place has a different rhythm to its growing season. In some places fruits and vegetables grow year-round, whereas other places have a definite season or seasons during which plants can grow, mature, and be harvested. Locally grown foods are also typically fresher (and more tasty!), but what's local for you? In this activity, the children explore the growing season in your area, and find out what foods are typically grown and harvested nearby.

Activity Goals

→ To understand the growing season

→ To identify foods that grow in the area

National Science Education Standards

Science in personal and social perspectives: personal health, characteristics and changes in populations, changes in environments

Life science: life cycles of organisms, organisms and environments

Materials and Supplies

☐ Maps of your country and state, province, or region

☐ Photographs of various kinds of fruits and vegetables

☐ Samples of those fruits and vegetables, if available

Procedure

1. Discuss with the children the variety of foods that are grown in your area. Show them your location on the map. Discuss the fact that different climates have different growing seasons, which means that different foods are available at different times of the year.

2. Explain that when we eat foods that are grown elsewhere, those foods must be brought to us on trucks, ships, or planes; sometimes on all three!

When we eat foods that are grown locally, those foods need less transportation, and the food is fresher.

3. Talk with the children about which local foods they have tried. Find out which are their favorites.

4. If you have samples of local foods, share them with the children.

TIPS

- Find out ahead of time the peak growing season in your area, which months it includes, and what crops are grown locally. If your area has a peak harvest season, do this activity during that time.

- Identify what you define as "local." For some regions, this might mean grown within twenty-five miles; for other regions, it might mean grown within two hundred miles.

- Consult a local agriculture organization to learn which food crops are commonly grown, harvested, or produced in your state. Find out if your region is known for certain foods or if your state's economy depends on certain foods.

- If possible, invite a local farmer or grower to talk with the children about farming and agriculture.

- Take a trip to a local farmers market to enhance this activity. Children will be exposed to local foods and meet local farmers.

- Use this activity as a springboard for kicking off a "local foods potluck" at your program (see chapter 9).

(continues on next page)

CONNECTIONS

Make a local foods calendar. Have the children draw pictures of fruits and vegetables that ripen during different seasons and use the artwork to create a calendar.

Ask the children why food might be considered fresher if it is grown locally. Discuss with them how long the growing season is in your area and what other factors in nature might affect a farm crop (factors might include weather, heavy rains, drought, fires, and pest infestation). Do some research on different plants and their life cycles, then determine their growing season. Encourage children to discuss why certain plants ripen at certain times of the year; for example, discuss what vegetable crop is the first to appear in the spring and why most apples ripen in the fall.

An Apple's Journey

Many foods are grown in multiple places to satisfy consumer demand. For this reason, you may be able to purchase an apple that was grown at a farm down the road, or one grown on an orchard in South America. In this activity, the children will explore the origins for different apples and use a map to find the locations where apples are grown.

Activity Goals

→ To understand why some food travels long distances

→ To read a simple map

National Science Education Standards

Life science: characteristics of organisms

Science in personal and social perspectives: science and technology in local challenges

Materials and Supplies

☐ A variety of apples, ideally from many different areas (Most apples at grocery stores have a sticker or label with the country or state of origin and the name of the apple variety on them. If you're unsure about an apple's origin, ask a produce manager for help.)

☐ A world map

Procedure

1. Display a variety of apples on a table, or pass one apple to each child.

2. Discuss the many differences among apples: the color, size, shape, toughness, scent, and so on.

3. Remove the sticker from one apple and read the name of the country or state where the apple was grown.

4. Work with the children to find that country or state on the map, and place the sticker there to mark the spot.

5. Repeat this process for all of the apples.

6. Ask the children where they live and mark this on the map too. Discuss how the various apples may have been transported to your local grocery store. Ask the children to identify any apples that came from a different part of the world, which apple traveled the farthest, how far the apple traveled, and how it got to your area.

TIPS

- Share the apples as a snack!

CONNECTIONS

Ask the children which apples tasted the best to them and discuss why. Many apples have interesting names, such as Golden Delicious, Zestar, and Fireside. Look at the names of the apples you've brought in and talk about them. Ask the children how they think the apples got their names. Invite the children to make up their own names for the apples they sampled.

Pass out small maps to each child and ask them to draw or paint the journey of each apple to your program.

Do this activity in the fall, and follow up with a trip to an apple orchard. Children can taste many varieties of apples grown locally.

Lunchtime Color Challenge

The United States Department of Agriculture (USDA) makes clear recommendations for healthy eating. This program, known as MyPlate, illustrates the components of a healthy meal (see page 97). Basically, a "healthy plate" should consist roughly of half fruits and vegetables, one-quarter grains—preferably whole grains—and one-quarter proteins. Dairy recommendations are also included.

The USDA program color-codes the different food groups in order to distinguish them. In this activity, children will use colored circles of construction paper to fill a lunch bag with different portions of food. As a group, you'll discuss what makes a balanced diet. Consider implementing this activity outside if the weather allows.

Activity Goals

→ To become familiar with a commonly used nutritional guideline

→ To have fun playing and collecting during an active game

National Science Education Standards

Science in personal and social perspectives: personal health

Materials and Supplies

☐ Three-inch circles of construction paper in red, brown, blue, purple, and green, at least five circles per child

☐ Small paper lunch bags, one per child

☐ A MyPlate poster or a color printout from www.choosemyplate.gov

Procedure

1. Give each child a lunch bag.

2. Scatter the circles around a large grassy area. Tell the children that they need to collect the circles. Ask them to try to get at least one circle of each color.

3. Children may run and scramble to collect as many circles as possible.

4. After all the circles have been collected, show the MyPlate poster and review with the children the different food groups represented. Tell them that each colored circle represents a different food group.

5. Have them remove the circles from their lunch bags and share with the group what they collected by naming a food from that color's food group. A red circle means the child should name a fruit, a brown circle equals a grain, a green circle equals a vegetable, a blue circle equals a dairy item, and a purple circle equals a protein.

6. Make some observations with the children. Ask them if everyone got at least one of each of the food groups, or if anyone collected a large number of one group. Discuss with the children what a lunch might look like if it was all dairy, for example, or all fruit. What do the children think a balanced lunch might look like.

TIPS

- Repeat this activity with new challenges. For example, challenge the children to crawl or to hop on one foot to collect the circles.

- As an additional challenge, remove one food group entirely and discuss what happens when people don't get enough of a certain food group. Alternately, spread out circles from only one food group, and discuss what might happen if someone only ate fruit, for example.

CONNECTIONS

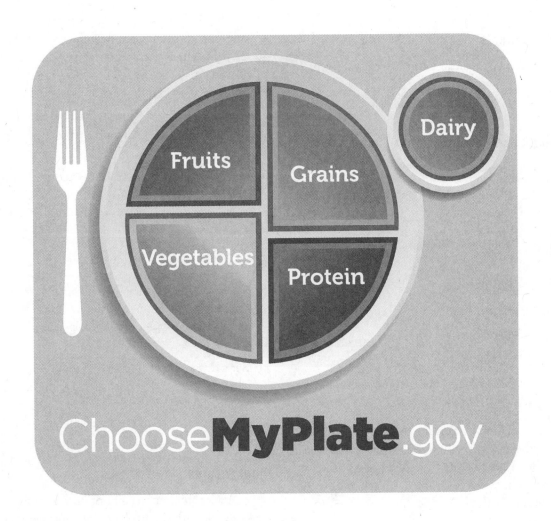

Attempt to identify the food categories during lunchtime. Make a chart or poster depicting the food groups, and have children identify the foods in their lunches and which groups they belong in.

Pass out paper plates and allow each child to draw, paint, or color foods from each of the food groups on the plate.

Refer to the MyPlate graphic and attempt to achieve the recommended proportions of the food groups while playing this game.

Rainbow on My Plate

AGES
3+

Every meal should contain a variety of nutrients in order to be the best it can be. The more colors we eat, the healthier we are. In this activity, the children will explore the many colors of fruits, vegetables, and other foods. You'll also provide children with a sense of the nutritive quality of their food. Concentrate on natural colors; artificially colored foods don't count when it comes to creating a colorful meal!

Activity Goals

→ To become aware of the variety of colors in our foods

→ To practice graphing and counting

National Science Education Standards

Life science: characteristics of organisms

Science in personal and social perspectives: personal health

Materials and Supplies

☐ Lunches, brought from home

☐ Chart paper and markers in red, orange, yellow, green, blue, purple, and black

Procedure

1. Ask the children to name the colors of the rainbow. Divide the chart paper into eight columns. Use each color of marker to write that color name at the top of a column, except for black; use black to label the last column "Other."

2. Ask, "What are some foods we might eat that are those same colors? Do you know what colors are in your lunch box for snacktime/lunchtime?"

3. While the children eat, ask them what colors they see in their foods and if the colors are there naturally or because the food has been colored artificially. Ask them to describe how they can tell. Talk about what colors are found in nature, and compare them with the colors of some of the foods.

4. As the children name the foods, write them in the appropriate color column. Some items will likely be white (such as crackers, white bread) or brown (bread crust, cookies). These belong in the Other column. If an item has many colors, such as soup or pasta salad, record each color the children see.

5. At the end of the meal, tally up the food items from each column.

6. As a group, continue this activity throughout the week (or month, or year!) and talk about the most frequently found colors and the least frequently found colors.

TIPS

- Enlist families to pack colorful lunches for their children. In your e-newsletter, mention the benefits of including a variety of naturally colored foods in each meal.

- Set a classroom goal of having every color represented by the end of one week. Do this activity as a group, tallying up the colors of foods at each meal and snack shared rather than singling out any specific children.

CONNECTIONS

Invite children to paint or draw a rainbow of foods with watercolor paints or crayons. This is a great complement to any classroom activities or unit you're doing on color.

Every Little Bit

This activity helps children become aware of the amount of food they are discarding on any given day. They will be more mindful about what they are discarding during snacks and lunches once they develop the habit of measuring and tracking it.

Activity Goals

→ To have fun measuring uneaten food

→ To become aware of food that goes uneaten

National Science Education Standards

History and nature of science: science as a human endeavor

Materials and Supplies

☐ Primary scale, with bowls or buckets

☐ A day's worth of uneaten food scraps

Procedure

1. Before eating, tell the children that you are interested in finding out how much food and liquid is thrown away each day in your classroom. Ask, "How do you think we could measure that?"

2. If they aren't already familiar with using a primary scale, demonstrate how it works, and allow time for each child to test it out.

3. After everyone has eaten, add all the leftover food and liquid to the bowl on one side of the scale.

4. Fill the bowl on the other side with the weight needed to accurately measure the weight of the food and liquid.

5. Record the weight.

6. Repeat this with all meals and snacks during the day.

7. At the end of the day, add the food to your compost pile and discuss with the children the amount of food that was discarded that day.

8. Ask them, "What do you think about that? Why did we throw away so much food? What can you do if you don't like your snack or lunch?"

9. Ensure that children wash their hands after placing food waste on the scale.

TIPS

- Be very careful to remain open-minded and non-judgmental during this activity. Resist the temptation to compare children's eating habits or to tell them to clear their plates or finish everything their parents packed. The intent of this activity is simply for children to learn to measure and become aware of how much food is being discarded.

- Provide gloves or tongs for children to place food on the scale if they don't want to touch the food directly with their hands.

- Publicize the results of your experiment to families. If they provide their children's food, this activity may help them reduce waste by evaluating whether they are providing portions that are too large or packing foods that their children don't eat.

- Explain that a leftover piece of food can be called an *ort* or a *scrap*.

CONNECTIONS

Measure food scraps each day for several weeks. Tally up the weight of food each week. Over time, students will naturally begin to pay more attention to the amount of food they discard.

Crazy Compost Mix-Up Dance

AGES 3+

For compost to "work," it must contain the right ingredients: green materials (such as food scraps and fresh grass clippings), brown materials (such as torn cardboard or dry leaves), water, heat, and air. *Microorganisms* in soil—as well as small insects and other critters—help break down the material by eating and digesting it. Through the composting process, waste materials in the pile are transformed into a rich, dark soil-like material that is great for plants and gardens. In this activity, children will have a chance to "become" a living compost pile. This is a great activity to conduct outside.

Activity Goals

→ To identify the different components that make up a compost pile

→ To play and be active in a fun, silly way

National Science Education Standards

Life science: characteristics of organisms

Materials and Supplies

☐ A large open outdoor area or a wide marked-off area inside

Procedure

1. Explain what a compost pile is and what happens to the things we put in it. Explain that we can put anything in the pile that once came from plants.

2. As a group, identify the main components of a compost pile (see the introductory paragraph).

3. Explain that you've marked off a designated area where you can do a crazy compost mix-up dance together.

4. Give each child a "role" to play in the compost pile. Try to have roughly the same number of children playing the roles of "critters," "greens," and "browns." Use whatever technique makes the most sense for your group: assign roles, pass out "job cards" you've made ahead of time, or let the children choose.

5. Invite all the children playing greens or browns to step into the circle.

6. Next, invite the critters to enter the circle and scurry around, moving and wiggling through the greens and browns. Remind them to be gentle with their classmates: no pinching or biting! You aren't really going to eat through this material!

7. When a brown or a green is lightly tagged by a critter, that child's role is to simulate the creation of heat in the pile, by jogging in place or hopping up and down, waving his hands in the air. As the critters continue to tag the browns and greens, you'll eventually have a crazy dance going on!

8. Make sure everyone stays within the borders you've set up. You may decide to play some fun music to get everyone moving.

9. Invite the browns and greens to move around randomly within the space after being tagged.

10. After a few minutes, encourage everyone to slow down and eventually stop. This happens in compost piles as the decomposition process slows. If you want to speed up the process, add water, mix the pile, or add green and brown material.

11. Have the children switch roles and repeat the game.

TIPS

• For very young children, simply lump the two categories together and call them materials that came from plants. There is no need to differentiate between green and brown materials.

• Allow plenty of time for this activity, and allow the children a chance to try all the different roles.

- Since a compost pile needs water, do this activity in the hot months, in swimsuits, with a teacher using a hose to supply the occasional bursts of water to the pile!

CONNECTIONS

Have the children draw labels for different elements in this game: the brown materials, the green materials, and the critters, worms, and microorganisms. (Microorganisms are too small to be seen with the naked eye, so children can draw them to look like beetles or other bugs, or anything they imagine!)

CHAPTER 5

Water, Water, Everywhere

Water is one of Earth's most important natural resources. It sustains all life on our planet. No matter who you are or where you live, you depend on it. Water makes up about two-thirds of the human body; each and every one of our cells is filled with it. Water is essential for the functioning of our bodies and organs. Without water, we—and all living things—can only live a short time. Nothing can grow or survive without water.

Water provides habitat for countless plant and animal species. Water has a profound effect on our weather and climate. Water has shaped, and continues to shape, our landscape. Features such as hills, valleys, canyons, and plains are often formed by water or ice, which is, after all, frozen water. Water provides power, cooling, and entertainment. The list of reasons for water's importance goes on and on.

Water is also a great tool for education, exploration, and fun in the early childhood classroom. Young children adore it. There are children who, if permitted, would spend hours at the water table sinking and floating objects, washing their hands, and splashing water around, delighting in the way it sparkles in the sun. Others will seize any opportunity to jump in puddles after a rainstorm, relishing their power to make a huge splash! Still others simply enjoy watching water and the way it shimmers and catches light, creating rainbows in the air. With water as your topic, you don't have to work hard to elicit a sense

of wonder in children. Water is an important subject and an easy one to start young children on the road to caring about the environment.

Water Is Special

So what is it about water that makes it so special? Water is truly a precious resource. Although 70 percent of Earth's surface is covered by water, most of that is ocean. Ocean water is salty, which means it's not suitable for drinking or for irrigating crops. Only 3 percent of the Earth's water is freshwater—or not salty. Of that freshwater, approximately 2 percent is currently frozen in *glaciers*, mostly at the Earth's poles. That leaves just 1 percent of the Earth's water available for drinking and irrigating vegetation. This 1 percent includes the water located underground—deep within aquifers. If we have only 1 percent of the Earth's water available to us, how is it that we don't simply run out? Good question. Before I answer it, I want to start with a basic overview of water and its unique properties. Please note that this is meant as an overview (or a refresher) for you, the educator. I am not suggesting you teach the scientific and technical details to the children in your program, although you might find it helpful in answering questions that children raise in the course of their explorations. As with the other chapters, the introductory material is intended for you—to review or strengthen your own understanding and help you develop further activities if desired.

WHAT IS WATER?

Water, like every living and nonliving thing in the universe, is made of tiny particles called *molecules* that are too small to see without the help of special instruments. Every molecule is made of even tinier particles called *atoms*. Atoms are the building blocks for all things, even air. A molecule can be formed by as few as two atoms and as many as millions of atoms or even more. A single water molecule is formed by two atoms of hydrogen (H) and one atom of oxygen (O), thus the scientific name H_2O.

Groups of molecules form different substances and materials, and depending on the substance and the *state* of the substance, the molecules are arranged in different ways. As we know, there are three common states in which materials and objects on Earth can exist: solid, liquid, or gas. Water is the only substance that naturally occurs in all three states at Earth's ordinary temperatures. This is important! It's one of the properties that makes water so special and so fascinating. In its *solid state*—ice—water molecules are arranged in an organized pattern and they have very little movement. In its *liquid state*, water molecules lose their organized pattern and they actually move, or slide around one another somewhat. As with the molecules themselves, however, you can't see the movement happening with the naked eye. When water turns into its *gas state*—vapor or steam—its molecules spread apart and move around even more. Each state is part of the water cycle, described next.

WATER CYCLE

Water changes from one state to another mostly in response to temperature changes. Heating or cooling water causes its molecules to change their arrangement. Have you ever watched steam billow from a boiling teapot? Or ice melt in the sunshine? Then you've watched water changing its state. You can also

imagine how much this feature of water affects the rhythms of nature on Earth.

In nature and all around our planet, water is constantly changing from one state to another, moving back and forth between the atmosphere and Earth. Along the way, it may pass through the bodies of living things. This constant and continuous journey of water is known as the *water cycle*. While it is impossible to describe every step or change that any given drop of water may undergo, I can summarize the basic ones.

The sun warms water on the Earth's surface. Heating water causes it to *evaporate*, or turn into a gas. Water vapor can rise up higher and higher into the atmosphere, where cooler temperatures cause it to *condense*, which means to turn from a gas into a liquid. In the atmosphere, liquid water droplets collect on tiny floating dust particles. These may clump together to form clouds.

When conditions are right, the droplets in clouds fall back to Earth as rain, snow, or sleet, otherwise known as *precipitation*. There are countless possibilities for where this water can then go. For example, some of it lands directly in bodies of water—such as rivers, lakes, or oceans—on the Earth's surface. Some of it falls on land and seeps down into the ground. Water underground is called *groundwater*. Some of the water falls on land and flows across the land until it enters the ground or a body of water. Water that flows across the surface of the land is called *runoff*.

However it lands and wherever it moves, water eventually returns to the atmosphere. Some of the water that seeps into the ground is taken up by plants. Plants turn it back into water vapor, which they emit through the surface of their leaves. This process is called *transpiration*. People and animals also emit water, in a gas form through our exhalations and in a liquid form through our bodily waste.

Now recall the earlier question "With so little of Earth's water available to us for drinking, why don't we use it up?" Thanks to the water cycle, we just keep reusing the same water, over and over again. We drink it, use it to grow food, swim and bathe in it, and water our plants and wash our cars with it. As we "use it up," it returns to the atmosphere, and the cycle goes on. The water cycle is continuous and constant. It has no beginning and no end. A single raindrop may fall from the sky and return to the atmosphere in a matter of hours, or the same journey for another droplet may take thousands of years. It is possible to drink water that was on Earth during the age of dinosaurs!

Watersheds

Liquid water on the Earth's surface has its own fascinating story in the journey it takes. That story starts with another basic, though abstract, property: gravity. Gravity is the force that pulls on every object or substance in the universe. Earth's gravity pulls everything downward toward Earth's center. Earth's gravity is responsible for water always running downhill. Water may seep downward into the ground, or it may flow across the land toward a body of water. It may move powerfully along riverbeds, sometimes crashing over rocks or cliffs, or it may meander slowly and peacefully, seeming almost still but moving nonetheless. Regardless of how it moves, water always flows from higher points to lower points.

A *watershed* is an area of land in which all the water that drains off it goes into a particular body of water such as a stream, river, pond, or lake. That body of water is the lowest point in that particular area of land. Watersheds vary greatly in size and nature. The watershed for a small lake could be just a few square miles, whereas the watershed for a major river could be hundreds of square miles. Keep in mind that most bodies of water flow into other bodies of water. For example, a stream flows into a river that ultimately flows into the ocean. In other words, smaller watersheds typically fall within larger watersheds, and so on; most of them ultimately connecting to the ocean.

No matter where you live, you live in a watershed. It has become commonplace in environmental circles to talk about one's "watershed address." But it can be confusing to determine exactly what that is, especially in areas where there are many bodies of water. In the continental United States alone, there are over two thousand watersheds (USGS 2012). Your watershed address most likely starts with the nearest major body of water. Because watersheds are nested one within another, your complete watershed address would include every watershed into which your watershed drains, ending in an ocean. For example, my watershed address is Minnehaha Creek, Mississippi River, Gulf of Mexico. This means that all the water that drains off my property (which doesn't evaporate, or get consumed by plant roots) winds up in the nearby Minnehaha Creek, where it flows downstream to the Mississippi River, which continues to collect water as it widens and grows, flowing on and on, all the way to the Gulf of Mexico. You can find your watershed by visiting the US EPA Surf Your Watershed website at http://cfpub.epa.gov/surf/locate/index.cfm. Type in your zip code or nearest body of water to find out which watershed you live in.

Why is it important to understand the watershed concept and know your watershed address? For one thing, it helps remind us that every place within our landscape is connected by our common contribution to, or impact on, a body of water and the ones beyond that one. Your everyday actions and decisions can have big consequences. For example, if you fertilize your lawn, some of the fertilizer will be taken up by the grass as nourishment, but some of it will likely be washed off by rain and will flow into a nearby storm sewer and into a nearby watershed. Recall that water flowing across the land's surface is called runoff. Runoff collects chemicals, sediments, and other substances as it flows along the surface. It carries these materials and deposits them into whichever body of water the runoff flows. Runoff happens all the time, but it is particularly problematic in times of big rainfalls, when the ground gets saturated and water that would normally seep into the ground can no longer do so.

In rural areas where there is a lot of agricultural production, farmers' decisions about how to manage their landscapes have negative effects on the quality of water in their watersheds and in the larger watersheds that hold theirs. Chemical fertilizers, pesticides, and contaminated soil can easily be carried by runoff into nearby watersheds. Agricultural runoff can disrupt the ecosystems of streams and rivers, making survival difficult for animals and insects. A stream that receives a lot of agricultural runoff may harbor little to no life. Here is where the watershed idea really starts to make sense. Take the Mississippi River watershed: Because it is so large, and many smaller watersheds flow into it throughout the Central States, it collects water (and agricultural fertilizers and chemicals contained in runoff) from 31 states, or approximately 41 percent of the surface waters in the United States (Mississippi River Gulf of Mexico Watershed Nutrient Task Force 2012). By the time the Mississippi reaches its destination in the Gulf of Mexico, it's carrying an enormous load of fertilizer and other agricultural waste. The agricultural waste enters the ocean and causes excessive algae growth. This algae growth leads to a condition known as *hypoxia*—extremely low levels of oxygen in the water. Recall that even aquatic creatures need oxygen to survive. Aquatic plants and animals cannot survive in a state of hypoxia. The area of hypoxia in the Gulf of Mexico is so large and so problematic that it has been called "the dead zone." In 2011, a year of record Mississippi River flooding, the dead zone was mapped at 6,765 square miles—an area larger than the state of Connecticut (LUMC 2011).

The impact on your watershed will vary depending on whether you live in an urban setting, a rural agricultural area, or a remote wilderness area. Getting to know your watershed and its main sources will help you understand some of the water- and Earth-friendly things you can do in your program and your community. This information might also spark curiosity among your colleagues about how you might partner with community organizations around water conservation. Water quality organizations include state natural resource or wildlife departments, city or county public works departments, parks and recreation organizations, and governmental agencies known as watershed districts. Many of these organizations will provide guest speakers or teaching materials on loan or for very little cost.

Human Impact on Water Quality

The sad truth is humans have contributed a great deal to endangering our precious water supplies. We've influenced the flow of the water cycle by altering our landscapes. We've vastly increased the amount of paved surfaces, which is significant because paved surfaces are *impervious*, or nonporous, so they cannot absorb water. When water cannot be absorbed, it runs off the surface, and as I mentioned earlier, collects materials along the way and deposits them into watersheds. Materials collected by runoff can include road chemicals, salts, sediments, gasoline, oil, and more. Anything that is found on impervious surfaces can get washed downstream into creeks, rivers, or lakes. Many of these substances can harm wildlife, plant communities, and overall water quality.

Humans have drained wetlands in order to expand agricultural fields and develop urban areas. Wetlands are natural areas that hold water—either in the soil or on the surface—for most of the year. They are home to an incredible variety of plant and animal species specifically adapted to such a watery habitat. From a water quality perspective, wetlands are extremely important because they hold water, allowing pollutants and sediments to settle out before the water moves on to streams, lakes, and rivers. By dramatically reducing the number and size of wetlands, we have reduced one of nature's most important water filters.

Humans have also affected water shorelines, removing or altering natural vegetation, adding homes and businesses, or otherwise developing them. In doing so, we've eliminated yet another natural water quality protection method. Natural shoreline vegetation, if left in place, helps filter materials carried in runoff so that those materials don't enter our waterways. Natural shoreline vegetation also stabilizes shorelines and makes them less vulnerable to erosion.

We've loaded our waterways with lawn, garden, and agricultural fertilizers. We've spilled oil and gas on the ground that gets picked up by rainwater and flows into storm sewers and into watersheds. Even small leaks from buses or vans leave motor oil and gasoline on the pavement, which eventually runs off and contaminates nearby waterways. If not properly disposed of, the oil used in an average oil change can contaminate one million gallons of freshwater (US EPA 2011g). In cold-climate winters, we use chemicals and salts to de-ice the roads. While helpful for making driving less hazardous, these materials unfortunately run off into watersheds and harm aquatic animals and plant life. Even the soaps, cleaners, medicines, and other personal care products we use every day can adversely affect water supplies. These products wash down our drains and wind up in our watersheds.

Industrial processes such as manufacturing, mining, and even commercial recycling facilities create wastewater, which can be hazardous to humans and animals alike. The burning of fossil fuels also can contribute to water pollution. Fossil fuel emissions include various pollutants that enter the atmosphere and can be carried back to Earth by rain. These pollutants are then washed into waterways, or they seep into the ground. This is known as *acid rain*, and it's very harmful to aquatic life (US EPA 2007).

Human Impact on Water Availability

Recall the statistic that only 1 percent of the Earth's freshwater is available for human and plant use. Although that's a lot of water (and because of the water cycle it is being recycled all the time), there are places on Earth where humans are using freshwater resources faster than that water is being replenished by the natural water cycle. Freshwater on Earth is not distributed evenly. There are many parts of the world where people lack access to clean water for drinking, cooking, or irrigation. The United Nations (UN 2012) asserts that over 700 million people in 43 countries are living in conditions of water scarcity. Because the Earth's population is constantly growing, this means that there will be an even greater need for clean freshwater in the future. Despite the continuous nature of the water cycle, conservation of water is of utmost importance. By conserving, we protect water for future generations.

But there's a positive story too. We can, and do, positively affect water quality in many ways. In addition to being mindful about big-picture issues, such as water-sensitive land-use planning and runoff management, we can consider the effects of our everyday decisions on water quality. We can pay attention to and try to reduce the potential pollution going down the drain in our homes, work facilities, and neighborhoods. The choices we make about soaps, detergents, and other cleaning supplies are important. In addition to taking steps to protect water quality, we can

also conserve water. That means using less water as well as being wise about how we use it. We can even pay attention to other consumer choices that may have a less obvious, but nonetheless important, impact on water. For example, buying recycled paper helps conserve water because less water is used in the production of recycled paper than in the creation of paper from virgin materials. Every drop makes a difference, and every little step we take toward caring for our water is important.

If you're using the *Go Green Rating Scale* by Phil Boise, you will find that scale 10 focuses on water conservation. You can use this scale to assess your facility's use of water for everyday purposes, such as sanitation and food preparation. You can also evaluate your use of water for landscape purposes, such as irrigation.

Teaching about Water in Early Childhood

Although I've said that getting into the topics of water pollution and water shortages in the early childhood classroom isn't necessary—or even encouraged—simple messages about conservation and water's unique role on Earth can be conveyed through your actions. You can also embrace children's natural love of water to foster their growing sense of stewardship. In subtle ways, you can make conservation a part of play. Consider all the things you already do with water in your classroom. From teaching toothbrushing and hygiene habits, to using a water table, to washing the classroom tables, toys, and vehicles, you can instill conservation messages by including children in activities, being mindful about how you use water, and discussing water's importance and your appreciation for it. When you teach toothbrushing or hand-washing habits, make turning off the water an important step in this activity. Instead of allowing the faucet to run, turn the water on only to wet the toothbrush and rinse hands. This will save a lot of water. When you hold a "car wash" for the tricycles and scooters on a warm spring day, consider filling buckets with water instead of allowing children to spray the vehicles directly with hoses. (And of course use nontoxic soaps or detergent.) Comment that using a bucket of water requires less water than spraying directly from the hose.

Remember to look at your indirect communication about water too. Consider how you use water in the classroom—what messages do you send the children about how you value water? Invite the children to help you wash the classroom furniture with water, and notice how the water makes things clean again.

And what is even more important, we must first ensure that the children in our programs have positive, joyful, and meaningful experiences with water. This lays the foundation for developing a sincere interest in conserving it. Ensure that you are offering children many opportunities to explore water and use it in new ways. Allow for open-ended play with water. Make sure you have a good collection of materials for exploring water, such as empty bottles, sponges, eyedroppers, milk jugs, tubes, funnels, and watering cans.

Don't let a lack of proper outerwear be a barrier to exploring water. Encourage families to send a change of clothes to school so children won't be afraid to get wet. Invest in extra rain gear to have on hand for children who lack it. A clothing swap, hand-me-down program, or donation program all provide good ways to procure children's clothing and gear.

Express gratitude about all that water can do, and the children will feel it too. Because of its unique qualities, universal appeal, and the incredible number of ways you can incorporate it into your classroom, water is a fantastic resource for the early childhood educator. Guided and open-ended experiences with water can enrich children's understanding of the properties of water and provide months of explorations and opportunities for discovery.

Although outdoors is by far the best place to experience water and do activities related to water, you

can even enjoy water within the comfort of the indoors. Invite the children to watch a rainstorm from inside, noses pressed to glass, as you observe water's path down the sidewalk, or notice where it creates puddles. Listen to the sound the raindrops make as they hit the roof. There is so much you can do to present opportunities for the children in your program to explore water, experience its properties, and develop questions of their own for teacher-supported investigation. Children are fascinated with water's ability to change states. This property alone offers many opportunities for exploration.

Water has unique and important properties that make it a perfect tool for exploring and enjoying nature and developing scientific-thinking skills through experimentation and exploration. Experiences using water as a medium can awaken artistic expression. Songs, poems, and stories about water can build literacy skills. The activities that follow will provide you with ideas for creating that all-important sense of delight and wonder—the first step toward conservation.

Water Words

Water is important for everyone! Plants need water in order to grow, and our bodies need water in order to work properly. Water also keeps us cool in the summertime when we can dash through the sprinkler. This activity allows children to creatively express their feelings and knowledge about water. Consider conducting this activity outside on a nice day. If you have an outdoor covered area available, you can even do this activity outside on a rainy day.

Activity Goals

→ To foster creative development and literacy skills

→ To encourage imagination

National Science Education Standards

Life science: organisms and environments

Earth and space science: properties of earth materials

Materials and Supplies

☐ Chart paper and a marker

☐ Assorted water-related photographs, such as bodies of water in nature, rain, glasses of water, animals that depend on water or live in wetlands

Procedure

1. Show the images to the children. Discuss what they have in common, and encourage the group to talk together about what they see. Ask the children how the images make them feel.

2. Have a brainstorming session and talk about all the great things the children can think of that pertain to water. For example, it helps plants grow, ducks can swim in it, and so on.

3. As the children share their words, record them on the chart paper for everyone to see.

4. Keep the paper posted in a highly visible location and refer to it often.

TIPS

- Encourage all kinds of contributions! To help younger children narrow their focus a bit, you might work together to choose a theme, such as "words that describe water." Responses might include "sparkly," "blue," and "wet." Or if your theme is "Who needs water?" responses might include "ducks," "birds," "frogs," "fish," and so on.

CONNECTIONS

Repeat this activity many times with different themes to help deepen the children's understanding of water. Example themes include "bodies of water near school," "animals that live in the water," and "how we use water."

 Use the words the children shared to make a list of cards and then pass them out. Encourage the children to make poems or tell a story using the words on their cards as prompts. Tell a story using the water words, or make up a story as a group, each child adding a little bit.

 Ask children to write or dictate poems using the water words.

Evaporating Art

AGES 3+

Remember that water is unique in that it can occur naturally as a solid, liquid, or gas, depending upon the temperature. *Evaporation* occurs when heat warms water and causes it to turn into water vapor. Water vapor is still water, it is just in the form of a gas. Some days there is more water vapor in the air than other days. We may be very aware of water vapor in the air on a humid day but not on a dry day.

Evaporation is an important part of the water cycle and it happens naturally all the time, all around us, as the sun warms water on our planet's surface. The process of evaporation can be difficult to understand, as it is not something that is visible to the eye. However, the result of evaporation can be seen when children "paint" with water on a warm sidewalk or rock during a sunny day.

Activity Goals

→ To see how the warmth from the sun causes water to evaporate

→ To enjoy being outside and playing with water

National Science Education Standards

Physical science: light, heat, electricity, and magnetism

Earth and space science: properties of earth materials, changes in earth and sky

Materials and Supplies

☐ A sunny day

☐ Buckets and bowls of water

☐ Assorted paintbrushes, including large ones used for painting walls

☐ A sidewalk, pieces of slate or stone, or large flat rocks

Procedure

1. Explain that the children will be doing an experiment to see the effects of evaporation. Ask, "Where does water go when it dries up and disappears?"

2. Invite the children to "paint" on a sunny sidewalk, rock, or other surface.

3. They can watch as their water paintings fade away, or evaporate.

4. Ask the children where the water has gone. Explain that it has evaporated, turning into a gas form that is now in the air all around them and invisible to their eyes.

TIPS

• Do this activity outdoors on a sunny day. Some children may want to try painting in the shade so they can compare the different rates of evaporation.

• Refer back to this activity in the future when children get wet or accidentally spill liquids in the classroom. This activity can also be a great experience for children with sensory integration issues, or for children who don't like to get wet. It can be comforting to see that water does evaporate and things do eventually dry.

CONNECTIONS

Compare what happens when children paint with water on a hot stone versus pouring water onto the grass. Discuss with the children what is different and what is happening. Do this activity at different times during the day. Notice that the pavement is cooler in the morning and that paintings last longer than they do in the afternoon. Ask the children for their ideas as to why.

Making a Cloud

Even when it's not raining, the air around us holds water. The air holds water in a gas form—called water vapor—and some amount of it is always present, even on days that seem dry to us. *Condensation* happens when a gas turns into a liquid—the reverse of evaporation. Clouds form when water vapor in the air condenses, or turns into tiny droplets of liquid water floating in the air. These water droplets clump together to form clouds.

In this activity, children are invited to think about the different states of water that occur naturally in the air. They will pretend to be the tiny bits of water vapor moving through the air and will have fun "linking up" with another child to form a liquid water droplet. Then they can clump together with a few more children to form a cloud.

Activity Goals

→ To have fun moving, playing, and imagining being water

→ To think about water and its different naturally occurring states

National Science Education Standards

Earth and space science: properties of earth materials

Materials and Supplies

☐ A large open space outside

Procedure

1. Explain to the children that water can occur in three forms—liquid, gas, and solid—and it can easily change form from one of these to another. We all know what water in liquid and solid forms looks like, but we can't see water in a gas form. Water in a gas form—water vapor—is always in the air around us, and sometimes that water vapor turns into a liquid and forms tiny droplets of water. Droplets of liquid water float in the air and clump together with other droplets to form clouds.

2. Invite the children to become tiny bits of water vapor, which means they are so small they can't be seen with our eyes. Ask them to dance around to symbolize that there is water vapor constantly in the air around us. Ask, "How might you move if you were very tiny?"

3. Tell the children that they will be joining another bit of water vapor to form a droplet of liquid water, and have each child find a partner.

4. Now tell the children that the droplets of liquid water will clump together to form clouds.

5. Encourage the pairs to wiggle and scramble around and connect with another pair of children.

6. Encourage the children to have fun trying to connect in as many ways as possible, linking arms, touching feet, and so on.

7. Invite the whole group to connect, forming one large cloud. As the group connects, they will likely stop moving or slow down.

8. Discuss with the children what happens to liquid water once it clumps together in a cloud. Mention that it often falls out of the sky as rain! Ask the children to "fall" like raindrops and sit on the floor.

9. After you've played this game for a while, reflect on the activity. Ask the children to tell you what happened.

TIPS

- For added fun, do this activity to music or to a recording of a storm.

- Use this activity as a complement to the Weather, Climate, and Energy chapter.

CONNECTIONS

Invite the children to write a description of the dance they just did, describing what happened in each step.

Have the children write stories from the point of view of a water droplet, describing what happens and the journey that water takes.

The Great Growing Water Drop

AGES
3+

One of water's special properties is that its molecules have a strong attraction to one another. This is a phenomenon called "cohesion," and it is an important force in causing raindrops to form. Observing the formation and movement of water droplets on a variety of surfaces can be a fun and interesting activity for children.

Activity Goals

→ To have fun making water droplets grow and move

National Science Education Standards

Physical science: properties of objects and materials

Earth and space science: properties of earth materials

Materials and Supplies

☐ Pipettes, eyedroppers, or drinking straws (see Tips)

☐ Squares of wax paper, approximately ten inches, one per child

☐ Paper towels or cloth dish towels, one per child

☐ A bowl of water for each child

Procedure

1. Tell the children that water is made up of tiny pieces called molecules that we can't see with our eyes, and that water molecules love to join together.

2. Instruct the children to take one pipette-full of water and drop it on the wax paper.

3. Have the children add another drop of water close to, but not touching, the first one.

4. Ask the children how they could get the water to form one bigger drop out of the two drops. (For example, they could move and bend the paper, or they could blow the water, or they could add more drops near the first one.)

5. Challenge the children to add the drops close to the others so they will connect either by manipulating the wax paper or by pushing the water drop with the pipettes rather than simply adding more drops to the others.

6. Invite the children to see how big they can make their water droplet without having it run off the wax paper.

7. Ask the children to explain their discoveries to the group.

8. Provide each child with a paper towel or dish towel. Invite them to repeat the activity with the towels. Discuss with the children what is different and why the water droplets don't bead up as they do on the wax paper.

TIPS

• Demonstrate the proper use of the pipettes and eye droppers, and allow the children time to practice before beginning this activity. To use pipettes or eye droppers, squeeze the bulb at the end before inserting the tip into a bowl of water. Release the pressure on the bulb and the pipette/eye dropper will fill with water. Alternatively, use drinking straws. Place the drinking straw in the water bowl; it will fill with a small amount of water. Place your finger over the end of the straw that is out of the bowl, and remove the straw from the bowl. When you remove your finger from the straw, the water will flow out.

• If a child's wax paper becomes really wrinkled, replace it; otherwise the water will not bead up as well.

• Place trays under the wax paper to help contain the water.

- Repeat this activity with many kinds of surfaces, including fabric, paper, and plastic.

CONNECTIONS

Ask the children how they got the water droplets to connect, what happens if they use plain paper or fabric, and why the wax paper is important.

Use watercolors or put food coloring in the water. Watch the colors mix as the water droplets combine. Allow the colored water to dry and see how it looks.

Catching Condensation on a Cup

As children begin to understand the water cycle, they may be curious to see evidence of condensation. You may have shared with them that clouds form when water vapor condenses into liquid water droplets in the sky, but grasping the concept of condensation can be difficult. Providing children with the opportunity to see the effects of condensation close-up can help them understand it. Through this activity, which uses only a cup of ice water and food coloring, children can see firsthand the result of condensation.

Activity Goals

→ To experiment with water and condensation

→ To test a common misconception about condensation

National Science Education Standards

Earth and space science: properties of earth materials

Science in personal and social perspectives: changes in environments

Life science: life cycles of organisms, organisms and environments

Materials and Supplies

☐ Paper or plastic cups, one per child

☐ Ice cubes

☐ Red, blue, or green food coloring

☐ Water

☐ Stir sticks or straws

☐ Light-colored cloths or white paper towels

Procedure

1. Review the concept of condensation with the children. Remind them that condensation is when a gas turns into a liquid. It happens in the air around us when water vapor—water in the form of gas—turns into liquid water droplets floating in the air. Floating liquid droplets clump together to make clouds. Condensation also happens closer to the ground when water vapor condenses on plants and forms the dewdrops we see on cool mornings. Condensation can even happen when we have cold water in a cup. Some children may already have noticed this phenomenon.

2. Pass out cups to the children, and fill them with ice cubes, water, and a few drops of food coloring. Invite the children to stir these together with the stir sticks.

3. Explain that the ice will cause condensation to take place faster than if the water were a warmer temperature.

4. Encourage the children to feel the cool air around the cup but to avoid touching the cup.

5. After several minutes have passed, the children can touch a small area on their cups. Does it feel wet? It should.

6. Ask the children where the water came from. Many will suggest that it soaked through the cup, which is not the case.

7. Pass out the cloths and have the children wipe the outside of their cups. There will be no color on the cloth. This indicates that the water could not have come from inside the cup.

8. Since we know that the water didn't come from inside the cup, discuss where it did come from: condensation. The water vapor gathered in the warm air surrounding the cup. Since the cup was cooler than the air, the water droplets settled on the outside of the cup.

TIPS

- Provide smocks and cover tables with newspaper, or do this experiment on trays to avoid staining clothes and tabletops.

CONNECTIONS

Experiment with different temperatures of water and compare condensation results. Experiment with different kinds of cups: plastic, glass, and paper.

Have children write or dictate a description of what happened during the experiment.

Wee Watershed

AGES
3+

A watershed is an area of land in which all of the water that drains out of it (both precipitation and ground-water) ultimately flows into the same place. Together with the children, you can create landforms—such as hills, valleys, and rivers—using sculpting clay. Use your fingers or sticks to create riverbeds and streams. Then allow the children to use watering cans to "rain" on the landscape and observe where the water goes and how it flows downhill. Watch how the water creates rivers and widens streams as it falls. All the water will collect in the lowest point of the watershed. This activity is fun to do outside on a nice day; you may even want to leave the landscapes outside and observe the effects of rain on them.

Activity Goals

→ To see how water moves to the lowest point in a landscape

→ To influence the way water moves

National Science Education Standards

Physical science: properties of objects and materials

Earth and space science: properties of earth materials, changes in earth and sky

Science in personal and social perspectives: changes in environments

Materials and Supplies

☐ Wide, shallow trays or pans (such as 9- by 13-inch baking pans), one per small group of children

☐ A large quantity of natural clay

☐ Filled watering cans, one per group

Procedure

1. Provide each small group of children with a mound of clay on a tray and invite them to create an area of land that includes hills, valleys, riverbeds, lakes, and streams.

2. Ideally, some children will make landforms with a flat topography and others will create very hilly landscapes.

3. Allow the children time to play with the clay and create their watersheds.

4. Pass out full watering cans and invite the children to experiment with the water as it moves across the landscape they've created.

5. When the activity is finished, ask the children what happened. Have them describe the paths the water took. Ask the children if it is possible to make the water flow uphill.

6. Note that the water all flowed downhill to the ponds, streams, and rivers they created.

TIPS

- Children love to experiment with clay, so plan on spending a lot of time on this activity.

- Provide an extra challenge by doing this activity in a sandbox. Because sand is so porous, water soaks in very quickly, making it difficult for children to observe the movement of water across the landscape. On the other hand, for those fortunate enough to have one close by, a beach can be a good setting for this activity because the water table is just below the surface, making it more possible for water to visibly pool on the surface!

- Add loose soil to the surface to observe runoff and sedimentation.

- Add animal replicas, small houses, or other figurines as appropriate for imaginative play.

CONNECTIONS

Allow the clay sculptures to dry completely, then repeat this activity. Ask the children if the water behaves differently and how. (Depending on the type of clay, some of the water may soak into the clay.)

Crumple aluminum foil or sturdy paper and drip watered-down paint on it using eyedroppers or spoons, or spray it with a spray bottle. Watch the water move in rivulets across the terrain of the paper.

Use sponges to simulate wetlands. Cut the sponges into various shapes and place them at the edges of the watersheds. Discuss with the children what effect this has on the land. You may wish to experiment with the effects of different topography on the flow of water in an area. For example, have children build a neighborhood in a valley, on the top of a hill, and on the side of a hill and experiment with water movement in these different settings. Ask the children how someone might catch water on a hill.

Puddle Hunters

As water flows across surfaces—such as rooftops, sidewalks, streets, and parking lots—it picks up chemicals, sand, silt, and other pollutants and carries them along to its destination in the nearest body of water. In this activity, there is no need to point out the specific pollutants being picked up and carried by runoff. Instead, use this activity to simply observe the phenomenon of water travelling across the pavement and collecting in puddles.

This activity is best done on a day when it's raining steadily but there is no danger of lightning or heavy winds. Use your best judgment when taking children outdoors on a rainy day. Follow all safety procedures, and return inside immediately at the first sign of thunder or lightning.

Activity Goals

→ To explore the environment on a rainy day

→ To discover where water flows

National Science Education Standards

Science as inquiry: abilities necessary to do scientific inquiry

Physical science: properties of objects and materials

Earth and space science: properties of earth materials

Science in personal and social perspectives: changes in environments

Materials and Supplies

☐ Rain gear for each person: waterproof pants, rain boots, and raincoats with hoods or rain hats

☐ Bucket, if desired, to collect water

Procedure

1. Ask the children where water goes when the rain falls. Most will say "on the ground!" Challenge them to think beyond that. Where does it go after it's on the ground? Sometimes it collects in puddles, sometimes it soaks into the lawn or garden, and other times it washes down the streets in gutters or along the edges of the streets.

2. Invite the children to take a trip outside to follow the path of water. Once everyone has put on their rain gear, go out the front door and turn to look at the building. Watch how the water moves off the roof and where it goes. The edge of a roof, where the water drips off, is called a "drip line." See if you can locate the drip line. If you like, you can put a bucket under the drip line to collect rainwater.

3. Does your building have gutters? Find them, and watch as the water comes out the downspout.

4. Next, walk slowly around your grounds. Do puddles collect in certain places on the sidewalk? Let the children splash and play in the puddles.

5. Depending on how hard it's raining, you may be able to see water actually flowing along the edge of the street or driveway. See if you can find any "rivers" of storm water moving. Follow the rivers.

6. Look for a storm drain near your site. If possible, watch the water flow into it, and see what materials the water is carrying as it does. Depending on the time of year, the water might be carrying leaves, sandy material, or even trash.

TIPS

• Ensure that all children have adequate rain gear, including rain pants and hats or jackets with hoods. Boots are a must! Many programs stock a "borrow basket" with rain gear from secondhand stores for children who need to borrow outdoor gear.

- Before doing this activity, locate the storm drains that are nearest to your site. Storm drains are most often located at the very side of the roadways or parking lots, so you can safely observe them without endangering anyone.

CONNECTIONS

 Collect rainwater in a bucket to use for watercolor painting. Take your painting materials outside to a covered location and paint on a rainy day. Paint watercolor pictures and put them outside in the rain while the paint is still wet. Observe the changes in the pictures.

If you have access to a local map, determine your program's proximity to the nearest body of water and visit it, if possible.

The Water Cycle Walk

The water on Earth is constantly moving through a cycle—air holds water in a gas form, called water vapor. Water vapor condenses, turning into liquid droplets that cluster into clouds in the sky. Most water falls to Earth as rain or snow. Some water lands on the Earth's surface, flows downhill, and collects in lakes, ponds, or rivers. Some water is absorbed into the ground, where plants can take it up through their roots. Plants release water vapor back into the atmosphere through the surface of their leaves. The sun warms water on the Earth's surface, causing it to turn back into a gas in the atmosphere. There it can condense into new clouds. This activity gets children up and moving as you venture through all the steps of the water cycle during a lively game.

Activity Goals

→ To have fun learning new words

→ To introduce the concept of the water cycle

National Science Education Standards

Earth and space science: properties of earth materials, objects in the sky, changes in earth and sky

Science in personal and social perspectives: changes in environments

Materials and Supplies

☐ Photographs showing rain, snow, clouds, cloudy skies, plants, and sunshine, at least one per child

☐ 10-foot sheet of butcher paper and a marker

☐ Adhesive putty or tape

Procedure

1. Draw a simple landscape line horizontally on the butcher paper, as shown in the rectangle below. The wavy line represents high and low points in the landscape.

2. Give the children a basic introduction to the water cycle, as described above, showing the photos to illustrate each stage and explaining the landscape line. Ask children to pretend the butcher paper is a landscape of the Earth with hills and valleys.

3. Pass out the photographs so each child has one. Ask them where in the landscape would be good places for their photos.

4. Have adhesive putty or tape ready and invite all the children with clouds, for example, to place their photos where they think clouds should go.

5. Invite all the children with rain pictures to place them on the landscape illustration.

6. Invite the children with pictures of bodies of water to think about where they should go, reminding them if necessary, that water flows downhill and collects in lower points in the landscape.

7. Continue until all the images have been posted on the paper.

8. After you've played the game awhile, ask the children to explain what they did and how they decided where to put the images.

TIPS

• Cut photographs out of magazines and laminate them or cover them with clear contact paper.

• For special fun, set this activity to music.

CONNECTIONS

 Use watercolors to paint a picture of the water cycle, or one part of it.

 Review the water cycle and discuss the different images. Ask the children to share what they think would happen if one set of images were removed (for example, if there were no wetlands). Ask them how the change would affect the water's journey through the cycle, which part of the cycle they think is most important and why, and how they think humans can affect the water cycle.

Absorb or Run Off?

Water that falls to the Earth as precipitation will either be absorbed into the ground, land directly in a surface body of water, or become runoff, traveling along the surface until it can be absorbed or join a body of water. In this activity, children will spray water on different surfaces (simulating rainfall) and observe its behavior.

Activity Goals

→ To experiment with different surfaces

→ To witness water's behavior on different surfaces

National Science Education Standards

Earth and space science: properties of earth materials

Materials and Supplies

☐ Chart paper and a marker

☐ Aluminum pie tins or baking pans, one per child or small group of children

☐ A supply of the following materials, enough so that each child will have one of each:

☐ Washcloths

☐ Wax paper

☐ Clay

☐ Aluminum foil

☐ Felt pieces

☐ Rubber scraps

☐ Filled watering cans or spray bottles

☐ Dry towels

Procedure

1. Lead a discussion about what water does when it rains (or when the snow melts). Ask the children where they think it goes and how they can find out.

2. Show the children the materials you've brought in and invite them to compare different surfaces by spraying water on them and watching what happens.

3. Ask them what they think the water will do on the aluminum foil, on the felt pieces, and on the other materials.

4. Pass out the pie tins and spray bottles and invite the children to choose from the collection of materials.

5. The children should place a material in the pie tin and spray it with enough water to see something happen. In some cases, the water will bead up; in other cases, it will soak into the fabric, slowly or rapidly.

6. Allow plenty of time for the children to test their predictions about what the water will do.

7. Discuss the children's observations and record the key words they use, such as "absorb" and "run off," on the chart paper. Use these terms to connect this experience with other discussions.

TIPS

• Have the children work in small groups rather than alone. Be sure to allow enough time for each child to have a turn experimenting.

• Make this activity particularly meaningful by doing it after the Puddle Hunters activity.

CONNECTIONS

With the children, investigate what makes the water soak in, what causes it to run off the surface, and where the water goes afterward.

Water Cycle Garden

AGES
4+

This activity enables children to make their own greenhouse or terrarium. They can observe the water cycle in action as water moves through the surface of the plants' leaves, condenses on the walls of the garden, and drips down into the soil, where it can be taken up again by the plants. Each child can make a water cycle garden that is easy to care for. You can readily take this activity outside on a nice day.

Activity Goals

→ To care for live plants

→ To discover how water moves through a cycle

National Science Education Standards

Science as inquiry: abilities necessary to do science inquiry

Life science: characteristics of organisms, life cycles of organisms, organisms and environments

Earth and space science: properties of earth materials

Materials and Supplies

☐ 2-liter bottle with top cut off and label removed, one per child

☐ Bag of pea gravel or aquarium gravel

☐ Bag of crushed charcoal

☐ Bag of potting soil

☐ Plastic spoons or scoops

☐ Small plants, such as ivy, philodendron, or sedum

☐ Spray bottles of water, one per child

☐ Plastic wrap

☐ Rubber bands, one per child

☐ Smocks

☐ Newspaper or other table covering

Procedure

1. Pass out one bottle to each child. Tell them that they will be making a garden so that they can see the water cycle in action.

2. Have the children scoop a half-inch layer of gravel into the container, followed by a quarter-inch layer of charcoal.

3. Next, fill the containers a little more than halfway with soil, and have the children dig a small hole using a spoon or their fingers.

4. Carefully remove the plants from their containers and gently spread their roots a bit. Place them into the holes. Gently refill the holes with soil and settle the plant by gently pressing the soil down.

5. Spray the plants and soil with the spray bottles. The soil should be moist but not soggy.

6. Cut a piece of plastic wrap and use a rubber band to secure it over the bottle's opening.

7. Everyone should wash their hands thoroughly after working with soil, gravel, charcoal, and plants.

8. Children can take the gardens home or keep them in the classroom to observe the water cycle in action.

TIPS

• A few weeks ahead of time, ask families to bring in empty two-liter bottles. Remove the labels, rinse them, and cut the tops off before this activity.

• Make the activity move more quickly by setting up stations: one for gravel, one for charcoal, one for soil, and one for plants.

(continues on next page)

- Keep the gardens out of direct sunlight.

- If the soil appears to be dry after a few days, or if water no longer collects on the sides of the containers, remove the top and squirt soil with water to make it moist. (But remember, moist *not soggy!*)

CONNECTIONS

To support children's inquiry during this activity, don't mention the water cycle. Instead, keep the gardens in the classroom and check the plants each day. Have the children note what they see inside the gardens. At first, there will be little condensation on the walls of the containers. Then they'll notice the water accumulating and dripping down the sides, back into the soil. Mention that the plants seem to be getting enough water and discuss as a group how this might be happening. See the description of the water cycle in the introductory paragraph and explain the cycle to the children.

Have the children draw their container gardens, including the different layers of materials. Have them make a picture using leftover soil, gravel, and charcoal.

Ask the children what happens when they put a container in direct sunlight, what happens if they over- or underwater a container, and why it is possible to leave the gardens alone and let them take care of themselves.

Float or Sink?

AGES 3+

Water play is made more meaningful in this activity as children make predictions and observations about the concepts of buoyancy and density. *Buoyancy* is the upward force exerted by a fluid that makes it possible for objects to float. It also refers to the tendency of an object to either float or sink in liquid. *Density* is the measurement of how much material an object contains compared to how much space it takes up (for example, a ball of steel is more dense than a Ping-Pong ball of the same size filled with air). An object that is more dense than a liquid will sink in that liquid. An object that is less dense than the liquid will float. These are not concepts you need to explain to very young children, but they are ones they can begin to observe and be curious about in the world around them. This activity also touches on another important scientific concept, *volume*, or the quantity of space enclosed by some structure or boundary. When a very dense object such as the steel hull of a ship holds a large volume of air, the overall density of the ship will be dispersed, so it can float. On the other hand, the same amount of steel compacted into a ball would immediately sink. Similarly, children can explore and discover on their own that changing the shape of a ball of clay so that it holds a volume of air can make the clay able to float.

Activity Goals

→ To explore the properties of buoyancy and density

→ To experiment with materials and discover how manipulating their shapes can affect their behaviors

National Science Education Standards

Science as inquiry: abilities necessary to do scientific inquiry

Physical science: properties of objects and materials

Earth and space science: properties of earth materials

Science and technology: abilities of technological design

Materials and Supplies

☐ Plastic tubs filled with two to three inches of water, one per small group of children

☐ Small balls of clay (about one ounce or the size of an apricot), one per child

☐ Assorted doodads, with different weights and densities

☐ Chart paper and a marker

Procedure

1. Show the doodads to the children and ask them to make predictions about which ones will sink or float. Record their predictions, and ask them why they think certain objects will sink or float. (Answers will include "it's heavy," "it's big," "it's a ball," and so on.) Record their explanations.

2. Provide one tub of water and a collection of doodads to each small group of children. Have them spend time experimenting.

3. Ask them to describe how the objects are behaving and if their predictions were accurate. Find out if anything surprised them or if they found similarities among the objects that sank, for example. Help the children generalize.

4. Now pass out the balls of clay and ask the children if the balls of clay will sink or float and why they think so.

5. Listen to their responses, and help them develop their predictions. (For example, they may say it will sink "because it is heavy.")

(continues on next page)

6. Have them drop the balls into the water. The balls should sink straight to the bottom.

7. Ask them if there is anything that might make the balls float. For example, if they change the shape of the balls, which shapes do they think will float.

8. Allow the children time to experiment with different shapes. Encourage them to think about things they have seen that float and talk about them. Challenge them to make a shape that floats.

9. When the children discover that if they flatten the balls and make them concave (like little boats) the clay will float, ask them if the clay still has the same weight as it did before.

10. When they answer yes, ask them what changed (the shape).

11. Allow them to play with the clay boats awhile and then have them add doodads to the boats. Ask them to describe what happens and whether they can affect the way the boats behave based on how many doodads they put in.

12. Explain that although they changed the shape of the clay, they didn't change the weight of the clay. The children designed boats with flat bottoms and high sides, both of which helps the boats float. (The change in shape affected the boat's density and buoyancy.)

TIPS

- Supervise children who might put small objects in their mouths or ears.

- Include small heavy objects and large lightweight objects in this activity. The discrepancy between size and weight might surprise and excite the children.

CONNECTIONS

Encourage the children to draw pictures of the balls of clay and then draw their boats with doodads in them. Let the clay boats dry and have children decorate them.

Discovering Dissolving

AGES 4+

Most substances dissolve in water. This means that substances break down into tiny particles and become a liquid solution. Water's ability to dissolve most substances is one of its most important properties. This means that water, all by itself, is an excellent cleaner! Water alone can break down a lot of grime and residue so we can wipe them away. However, water's ability to dissolve substances can also generate some tricky problems for our environment. Once a substance dissolves in water, it can be very difficult to remove it. Dissolved substances can drastically lower the quality of water and can even make it unusable for plants and animals. In this activity, children will observe the phenomenon of dissolving. They will experiment with different substances and observe how quickly they dissolve in water (or not).

There is a limit to how much of any substance can dissolve in a given quantity of water. This limit is called the *saturation point*. If you add more of the substance after that point has been reached, the additional material will not dissolve. You may have observed this phenomenon if you've ever added too much sugar to a cup of tea and found that a pile of sugar settles at the bottom of your cup. The saturation point for a given substance in water will depend on a number of factors, principally the temperature and quantity of the water.

Activity Goals

→ To discover how water can change certain materials

National Science Education Standards

Physical science: properties of objects and materials

Earth and space science: properties of earth materials

Materials and Supplies

☐ Clear containers filled two-thirds full of water, six per child

☐ Stir sticks or spoons, one per child

☐ Measuring spoons

☐ Bowls of a variety of materials, including dried leaves and grass, salt, sand, soil, and flour

☐ Marker

Procedure

1. Tell the children that they are going to experiment with different substances in water to learn about how things change when mixed with water.

2. Start with the salt, adding just a teaspoon to each child's water. Invite them to watch as the salt slowly mixes with the water. Have them stir the water and notice how the salt "disappears" into the water. The water may appear cloudy.

3. Invite the children to dip a clean finger into the salt water and taste it. (Tell them not to drink the water—just take a small taste). The water will taste salty. Ask the children where the salt is and how they know it's there if they can no longer see it. Explain that the salt dissolved into the water. Although they can't see it, it's there.

4. Ask the children to predict what will happen to the other materials if they add them to water. Record their predictions for each substance.

5. Continue to mix materials, one by one, into separate containers of water. Begin with the soil. Add a scoop of soil, and stir it into the water. Ask the children to describe what happens.

(continues on next page)

6. Continue to ask for observations about how the water affects the substances. Record the children's observations.

7. Ask the children for ideas about how to remove the materials from the water once they have dissolved. Note that many substances are very difficult to remove from water.

8. Allow the materials to settle in the cups of water over time. Continue to make observations throughout the day.

9. At the end of the day, ask the children to describe what happened in the various containers.

TIPS

- Help children add their substances to water slowly, little bit by little bit, so as to better observe the dissolving phenomenon and not get confused by substances settling out too quickly.

- Explain that even though scientists are trained never to taste their solutions, this activity can help children comprehend the phenomenon of dissolving if they are allowed to taste the water with dissolved salt. Instruct them to simply dip a finger into their container for a taste. If they do not want to taste it, that is fine.

Do not allow children to drink the saltwater; permit only a small taste. The saltwater solution is the only water that should be tasted during this experiment.

CONNECTIONS

Invite children to try different ways of removing the materials from the water. (Ideas might include using filters, letting the water evaporate, adding more water to dilute the materials, and so on.) Record children's observations.

Determine the saturation point of salt in water. Measure how much water is poured into the containers, then record how much salt can be introduced to the water before it reaches a saturation point. Try the other materials too. Ask the children to predict whether the other materials will be the same as or different from the salt. Ask them to explain how they know. Have the children test their theories.

Oil and Water

Oil and water don't mix, oil being one of the few materials that does not dissolve in water. The oil molecules cling together or *adhere*, which holds the oil together. This activity lets children try mixing the two substances and observe what happens when they try.

Activity Goals

→ To have fun trying to mix substances

National Science Education Standards

Physical science: properties of objects and materials

Earth and space science: properties of earth materials

Materials and Supplies

☐ Small clear containers with lids that can be securely attached, one per child

☐ Pitcher of water

☐ Vegetable oil

☐ Measuring spoons

☐ Food coloring

☐ Chart paper and a marker

Procedure

1. Add food coloring to a pitcher of water and stir. Fill the clear containers two-thirds full with the colored water.

2. Show the containers to the children and explain that you are going to add oil. Ask them what they think will happen to the oil, and record their predictions.

3. Pass out the containers of water and add several spoonfuls of oil to each container while the children watch. Secure the lids.

4. Have the children observe the oil without moving the containers.

5. Ask them if there's any way to mix the oil and water. Invite the children to shake the containers vigorously and observe the change.

6. Have them set the containers down and watch the oil and water separate again. (It may take several minutes.)

TIPS

• Enhance the significance of this activity by doing it subsequent to the Discovering Dissolving activity on page 129.

• Use food coloring with care. It will stain clothing and skin.

CONNECTIONS

Add some shiny sequins, pretty buttons, or a little glitter to the water in the containers and children will have their very own shaker jar.

Experiment with how the materials behave when children shake the jars, or roll them. Ask the children why the materials behave the way they do. Discuss the children's observations.

Clean Water

We are very lucky if we live in areas where the water we use is treated and cleaned to very high standards. We can turn on the faucets in our homes and schools and clean, fresh water flows out. Most of us depend upon human-made filtration and treatment facilities to purify our water. But nature has ways of cleaning and filtering water too. For example, wetlands serve as giant water filters. They slow runoff, allowing soil and particulate matter to settle out as the water returns to watersheds. Wetlands absorb and filter rainwater and snowmelt before it reaches larger bodies of water. Sand and gravel in soil also help filter water. As water flows through layers of sand and gravel, large particles—as well as chemicals and other pollutants—can settle out. In this activity, children will learn a bit about the ways that nature filters water.

Activity Goals

→ To experience filtering water

→ To understand the way water percolates through soil systems

National Science Education Standards

Physical science: properties of objects and materials

Earth and space science: properties of earth materials

Science and technology: ability to distinguish between natural objects and objects made by humans, abilities of technological design

Materials and Supplies

☐ Small flowerpots with holes in the bottom, one per child

☐ White basket-type coffee filters, one per child

☐ Bag of gravel or small pebbles

☐ Bag of coarse sand

☐ Large handful of crumbled dry leaves and grass

☐ Bag of potting soil

☐ Two to three large, clear pitchers

☐ Water (can be tap water or lake/pond water)

☐ Plastic container, slightly larger than the flowerpots, one per child

☐ Scoops or spoons

☐ Chart paper and a marker

Procedure

1. If you are using tap water, fill the pitchers with water and mix in soil and crumbled leaves and grass. Your mixture should be very muddy and hard to see through.

2. Show the muddy water to the children and explain that this is what happens to bodies of water, such as streams, rivers, ponds, and lakes, after a heavy rainstorm as water mixes with loose organic matter.

3. Pass out the flowerpots, coffee filters, and plastic containers. Have children place a filter in their flowerpot and then place the flowerpot into the plastic container to catch the filtered water as it drains through the pot.

4. Next, scoop a small amount of sand into the filter. The sand should fill the flowerpot about one-third of the way to the top.

5. Then scoop a small amount of gravel into the filter. The gravel should just cover the sand layer.

6. Very carefully pour a small amount of water into each child's flowerpot.

7. Ask the children what they think will happen to the water. Record their responses on the chart paper.

8. Watch as the organic material (leaves and grass) is filtered out and stays on top of the gravel. The tinier pieces of material seep through the gravel and sand, and cleaner water comes through the filter.

9. Have the children describe the process they used to create the filters. Invite them to share what happened, as well as their theories about how the filters work.

10. Discuss how in order to obtain clean water for drinking, water needs to be filtered even more. Chemicals and heavy-duty filtration processes are required to make water safe for drinking.

TIPS

*Be aware that, although nature's water filters are effective at keeping some sediments and chemicals from reaching other bodies of water, this is **not** an effective method of filtering out microscopic bacteria or other potentially harmful substances. It is very important to make this distinction. Do **not** allow the children to drink this water.*

• Allow the water to settle for several hours or even days. Observe the changes in the amount of filtration that has occurred.

CONNECTIONS

Have children empty their filters onto trays and examine the size of the materials that made it through. Ask the children if any small particles made it through the sand, why the different layers of materials are important, what the coffee filter looked like after the experiment, and what would happen if the layers were in a different order.

Visit a wetland area and invite the children to draw or paint what they see. Take samples of these different layers from the Earth and use them to create a picture.

Ask the children what they would do if they wanted to design a better filter.

Have the children discuss what would happen if they took out one of the layers.

Rain Gauges

Rain gauges allow us to measure the amount of rain that falls in a given rain event. This can be important for many reasons, including predicting floods, planning agricultural production, and even taking care of our gardens and deciding whether and when to water them. Rain gauges are simple, easy to use, and fun to make. As a group, you can make your own rain gauges to measure rainfall at your program or for children to take home.

Activity Goals

→ To create measuring devices

→ To explore the concept of water measurement

National Science Education Standards

Earth and space science: properties of earth materials, objects in the sky, changes in earth and sky

Science in personal and social perspectives: changes in environments

Materials and Supplies

☐ Small clear-plastic containers, one per child

☐ Permanent markers in a variety of colors

☐ Liquid measuring cups, one set per small group of children

☐ Ruler or measuring tape, one per small group

Procedure

1. Discuss with the children that you would like to come up with a way to measure the amount of rainfall, and elicit their suggestions for how you might do that as a group.

2. Explain to the children that rainfall is measured in inches rather than in cups or teaspoons, which is another way to measure liquids.

3. Divide the children into small groups and provide each group with a ruler and a set of measuring cups.

4. Provide each child with a small container and a marker.

5. Demonstrate how to find and mark a half-inch on the container by holding the ruler inside the container and drawing a two-inch line on the outside at the half-inch ruler line. Encourage the children to help each other in this work.

6. Have the children find and mark the one-inch point in the same manner, but with a marker of a different color. They should continue marking half-inch increments for five inches or to the top of the container.

7. Children can then use the measuring cups to fill their rain gauges and determine how much water is in one inch, two inches, and so on. The amount will vary if the diameter of the containers differs.

8. Place the rain gauges in different locations outside your school, or have the children take them home.

TIPS

• Use permanent markers for the rain gauges; otherwise, the ink will soon wash away! Remember, however, that permanent ink will stain clothing and skin. Take precautions to ensure children use the markers properly.

• Use this activity as a complement to the activities in chapter 7: Weather, Climate, and Energy.

CONNECTIONS

Ask the children what changes they can observe over time. If you live in a snowy area, collect snowfall in a rain gauge and then bring it inside. As the snow melts, the amount collected appears to shrink. Ask the children why they think this is.

Catch It If You Can!

As we go about normal, everyday routines—such as brushing our teeth or washing our hands—we often don't think about how much water we're using. If we aren't mindful of our consumption, a lot of perfectly good water simply goes down the drain. This activity helps children (and adults!) gain awareness of how much water can be conserved by simply turning off the faucet during these daily routines.

Activity Goals

→ To develop an awareness of one's own water use and waste

National Science Education Standards

Science in personal and social perspectives: personal health

Materials and Supplies

☐ Sink with handles to turn water on and off (not an automatic faucet)

☐ Plastic tub that fits inside the sink

☐ Clear container, such as a storage bin, with volume measurements marked clearly on the outside (see Tips)

Procedure

1. Before eating, invite the children to wash their hands as usual and explain that you are placing a tub in the sink to catch the water as they wash their hands.

2. As the children wait in line, ask them if they think the tub will collect a lot or just a little water.

3. When the tub is full or when all of the children have washed their hands, remove the tub from the sink and pour the water into a clear bin so the children can see how much water was used.

4. Ask them what they think about how much water was collected and if they were surprised.

5. Repeat this activity the next time the children all wash their hands. This time, designate a child to turn off the water as each child scrubs her hands, and then turn it back on to rinse.

6. Again, pour the contents of the tub into the clear container and compare your results.

TIPS

- If your container is not already marked with volume measurements, pour measured amounts of water into the container and use a permanent marker to indicate that amount's level on the outside of container before beginning this activity. For example, mark one cup, two cups, and up to a gallon, which is sixteen cups.

- Remember to be very matter-of-fact as you observe the amount of water collected. The goal is not to shame children or make them self-conscious in any way about the amount of water collected.

- Explain to the children that even though it is important to conserve water, it is also extremely important to do a thorough and complete job of hand washing. If your class uses a song, such as "Twinkle, Twinkle, Little Star," to mark the appropriate amount of time to spend rubbing soapy hands together, this is a great opportunity to reinforce that. Doing so will minimize children feeling rushed during the process. The children will learn that they *can* wash hands well and conserve water.

CONNECTIONS

Invite the children to challenge the adults in the building to do this same activity. Then compare results. Additionally, track this kind of water usage for a week or longer.

CHAPTER 6

Air Is All Around Us

Air can have an enormous impact on people and places. Consider tornadoes, hurricanes, and temperature extremes. The fact that air is invisible, yet its effects are so tangible, makes it especially intriguing for young children, fun to explore, and prime for learning opportunities. Children can make and fly kites, watch wind blow through the trees, and play with air pressure. Air is everywhere, and so are opportunities for exploring it. Like water, air is also a natural resource on which we all depend for survival as well as an environmental issue with many challenges. So exploring it, and learning more about it, is very important for environmental stewardship.

This chapter offers you two things: One, it will help you understand the basics of air as well as air pollution and its impacts on young children. Two, it will offer you activities and ideas for exploring air and its basic properties with the children you teach. The activities focus on helping children have fun with air and explore its qualities: how it moves, what it can do, and how it can affect things. Above all, I urge you to go outside with the children and experience air. Enjoy being outdoors when the temperature is warm, cool, and somewhere in between. Encourage the children to notice the breeze, feel the air moving across their skin, and watch leaves flutter in the wind. Feel air's power on a windy day. Notice what stillness—the lack of moving air—feels like.

What Is Air?

Our air is one of the things that makes our planet so special. But what exactly is our air anyway? Air isn't just emptiness, it is a real substance that takes up space around us. Pass any child a cup of milk and a drinking straw to see some evidence: the child will blow air into the milk, which will bubble up to the surface of the milk to escape. Our air is actually a mixture of gases, the two biggest ingredients being nitrogen and oxygen. Oxygen, of course, is the gas that all humans and animals need to breathe, but both oxygen and nitrogen are essential for supporting life. Air also includes a number of other gases that occur in smaller relative concentrations. One of the most well known of those is *carbon dioxide*, which all animals exhale, and plants take in and use to grow. Another small but extremely important component of air is water vapor, which—as described in detail in the previous chapter—is water in its gaseous form.

Air fills the space surrounding our planet, forming a layer called the *atmosphere*. In the atmosphere, air flows and swirls constantly, redistributing heat and moisture around the globe. The atmosphere is hundreds of miles thick and comprises several distinct layers. The layer closest to Earth is called the *troposphere*, and this is where all the weather that we experience develops and occurs.

The air in our atmosphere can vary greatly in temperature. The sun's rays warm the air, but they do so unevenly, heating areas near the equator much more than areas near the Earth's poles. Since warmer air rises, the sun's uneven heating contributes to air's constant movement and mixing within the atmosphere. And even though we can't feel it, air has weight. This weight puts pressure on Earth and on everything found on Earth. This is called *air pressure*. The degree of air's pressure changes constantly from place to place and over time. Air moves from places of high pressure to low pressure, and this movement of air is wind. In fact, the variations in air pressure from place to place and over time play a big role in creating all the weather conditions we experience. Many a grandparent claims to predict weather based on the changing stiffness in a "bum knee." Well there's truth to that. Most likely those grandparents are feeling the effects of changing atmospheric pressure in their joints. Learning about and paying attention to changing air pressure and its association with weather patterns can be a great way for all of us to become more attuned to our environment.

Air Pollution

Unfortunately, most people have come to be familiar with *air pollution*. This refers to the presence of airborne substances that are harmful to the environment. There are hundreds of different kinds of pollutants. Some are in the form of a gas, such as *carbon monoxide*, a highly toxic gas emitted from vehicle tailpipes, among other sources. Some have strong odors, while others have no odor at all. Pollutants can also be solid or liquid particles suspended in the air, known as *particle pollution* or *particulate matter*. In some cases these particles are big enough to be seen with the naked eye, such as dust, smoke, soot, or volcanic ash. Other kinds of particulates are too small to detect without special instruments.

Air pollution can come from either natural or human-made sources. Natural sources include erupting volcanoes that send ash, sulfur, and nitrogen gases into the atmosphere. Forest fires (which can occur naturally or be caused by humans) put smoke and ash into the air. Domestic livestock cause air pollution by emitting methane gas. Pollutants can be substances that are harmless in the air at certain low or moderate levels but become problematic—and thus considered pollutants—at more elevated levels. In fact, even *pollen*, the tiny reproductive grains or spores that come from plants, trees, and grasses, can be a source of air pollution when it accumulates in the air to a sufficient level. Pollen is found anywhere plants are found and can exacerbate allergies. Even for people without allergies, pollen can be an irritant and cause sneezing.

HUMAN IMPACT ON AIR QUALITY

Though natural sources of air pollution are not insignificant, human sources of air pollution are unfortunately even more common and widespread. For example, burning *coal*—a combustible rock composed mostly of carbon—for energy production is one of the biggest sources of air pollution in the United States today (UCS 2012). While generating over 50 percent of the electricity used in the United States today, the burning of coal also produces extremely high levels of pollutants, including sulfur dioxide, carbon monoxide, and carbon dioxide gases; mercury (a known *neurotoxin*, or poisonous compound that acts on the nervous system) and other heavy metals; and particulate matter such as soot. The toxic emissions generated by coal burning are equal to the emissions generated by all the cars, buses, and trucks on US roads *combined* (UCS 2008). Although you may hear people talk about "cleaning" coal emissions with technology and tools, most air-pollution scientists agree that it is not presently possible to eliminate or even significantly reduce coal's harmful environmental impacts. Even if highly effective technology were ready, available, and affordable, truly reducing the harmful impacts of this industry would still require drastically cutting our society's consumption (UCS 2007).

Coal, oil, and natural gas are among the world's *fossil fuels*. They are called this because they are derived from fossilized plant and animal material found deep within the Earth. Fossil fuels are burned to provide power for factories, power plants, and vehicles. In fact, fossil fuel usage is so widespread and central to all human activities that you might say fossil fuels run our modern world. Vehicles running on fossil fuels emit tremendous amounts of air pollutants. For example, they are the main source of the highly toxic carbon monoxide in our air (US EPA 2012d).

The burning of fossil fuels also creates *greenhouse gases*—which are gases in the atmosphere, such as carbon dioxide—that trap the sun's heat near Earth's surface. This trapping of heat is causing our planet's air, water, and surface temperature to warm and our global climate to change. I go into more detail about fossil fuels, global warming, and climate change in chapter 7, but this phenomenon is also pertinent in the discussion of air pollution. Greenhouse gases are somewhat different from the other pollutants that can have immediate harmful effects on the environment and living creatures. Most—though not all—greenhouse gases are naturally occurring and not immediately harmful to human health. But the burning of fossil fuel is resulting in greenhouse gases accumulating at a far faster and far greater rate than has ever occurred in human history. The global warming and climate change caused by greenhouse gas accumulation presents enormous threats to our planet, influencing such events as changing weather patterns, rising sea levels, changing habitats, expansion of conditions favorable for disease-bearing insects, and more. Given the very real environmental and human health threats posed by greenhouse gas accumulation in the atmosphere, these gases have come to be considered pollutants by the US Environmental Protection Agency. Again, see chapter 7 for a more thorough discussion of fossil fuels and climate change.

Unfortunately the examples of human-sourced air pollution go on and on. Let's look at *smog*, a well-known and commonly experienced form of pollution that is a combination of gas and particulate matter. While many types of air pollution are invisible and odorless, smog can be seen as a brownish, grayish haze hanging over large cities but also found in natural areas. Smog occurs when certain gases and particulate matter in the air react to the presence of sun

and heat. Smog is present year-round in some cities. It can irritate the eyes and throats of humans and is especially hazardous to children because of their very delicate mucous membranes.

Pollution produced in one place can travel over many miles to create problems far from its original source because air moves so easily through the atmosphere. In fact, pollution levels have even been detected in the Arctic Circle, where there are no large immediate sources of pollution (AMAP 2011)! Pollutants also create severe problems in the areas closest to its sources. For example, people living near factories or oil refineries have greater exposure to toxic chemicals produced by these industries simply due to their proximity to the pollution source. Locations near busy streets have higher levels of particulate-matter pollution from automobile exhaust, which can result in respiratory challenges for children (NIEHS 2008). If a long line of school buses visits your site each day, you will have higher levels of diesel exhaust fumes near your site as well. Small children, who are taking their breaths of air right at the same level as vehicle exhaust pipes, are particularly vulnerable to the effects of exhaust (Wargo 2002).

INDOOR AIR POLLUTION

All of this talk about air pollution is enough to make a person want to stay inside with the windows shut tight to escape the nasty stuff in the air, right? Unfortunately, in some cases indoor air can be more polluted than outdoor air! Due to the relatively small volume of air inside closed quarters, there is potential for higher concentrations of pollutants indoors. With limited openings to the outdoors, fumes, chemicals, and particles can accumulate in indoor air. In many early childhood programs and schools, windows are inoperable or locked for safety reasons. This may make sense from a safety perspective, but this practice can reduce overall air circulation, which also contributes to poor indoor air quality.

There are many sources of *indoor air pollution*. Common ones include mold, mildew, pet hair, and dust from air vents and circulation systems. Unfortunately, cigarette smoke is still a source of indoor air pollution, generating toxic carbon monoxide. Unintentional inhalation of cigarette smoke occurs when children are playing in a room where adults are or have recently been smoking. Chemicals and residue from smoke can persist on walls, furniture, clothing, and other surfaces. This is known as *thirdhand smoke*, yet another form of air pollution. The chemical residue left behind from cigarette smoke can actually be reemitted or react with other chemicals or pollutants in the indoor air and form new toxins (Protano and Vitali 2011).

You know that smell of fresh paint, new furniture, and new cars? That's a result of something known as *off-gassing*, which occurs when chemicals dissipate from a material and enter the air. Those scents that some people associate with a new or clean room can actually indicate that there are chemicals in the air. Some of the off-gassing chemicals are VOCs, or *volatile organic compounds*. VOCs are defined as "carbon-based chemicals that easily evaporate at room temperature" (MDH 2010, 1). VOCs are generated from many industrial sources, such as coal burning, and also come from natural sources. Many synthetic VOCs are thought to be harmful to human and animal health (US EPA 2012c). Once they enter your body through inhalation, they can persist there for days, weeks, or in some cases even longer. Today's paint, plastics, carpets, wood products, and even books frequently contain VOCs. One example of a VOC is the chemical *formaldehyde*, which is an adhesive commonly used in the manufacturing of particleboard, a wood composite material used to make inexpensive furniture and cabinets or shelves. Formaldehyde is also found in carpets, flooring, paint, and varnishes. Formaldehyde is a known *carcinogen*, a substance that causes cancer (IARC 2004). Formaldehyde and other VOCs used to manufacture products can easily dissipate from the materials and enter the indoor air.

In recent years, many paint, carpet, and furniture manufacturers have become more sensitive to the need for producing low-VOC paints and furniture. However, as with all green or eco-friendly products, it's important to do your homework before purchasing. Because of the potential for VOC emissions, it is wise to keep children away from areas that have been freshly painted. When you purchase new furniture, allow it to off-gas (air out) for several days before exposing children to it. This gives the fumes found in the adhesives, foam, and paint time to dissipate. If you have carpeting or flooring installed at your site, try to do it before a lengthy break so that the children aren't exposed to the hazardous fumes from the glues or adhesives used.

Other common sources of indoor air pollutants include dust mites found in bedding, curtains, carpets, and plush toys. Although they are invisible, dust mites frequently cause watery eyes, runny noses, and sneezing in children and adults. Pet dander—tiny flakes of skin and hair that come off pets and animals and that stay in carpets and on fabrics such as upholstery or curtains—can also pose problems.

Mold and mildew, the results of moisture, are also common in homes and child care facilities. Mold and mildew are particularly hazardous and can grow on damp surfaces and fabrics. They release tiny spores into the air, spores to which many children are especially sensitive due to their delicate mucous membranes. Sometimes mold and mildew are invisible. Most often, people can detect the presence of mildew or mold by the strong odor, but in some cases they can't be detected. Mold and mildew can often be removed by thoroughly cleaning the affected surface and drying it to prevent recurrence, but in some cases major repairs or refinishing work is necessary to combat the source of the moisture. Furniture, walls, windowsills, and even books, clothing, plush toys, and bedding are all susceptible to mold and mildew.

HEALTH IMPACTS

Children and adults can be sensitive to everyday chemicals, such as the fumes from cleaning supplies or aerosols, and even the scents from perfumes, shampoos, and soaps. Sensitivity reactions can range from hives to headaches. Some children may sneeze or cough and have a runny nose. Because we come into contact with so many chemicals every day, it can be difficult to determine the cause of a reaction. Also, because many sensitivity reactions may be relatively subtle, it can sometimes be difficult to know if someone is having a reaction to chemicals, foods, or something else. In some cases, the sensitivity reaction may resemble a common cold, further adding to the confusion.

Exposure to air pollutants can cause a wide range of health effects. In addition to the everyday irritation that may be caused by both indoor and outdoor air pollution—such as itchy, watery eyes, burning throat, or coughing—air pollution can irritate or harm our delicate lung tissues. Air pollutants can cause diminished lung capacity and inflammation or damage to tissues and mucous membranes. When we inhale particulate matter and harmful vapors, the chemicals can enter our lungs and move into our bloodstream, which may result in endocrine or nervous system disruption (Landrigan, Garg, and Droller 2003). Even routine outdoor maintenance, such as mowing grass or using a leaf blower, can put tiny particles into the air that can irritate people's lungs.

Air pollution can be particularly hazardous for children and adults with acute respiratory conditions such as asthma. While some people dispute a direct causal relationship between pollution and asthma, there is most certainly evidence to support the claim that air pollution can exacerbate asthma (Leikauf 2002). Asthma is a chronic health condition that involves respiratory sensitivity and swelling of the bronchial airways in the lungs, making breathing difficult. It is the most common chronic health disorder in childhood, and its incidence is on the rise. Over seven million children under the age of eighteen are affected by asthma. That's 9.4 percent of all children in the United States (Bloom, Cohen, and Freeman 2011). Children in lower-income communities and children of color are more likely to be afflicted with asthma (US EPA 2003). One possible explanation for this is that low-income communities tend to be closer to major highways, industrial areas, and other sources of air pollution. Asthma is still being studied, but while it is known that genetic factors and allergies are risk factors in the development of childhood asthma, exposure to air pollutants is a risk factor as well. For those children already diagnosed with asthma, any airborne contaminants can be very troublesome, especially pollen, dust, mold, and smoke. Many educators coordinate their outside time around the needs of children with asthma to avoid exposing those children to conditions that will aggravate their breathing. However, a child doesn't have to have asthma to be sensitive to air quality. Indeed, many pollutants can affect a child's ability to breathe, to fight off illness, or to simply be comfortable (US EPA 2003). It's important to know if and how children in your program are susceptible to air pollutants so you can provide them with the best possible care.

The Importance of Clean Air in Early Childhood

Air quality can, and does, vary from place to place and from day to day and is affected by weather, temperature, industrial activities, and many other factors. Pollution levels can be affected by natural conditions, including changes in temperature, weather, and seasonal elements such as pollen levels and leaf mold. Levels can also be affected by human-made conditions such as excessive traffic or chemical outputs from factories. And since air pollution is especially problematic for the elderly, young children, or those with compromised immune systems, it is an issue of great concern for early childhood educators. How do we make sense of it all in order to make choices that support children's health?

To the extent possible, it makes sense to pay attention to the air quality in your area. In many parts of the world, scientists measure levels of air pollution to better understand human impacts on air quality and to try to help people understand the associated health effects. The Air Quality Index (AQI) is a tool developed by the United States Environmental Protection Agency to help cities report on local air quality conditions within the United States. It is designed to measure five major pollutants and rate air quality according to measurements on a scale of 1 to 6. Each level corresponds to a different level of health concern, from "good" to "hazardous." Because the AQI is a national tool, the ratings and color-coding system used to communicate about air quality are the same for all cities throughout the United States. Many cities publish air quality ratings on a regular basis, particularly when conditions are poor. Since smog and pollen aren't explicitly included in this index, some cities also publish separate smog and pollen reports. This information often can be found in your local newspaper or weather forecast. This information is very useful for helping those with allergies (or their caregivers) plan their activities so as to be prepared and take measures as needed for comfort.

Many early care and education providers are familiar with the AQI due to the prevalence of children with asthma and allergies. Air quality warnings now appear with some frequency in some areas, particularly urban areas. An air quality warning helps you know when to take special precautions, such as staying indoors, limiting aerobic activity, or—for those with respiratory conditions—using supplemental oxygen, medications, or asthma inhalers. If there are children in your program with asthma or other respiratory conditions or sensitivities, you most likely already pay attention to air quality reports, smog reports, and pollen counts and may limit your outdoor activity to certain times of the day.

It is important that you are aware of air quality reporting to ensure the health and safety of the children in your program. By paying attention to these reports, you can take necessary measures to protect susceptible children, such as by minimizing outdoor time during afternoons in response to pollen counts or playing outdoors in the morning rather than in the afternoon, when air quality is usually poorer. Of course, you may also plan your outdoor time around maintenance activities so children are not exposed to exhaust, fumes, and particulate matter from machines such as mowers, leaf blowers, or other landscape or construction equipment. The *Go Green Rating Scale* by Phil Boise is a good resource to help you carefully examine your program's potential for harmful indoor air as well as your response to air quality concerns outdoors. Refer to scales 20–25 for further information.

Teaching about Air

Whew! That's a lot to take in. Just remember, there is no need to delve into this level of detail about air pollution with children. Imagine being told you're breathing in something that you can't see, feel, or smell, but that could be harming your body? That would be frightening indeed! Remember that the early years are not the time for overly technical information, nor is it the time for scary and abstract discussions of environmental problems. Instead, stick to the basics, the fun stuff: air is vital to living things, and although invisible, it is an actual substance that takes up space, can move and carry objects, and plays a big part in the weather we experience.

Exploring air's properties and behavior offers interesting, exciting opportunities and fun for young children. In the activities that follow, children will have the opportunity to play with air, to explore how air behaves through flying objects, and to experience the qualities of air. As with all the environmental topics in this book, these creative explorations will lay the groundwork for understanding more complex topics in later years as well as for developing feelings of stewardship.

There are all sorts of ways to experiment with air and to create objects that clearly demonstrate air's ability to move things. Children take great delight in making toys and simple objects that can float or fly, and these experiences help them learn how air moves, and how we can experience air. You can help develop their observations and learn more about their experiences with air by asking questions such as "How would you describe air?" "How do you know air is all around us?" and "Could you 'show' air to someone?"

Hopefully you're aware of some resources to help you understand the risks and issues related to air quality and children's health, and you can take the necessary measures to protect children from exposure to poor quality air. Now that you're armed with information and can make informed choices, it's time to simply take a deep breath and enjoy exploring the wonders of air together. Consider how you can foster a sense of joy and curiosity around air for the young child. Enjoy the activities that follow!

Deep Breathing

AGES 3+

This activity, while very basic, is great for helping children get in touch with how air feels inside their bodies. Deep breathing can help children and adults relax and refresh. During the course of a normal day, our breathing is relatively shallow; we often don't fill our lungs to capacity. When we are excited, nervous, or afraid, our breath may be even shallower, or we may feel short of breath. Deep breathing—the process of filling one's lungs completely and then emptying them—replenishes the body's supply of oxygen, the component of air that our bodies need to function. When we exhale, we breathe out carbon dioxide, a waste product generated by the normal functioning of our cells.

Activity Goals

→ To experience the difference between deep breathing and shallow breathing

→ To control one's own breathing

National Science Education Standards

Science in personal and social perspectives: personal health

Materials and Supplies

None

Procedure

1. Invite the children to stand in a circle and think about their breathing. Allow a few seconds to pass while the children feel their breathing.

2. Invite them to take a big breath in, and to feel it filling their lungs, then to exhale slowly until they feel they can't exhale any more.

3. Inhale again, and try to inhale a second time. Try to breathe as deeply as possible, and then breathe in some more. Ask the children why they can't fit any more air in their lungs.

4. Continue practicing deep breathing. Ask if they can feel their chest rise and fall. Explain that the movement of their chest is actually their lungs filling with air and then emptying.

TIPS

- Use deep breathing as a "centering" activity when you need to calm the energy of the classroom. It is also helpful for children who are scared or nervous.

- Remember that this activity is also a great way to beat the midday blahs, since getting more oxygen to our cells can increase our energy.

CONNECTIONS

Provide a diagram of the body's anatomy for the children. Point out where the lungs are, and show how air travels through the mouth and nose to the lungs. You may also wish to explain how blood carries oxygen through blood vessels to all parts of the body.

Blow up a balloon and show the children how our lungs fill with air and expand. Explain that although lungs don't expand and contract to the extreme of a balloon, the basic idea is still the same.

Air Is Real

<solem
>This activity helps children visualize that air is not just emptiness; it actually is a substance (though invisible) that takes up space. Air has weight and mass. This activity will help children "see" air as it fills an empty space in a drinking glass.

Activity Goals

→ To understand that air, although invisible, still takes up space

→ To play with air and water

National Science Education Standards

Physical science: properties of objects and materials

Materials and Supplies

☐ Tissue paper, one sheet per child

☐ Drinking glasses, one per child

☐ Plastic tubs filled halfway with water, one for each small group

Procedure

1. Pass out the drinking glasses and ask the children what's inside ("nothing" will likely be the answer).

2. Pass out the tissue paper and show the children how to wad up some tissue and stuff it as tightly as possible in the bottom of the glass so that the tissue does not fall out when the glass is turned upside down.

3. Have children turn their glasses upside down and push them straight down into the basin of water. Then look for the top line of the water inside the glass and compare it with the top of line of the water outside of the glass.

4. Have children remove their glasses and look at the tissue. It should still be dry. Ask the children to describe what happened and how the tissue stayed dry. Explain that the tissue stays dry because there is air inside the glass. Remind them that you asked them what was inside the empty glasses. The real answer was air. Air takes up space inside the glass, and when the glass is upside down the water cannot push the air out. So the air is trapped inside the glass and keeps the tissue from getting wet.

5. Ask the children to predict what would happen if they tilted the glass just slightly while it is in the basin.

TIPS

- Instruct the children to pack the tissue very tightly in the glass so it stays in place when the glass is upside down.

- Invite children to plunge their glasses down quickly into the basin. They will find that bubbles are forced out of the glass and rise to the surface of the water. Ask them what is causing these bubbles. Explain that bubbles are bits of air being forced out of the glass when it is plunged downward.

CONNECTIONS

Try a variety of materials other than paper. Ask the children if the experiment will work with scraps of fabric, dry beans, or cotton balls and why or why not. Document their experiments.

Air Is Everywhere

Air is all around us. There are lots of ways to learn about this amazing thing called air. Although we can't see it, we can observe and feel its effects when we notice how differently things behave when air moves. In warm or cold months, children are very aware of air temperature. During very windy days, or when they blow on the backs of their hands, they are also aware of air's movement. This activity helps children build their awareness of air, even on days when the air is not so noticeable!

Activity Goals

→ To explore air using one's body

National Science Education Standards

Earth and space science: properties of earth materials

Science as inquiry: abilities necessary to do scientific inquiry

Physical science: properties of objects and materials

Science and technology: abilities of technological design (if challenge extension is done)

Materials and Supplies

☐ A windy day

☐ A clear container with a cover

Procedure

1. First, show the children the empty container and ask them what's inside. Pass the container around for them to examine. When they say "nothing," remind them that the container holds air. Tell them that although air is invisible, it is a real substance that fills the space all around us.

2. Ask if there are ways to experiment with air even though it is invisible. Allow time for the children to brainstorm answers.

3. Ask them for some ideas about how they could use their senses to explore air. Ask how they might be able to hear, feel, taste, see, and smell air.

4. Explain that although we can't see or hear air, we can see the effect that moving air can have on things. A flag moves in the wind and leaves rustle when the wind blows.

5. Invite children to use all their senses to make discoveries about air. Have them list objects they can see moving in the air.

6. Challenge them to discover how they can feel air. Let children experiment with blowing on their hands or arms, running through the air to feel wind in their hair, and waving their arms through the air.

7. Ask the children if it is possible to hear air and what needs to be present to hear air. Have them list the sounds that air makes. The sounds they hear are actually vibrations caused by air moving past objects.

8. Invite the children to stick out their tongues. Can they taste the air?

9. Invite the children to identify smells in the air. If there are scents in the air, you may have to explain to them that it is not the air itself they are smelling but rather tiny particles coming from different objects and traveling in the air and into their noses.

TIPS

 Use caution when handling glass containers.

• Do this activity on a windy day, and record your observations and experiences. Repeat the activity on a day when there is no wind, and compare the observations.

• Try this activity during different times of the year.

(continues on next page)

CONNECTIONS

Ask the children to list some words used to describe the sounds that air makes (whistling, roaring, blowing, squeaking), then write poems about air and wind.

Provide a variety of materials such as fabric scraps, plastic bags, straws, and so on. Tell the children you want to learn about air using a new tool. Allow the children to work in small groups or pairs to design their own tool for learning about air. Have them demonstrate their tool and describe the process they used to invent it. Ask them how their tool can be used to teach others about air.

Bubbles!

Children adore soap bubbles. Bubbles also happen to be a great tool for exploring air, since they move so freely in response to subtle shifts in air movement. In this activity, children will watch as bubbles float on the air, and they'll try to make them move using their arms and hands.

Activity Goals

→ To have fun blowing bubbles

→ To explore air's effect on soap bubbles

National Science Education Standards

Physical science: properties of objects and materials, position and motion of objects

Materials and Supplies

☐ A large quantity of soap bubbles (see recipe below)

☐ A variety of bubble wands

☐ Aluminum pie tins

Procedure

1. Explain to the children that because bubbles are so light, they will seem to float on the air.

2. Pour a half-inch of bubble solution into each pan and tell the children they can use bubbles to observe how air moves.

3. Pass out the wands and allow the children plenty of time to blow bubbles and watch where they go.

TIPS

- Invite children to help make the soap bubble solution.

- Suggest that children use their arms and hands to fan the soap bubbles to move them. This demonstrates one way air can move things. Challenge the children to move a bubble without popping it!

- Use this as a way to explore breathing. The slower children breathe, the bigger the resulting bubbles will be.

- Do this activity following the Deep Breathing activity on page 143.

- Make bubble wands from pipe cleaners.

- Experiment with different brands of liquid soap; some work better for bubble-making activities. Though it's not my intention to promote a particular brand, Joy and Dawn have worked well for me.

CONNECTIONS

Invite the children to make bubbles in a variety of shapes. Have them explore what happens when they use a star-shaped wand or a square one. Ask them to observe whether large bubbles move at the same speed as small bubbles. For some practice with measuring and counting, have the children mix up the bubble solution themselves.

Add several drops of food coloring to the bubble solution. Hand out pieces of watercolor paper and have the children catch the bubbles on the paper. When they pop on the paper, they'll turn into one-of-a-kind bubble art! Be aware that food coloring can stain clothing. You may want to have the children wear smocks during this activity.

Bubble Solution

¼ cup liquid soap
1 tablespoon glycerin
8 cups water
Few drops food coloring (if desired)

Using Air to Move Things

In this activity, children use the air in their own bodies to move objects. They will see that some objects respond to puffs of air differently than others. They will also have a chance to experiment with how to control air.

Activity Goals

→ To have fun playing with objects that respond to puffs of air

→ To blow hard and softly and see the result of these efforts

National Science Education Standards

Physical science: properties of objects and materials

Materials and Supplies

☐ Drinking straws, one per child

☐ Trays or cookie sheets, one per child

☐ A variety of small objects—such as scraps of felt, feathers, Ping-Pong balls, marbles, poppy seeds, and cotton balls—one handful of objects per child

☐ Chart paper and a marker

Procedure

1. Present each child with a tray and a handful of objects and ask them what kind of experiment you might conduct with these objects to learn about how air can move things.

2. In response to their suggestions, encourage them to make predictions about how air might affect each different object. Ask them to explain their ideas; record their predictions on the chart paper.

3. Encourage them to experiment with air movement by using their straws to blow different objects across their trays. Some items will move quickly, others less quickly. Some will not move at all.

4. Show them how to blow both forcefully and softly to control the speed with which things move.

5. After some time experimenting, gather the children and ask them what they did to make the objects move, how they controlled the way things moved, and if any of the experiments surprised them. Compare their observations with their earlier predictions.

TIPS

- Providing a tray for each child helps prevent them from blowing germs into each other's faces.

- Add to the trays some heavy items that will not be affected by the children's blowing.

CONNECTIONS

Plug in a fan and invite the children to make predictions about how far objects will travel. Invite them to stand next to the fan (or on a chair behind the fan) and drop different objects to see how far they travel. Mark a line on the floor where each object lands. Encourage the children to observe which object went the farthest and why. Have them experiment with different kinds of paper and fabrics.

Water down some tempera paint and put a few drops on a piece of paper. Put the paper on the trays, and invite the children to create art by blowing on the paint drops. Ask the children if the pictures will be different if they blow forcefully rather than softly. Have them describe how the rate at which they blow affects the picture. Also experiment with how changing the water content affects the movement of the paint and the picture.

Air Traffic

AGES 4+

Wind is very important for many plant species. It carries their seeds to new locations where they can embed in the Earth and begin to grow. Being carried on the wind often takes seeds far from their "parent plant." This helps plants spread and can even be important for their survival because it can allow a seed to take root and grow in an area where it doesn't have to compete with a larger plant for food, sunlight, and water. This act of carrying seeds to new locations is called *wind dispersal*. Conduct this activity on a windy day so the children can examine how dandelion seeds travel through the air.

Activity Goals

→ To have fun outside observing how the wind can carry lightweight seeds

National Science Education Standards

Physical science: position and motion of objects

Life science: characteristics of organisms, organisms and environments

Materials and Supplies

☐ Dandelions that have gone to seed (the white, puffy globe-shaped flowers are the ones that have gone to seed)

Procedure

1. Ask the children what things can travel on the air. (They will likely respond by saying "birds," "airplanes," "helicopters," and so on.) Explain that they will be looking for plants and seeds that can travel on the air.

2. Discuss how there are many seeds that travel on air. Different seeds travel on air in different ways. Some seeds drift on the wind (like dandelion seeds) and others (such as maple seeds, commonly known as "helicopters") will spin and fly through the air. Seeds that travel on air usually have a shape or form that helps them do so.

3. Explain that having their seeds carried away by the wind helps plants spread. See the introductory paragraph for information.

4. Pass out the dandelions, or invite children to pick dandelions and then blow the seeds into the air to see how the wind carries them.

TIPS

• Do this activity outdoors in late spring, when there are numerous dandelions that have gone to seed. The children will enjoy blowing the seeds.

• Find species in your area that utilize wind dispersal, such as milkweed and thistle, which go to seed in late fall; repeat the activity above with these other plants.

(continues on next page)

CONNECTIONS

Discuss with the children the characteristics of the shape or design of some seeds that helps them travel through the air. For example, some tree seeds are shaped like helicopter blades (certain maple and ash species), some are shaped like flags (linden trees), and some are shaped like gliders (milkweed plants).

Ask the children to design a seed of their own that would travel through air. Have them describe what it would look like.

Wind Ribbons

An *anemometer* is a simple device that measures the wind's speed and pressure. In this activity, children will make simple anemometers using ribbons and fabric. Setting up a simple wind station can make it easy for children to turn observing the wind into a natural part of the day's routine. By hanging lightweight ribbons where children can see them from indoors and out, they will notice even a light breeze.

Activity Goals

To create a simple, beautiful tool for measuring wind

National Science Education Standards

Physical science: properties of objects and materials, position and motion of objects

Science and technology: abilities of technological design

Materials and Supplies

☐ Colorful, lightweight strips of fabric or ribbon at least one foot in length, one for each child

☐ A tree or outdoor post, near a window if possible

☐ Chart paper and a marker

Procedure

1. Provide each child with a strip of fabric or ribbon and invite the children to find a place on the tree or pole where they can tie their ribbons. Assist as needed to secure the fabric or ribbons so they have long "tails" hanging.

2. Ask how the ribbons can help monitor and measure the wind. Record the ideas on chart paper; then, over the course of a few days, try each idea.

TIPS

- Check the ribbons throughout each day. Before going outside, ask the children to take a look at the ribbons and predict how windy it will be.

- For added fun, attach a Ping-Pong ball to the end of each ribbon. This may make the ribbons easier to see. Simply tape the ball to the ribbon using masking tape or other strong tape. Note that Ping-Pong balls are heavy enough that they will keep the ribbons from blowing in a soft breeze.

CONNECTIONS

Hang ribbons in a variety of locations on the schoolyard. Invite the children to predict whether there are areas that are more windy than others and why this might be so.

Hang some ribbons with Ping-Pong balls, others without. Compare the differences. If there is a difference, invite the children to speculate as to why that might be.

Simon Says South

Children love to learn about the four directions. Having a solid understanding of the four directions is essential for navigation and reading maps, and as children get older they often become fascinated with these things. This activity introduces the directions in a playful way. If you leave the directional labels posted, children will begin to internalize a sense of direction over the course of the year. This activity also helps children pay attention to wind direction, which is the direction *from which wind comes*, as opposed to the direction in which it is blowing. Wind direction is a very important concept in understanding and learning about weather.

Activity Goals

To become familiar with the concept of the four directions

National Science Education Standards

Physical science: position and motion of objects

History and nature of science: science as a human endeavor (if challenge extension is done)

Materials and Supplies

☐ A compass or map

☐ Cards with North, South, East, and West written on them

☐ Twine or tape

Procedure

1. Start by introducing the four directions: north, south, east, and west.

2. As a group, use a compass or map to identify the directions in your play yard.

3. Use the twine or tape to hang or post the cards indicating each direction in a prominent location.

4. Play a simple game of Simon Says, asking the children to move or point to one of the four directions. For example, say, "Simon says, point in the direction of the corner store and name

that direction," or "Simon says, walk south." You can even ask them to point in the direction of landmarks that are not visible to them, such as a nearby park or their homes. Many children will remember which direction they came from on the way to school. Some will not. This is okay!

TIPS

- To use a compass, stand outside and look at the small (usually red) arrow inside the compass. It will point north. Turn your body a bit to see how the compass needle moves. It will always point north. You can use this to determine the four directions. If you are facing north, east will be on your right, south will be directly behind you, and west will be on your left.

- After the children are familiar with the four directions, incorporate discussions of wind direction into your everyday activities and outings.

- Use this activity as a complement to the previous activity, Wind Ribbons. Once you've marked out the four directions, you'll be able to observe wind direction.

CONNECTIONS

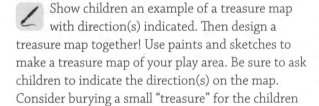 Show children an example of a treasure map with direction(s) indicated. Then design a treasure map together! Use paints and sketches to make a treasure map of your play area. Be sure to ask children to indicate the direction(s) on the map. Consider burying a small "treasure" for the children to find.

Design an obstacle course for the children. Create cards with directional instructions; for example, "Take twenty steps to the north, then clap your hands." "Take one big jump to the west, then spin around." Beginning readers can read the cards, or you can create pictures to say the same things. Make the clues appropriate to the children's level of reading and understanding.

Work together to make a map of your school and neighborhood. Make this a long-term project. Go out often as a group to explore the area on foot, and add to the map each time.

Let's Go Fly a Kite

AGES 3+

Children love kites, which are delightful and fun to play with and can easily be made from a variety of materials that would otherwise be thrown away. In this activity, you'll work with children to reuse plastic shopping bags and make them into colorful kites that catch air beautifully. In flying kites and playing with them in the wind, children gain experience with the properties of air and how it affects things.

Activity Goals

➜ To experience playing with air

➜ To test out different materials and how they move through air

National Science Education Standards

Physical science: properties of objects and materials, position and motion of objects

Science and technology: abilities of technological design

Materials and Supplies

☐ Assorted plastic grocery bags, one per child

☐ Construction paper scraps

☐ Pieces of lightweight fabric or ribbons

☐ Kite string cut into twelve- to eighteen-inch lengths, one per child

☐ Tape or glue

Procedure

1. Explain that one of the many ways that scientists and others learn about air is by tracking its movement. Some of the questions scientists ask include, "How hard is the wind blowing?" and "What direction it is coming from?"

2. Tell the children that watching a plastic-bag kite fly in the air can help them observe wind by "catching" wind in it.

3. Pass out the plastic bags and let the children have access to construction paper scraps, fabric, and ribbon to decorate their kites.

4. When the kites are decorated, tie one length of string to each bag's set of handles.

5. Spend time flying the kites. If it's not a windy day, children can run with the kites behind them to try to harness the wind.

6. Ask the children to make observations about what's happening. Ask them if it is easy or difficult to fly the kites, why the bags seem to "puff up," and how the bags behave differently if they simply walk or if it's not a windy day.

7. Discuss how air is filling the bags as they run or hold them in the wind. The air fills the bag completely, causing it to puff up.

TIPS

• Allow ample time for children to decorate their kites. If you are using glue sticks to affix the decorations, plan enough time for the glue to dry before taking the kites outside.

• Long, narrow plastic bags—such as those newspapers are delivered in—work especially well for this project.

• Experiment with how much decorating the kites can handle. A lot of construction paper scraps will make a plastic-bag kite heavier, so flying it will be more challenging.

• Use this activity with the family kite-making and kite-festival activity in chapter 9, Greening Your Program.

- Keep in mind that the kite flying will probably be most successful on a moderately windy day, although it is worth trying in varying weather and wind conditions.

Be sure that an adult is supervising children at all times when they are making and flying the kites. The plastic bags should never cover a child's face, and the strings should never be wrapped around anyone's neck.

CONNECTIONS

Research different shapes and materials for kites. Have the children experiment with how the shapes make it easier or more difficult to fly the kites. Invite the children to make kites with paper or with fabric and to notice how the different materials affect the kites.

Air Has Weight

AGES
5+

Although we can't see air, we know it takes up space and we know it has weight. One way to demonstrate this is to blow up two balloons equally and balance them. As one balloon loses air, the children will see quickly that air has weight.

Activity Goals

→ To understand that air has weight

→ To play with balloons and experiment with air pressure

National Science Education Standards

Physical science: properties of objects and materials, position and motion of objects

Materials and Supplies

☐ Party balloons, two per child

☐ String, cut into six-inch lengths, two per child

☐ Wooden rulers or sticks, at least six inches long, one per child

☐ Safety pin, for adult use

Procedure

1. Prior to working with the children, blow up the balloons equally and tie a knot to seal them. Then, use the string to attach the balloons to the rulers, one balloon per side.

2. Have the children stand behind a child-size chair and explain that they are going to see how air has weight.

3. Pass out the balloons on the rulers.

4. Ask the children to balance the rulers on the pivot point at the back of the chair. The balloons should hang equally and the ruler should balance.

5. Use the safety pin to carefully make a small hole near the tie of one balloon from each pair. The balloon will not pop, but air will slowly leak out.

6. As the air leaks out, the balloons that are losing air will appear to rise. What is really happening is that the balloon with more air is heavier, causing it to pull on the end of the ruler.

7. Discuss the children's observations and dispose of the balloons.

TIPS

• Keep in mind that this activity works best when there is plenty of space for each child (or teams of children) to conduct this experiment, rather than observing the teacher conducting it!

✋ ***Be sure there is no one with a latex allergy and that all balloons are disposed of after the activity, as balloon pieces can be a choking hazard.***

CONNECTIONS

🔍 🎖 Use coins or other small objects on the rulers to try to balance the balloons. Ask the children to make predictions about how many coins it will take, and test their predictions.

Rocket Balloons

One way to understand air is to watch how it affects things. In this activity, children will fill balloons with air, mount them to a straw on a string stretched across the room, and watch as the balloon races across the string as the air is expelled.

Activity Goals

→ To discover that air pressure forces the air out of a balloon rapidly

→ To experiment with different amounts of air pressure and observe its effects on the balloon

National Science Education Standards

Physical science: properties of objects and materials, position and motion of objects

Science and technology: abilities of technological design, understanding about science and technology

Materials and Supplies

☐ Party balloons, at least one per child

☐ Small air pump for blowing up balloons, optional

☐ Drinking straws

☐ Clear tape

☐ String

☐ Chairs

☐ A large empty space

☐ A measuring tape

Procedure

1. Prepare the balloon track ahead of time: Place two chairs at least five feet apart. Secure a piece of string to the top of one chair. Slide the drinking straw onto the string and secure the other end of the string to the other chair.

2. Tell the children you'd like to experiment with how air can make things move.

3. Blow air into a balloon, but do not tie it.

4. Ask the children where they think the air will go if you let go of the balloon. Also ask what they think will happen to the balloon (it will race around the room) and why (air is being forced out of the balloon as the latex retracts). Because there is such a small opening for the air to come out, it rushes and causes the balloon to race around erratically.

5. Tell the children to sit still, and begin by letting go of the balloon.

6. Explain that you want to control the balloon a little better so you can measure how far air can push a balloon.

7. Blow up the balloon again, but do not tie the end.

8. Keeping the balloon pinched closed, tape the opening of the balloon to the drinking straw. Do not tape the balloon closed; you need a small opening for the air to come out.

9. Release the balloon and watch it race across the string as the air rushes out.

10. Allow children time to blow up their balloons and measure the distance they travel. Challenge the children to make their balloons travel farther (by adding more air).

11. Reflect on the experiments. Invite the children to describe the process from beginning to end.

(continues on next page)

TIPS

- Set up a few tracks so children do not have to wait so long for a turn.

✋ *Be sure that no one is allergic to latex and that all balloons are disposed of after the activity, as balloon pieces can be a choking hazard.*

CONNECTIONS

🔍 Measure the distance each balloon travels. Experiment with different amounts of air and how that affects the distance traveled.

🔍 Change the angle of the string so that the balloons travel "uphill" or "downhill." Have the children describe the change in how much air is needed to move the balloons.

Paper Pinwheels

Children will enjoy making their own pinwheels and watching them spin when the wind blows. This experience will show them how wind can be used to move things. Wind is a form of energy, and it can make things move, work, and change. Wind (created by blowing on the pinwheels) will make the pinwheels spin and demonstrate the principle that we can harness the energy created by wind to do work.

Activity Goals

→ To explore air and the way it moves

National Science Education Standards

Physical science: position and motion of objects

Materials and Supplies

☐ Paper, cut into approximately five-inch squares, one per child

☐ Art supplies

☐ Glue sticks

☐ Thumbtacks, for adult use

☐ Unsharpened pencils with erasers

☐ Children's scissors, one per child

☐ Hole-punch that will create an eighth-inch hole

Procedure

1. Pass out the squares of paper, and have the children fold them in half diagonally, corner to corner, and then unfold and fold the paper in the other direction to create four triangles.

2. Using the fold lines as a guide, have children cut toward the center of their squares from each of the four corners—they should leave a half inch uncut at the center.

3. Use the hole-punch to make a hole in the center of the square.

4. Bring all four corners to the center of the square. Match up the corners, and secure them in place by pushing a thumbtack through the corners, through

the punched-out hole, and into a pencil eraser behind the pinwheel.

5. Decorate the pinwheels as desired.

6. Encourage the children to blow on the pinwheels to make them spin. Take the pinwheels outside and see the effects of wind on the pinwheels.

TIPS

• Use construction paper, reused art paper, or magazine pages to make the pinwheels.

• Provide assistance with the hole punch, if needed.

• Have younger children decorate the paper before cutting, and offer assistance in folding the paper.

(continues on next page)

Be sure to supervise closely and make sure the thumbtacks stay connected to the erasers so they do not hurt anyone.

CONNECTIONS

Invite a wind industry representative to visit and speak to the children. Ask the person to show pictures of windmills and talk about how wind can be used to generate electricity. In some parts of the United States, windmills are becoming increasingly common on the landscape, and they can be very exciting to see in operation. Investigate whether there might be a working windmill somewhere nearby. If by chance there is, perhaps you can find a way to see it or encourage families to take field trips to see it.

Scent Chase

The air we breathe has no scent of its own, but it can carry scents. Scents are created by tiny, invisible particles that come from foods, flowers, chemicals, and many other things. These particles float and travel along with air, but they are so tiny that we can't see them with our eyes. These particles enter our noses. Special sensors in our nasal passages send messages about the particles to our brains. Our brains receive the messages and we experience the scents. In this activity, children will play a simple game to learn how scents travel through air.

Activity Goals

→ To use one's sense of smell

→ To have fun trying to match scents

National Science Education Standards

Science as inquiry: abilities necessary to do scientific inquiry

Physical science: properties of objects and materials

Materials and Supplies

☐ Clean opaque containers with lids, such as small yogurt cups with lids or 35mm film containers or baby food jars or prescription bottles that have been painted opaque, one per child

☐ Cotton balls

☐ A variety of nontoxic substances with strong scents, such as cinnamon, mint, or vanilla extract; lemon, orange, or lavender oil; and vinegar, one for every two children

Procedure

1. Prior to the activity, make two matching sets of "scent jars" by placing cotton balls that have been soaked in extract, fragrant oil, or vinegar into the containers; one scent goes into two containers.

2. Tell the children they are going to play a game to learn how scents travel through the air.

3. Randomly pass out the closed containers and invite the children to open them and use the wafting

technique to smell the contents—but they should not announce what they smell.

4. Ask them to try, without talking, to find the child who has the matching scent.

5. Explain again that, although these scents can't be seen, they are traveling through the air as tiny molecules, smaller than anything we can see. The molecules travel through the air and enter our noses, where we register them as a scent.

TIPS

- Teach children the wafting technique for smelling contents: Open the jar, place it four to six inches from your nose, and gently fan the air above the jar toward your nose. This will cause the scent to waft upward, enabling you to smell it without overpowering your nostrils or harming your nasal passages.

- Try doing this activity indoors and outdoors. Ask the children if it is easier to detect scents in one place or the other.

CONNECTIONS

Invite the children to close their eyes and do this activity. Ask them if their experience of the scents changed and, if so, how. Also ask how many scents they can identify and when they have noticed these scents in the past.

With older children, do this activity as part of a more comprehensive investigation of the senses.

Playing with Pollen

Many plants reproduce by creating a fine powder called *pollen*. Flowering plants reproduce, or make new flowers, by sharing their pollen with other flowers of the same kind. Many flowers (though not all) spread their pollen on the wind. The tiny grains are carried by the wind, and when they land on other flowers of the same species, the plant can reproduce. In this activity, children play a simple game to capture pollen from a plant.

Activity Goals

→ To learn about pollen in a fun, playful way

National Science Education Standards

Life science: characteristics of organisms, life cycles of organisms, organisms and environments

Materials and Supplies

☐ Construction paper, torn into very small pieces (used construction paper works great for this activity!)

☐ Card stock

☐ Clear double-sided tape

☐ Real flowers, such as tulips or lilies, that have wind-carried pollen

☐ Magnifying lenses, one per child

☐ Art supplies

Procedure

1. Prior to the activity, make one paper flower for each child by cutting the card stock into a simple flower shape.

2. Explain to the children that pollen is a fine powder found on some flowers.

3. Invite the children to look closely at real flowers with pollen. The pollen will be located on the stamens (see image on next page).

4. Pass out the paper flowers and provide art supplies.

5. Allow the children time to color and decorate the flowers. As they are working, explain how some plants use pollen to reproduce, as described in the introductory paragraph.

6. As the children finish decorating their flowers, affix a piece of double-sided tape to the center of each one. For younger children, use a bigger piece of tape.

7. Invite the children to sit in a circle on the floor, while you stand in the center. Let them know that you are going to "shed your pollen" on the wind as many flowers do. Their job as flowers is to try to catch the pollen without getting up from the floor.

8. Scatter the scraps of construction paper in the air as the children hold up their flower blossoms, trying to catch the pollen. Not all pollen grains make it to another flower (as evidenced by the many construction paper scraps on the floor!) but this is a good approximation of actual wind pollination.

TIPS

• Make sure each child has a chance to catch at least a few of the "pollen grains."

CONNECTIONS

Explain that some plants are pollinated by wind and some by insects. Discuss with the children what characteristics would indicate that a plant depends on the wind to spread its pollen and what characteristics would indicate that a plant depends on insects for this job.

Take magnifying lenses outside and encourage children to gently examine flowers for pollen.

See the Plant a Sensory Garden activity on page 30. Ask the children to identify which plants use the wind to reproduce and to notice the wind's effects on these plants. The wind might help to transport seeds, or in autumn or winter it may rattle dry seed-pods or dry leaves, creating a nice sound.

Pollen

Stamen

CHAPTER 7

Weather, Climate, and Energy

These days everyone seems to be talking about climate change—polar ice caps melting, sea levels rising, weather systems changing, and species going extinct—and for a good reason. There is now widespread agreement among scientists that Earth's climate is changing and that the current trajectory and pace of change presents incredibly serious problems for our planet (IPCC 2012). It is truly one of the most challenging issues that humankind has ever faced, and one that affects everyone on Earth.

Many educators are already paying a lot of attention to this issue and have a natural urge to involve children. As with other environmental topics, it's also important to keep the developmental readiness of young children in mind. Perhaps even more than the other topics covered in this book, this one can be overwhelming to young children. The idea of Earth's temperature changing, sea levels rising, and animal populations going extinct can be terrifying. Children can so easily and justifiably feel out of control and helpless to do anything about the issue. As I've said, I recommend that you focus on providing opportunities for children to feel love and a sense of wonder about nature. Trust that the motivation for stewardship will emerge naturally from the base of joy you're building in the early years.

In reality, some children will enter the classroom having already heard rumors or scary stories about global warming or climate change, so I hope this book can be a valuable resource to those of you who want to be prepared to respond to those legitimate and important questions children have. While I'm not suggesting you dodge the issue completely, be mindful of the information you present and how you present it. Remember that you can also steer children's awareness away from the unsettling and scary parts of what they've heard to more joyful, tangible experiences—both indoors and out—that connect them to nature and to the concepts of weather and climate. Finally, remember that your actions speak volumes. When children see adults engaged in "positive" environmental behaviors—drinking from reusable water bottles, reducing fossil fuel consumption, composting—it normalizes those behaviors. In this way, you're also teaching children to be responsible stewards of our planet.

As with the other environmental topics, it's not my intention—nor would it even be possible—to cover this one comprehensively. My hope is simply to assist you in laying a foundation for understanding these issues and perhaps to interest you enough to pursue further knowledge on your own. For now, let's start with the basics.

What Is Climate?

First and foremost, when talking about climate change it is essential to be clear about the distinction between climate and weather. Weather refers to the conditions and patterns of temperature, precipitation, wind, and clouds that we experience from day to day. *Climate* refers to weather patterns and trends over an extended period of time, thirty years or more (WMO 2012). Weather can fluctuate daily, often even hourly. Climate may include seasonal variations, but it's the big picture of average weather and patterns over the long haul that matters. This is important because it is not possible to judge or evaluate the occurrence of climate change by looking at daily changing weather.

People often talk about the climate of a particular region. For example, the state of Florida has a sunny and warm climate. Remember that climate is the long-term picture. So by saying Florida's climate is sunny and warm, we are not saying that it *never* rains or gets chilly. As those who live there will attest, rainy, chilly days certainly occur, but we use the overall pattern of sun and warmth to describe its climate.

We can also talk about the climate of Earth as a whole. Earth has a climate unique in the solar system—one that supports life! What makes Earth's climate so special? Well, for one thing, its temperature. Averaged across the whole planet, Earth's temperature has held steady at around sixty degrees Fahrenheit for about the past ten thousand years; in other words, most of human civilization (Center for Climate Change Communication 2012).

Greenhouse Gases

Earth's climate is also unique in having an atmosphere with a mixture of gases that its inhabitants can breathe. That mixture consists predominantly of nitrogen and oxygen, the latter of course being what humans and animals need to breathe, but both being essential for sustaining all life. Beyond those major ingredients, there are a number of other gases present in relatively much smaller amounts. These include both naturally occurring and human-made gases. Among those lesser gases, there is a group that has come to be called *greenhouse gases* because they trap heat near the Earth's surface, acting in a way similar to the clear

glass of a greenhouse. Well-known greenhouse gases include methane (CH_4) and carbon dioxide (CO_2). It's important to know that by their presence, these greenhouse gases actually keep our planet from getting too cold; without them, life on Earth would not be possible. On the other hand, increasing the levels of these gases in the atmosphere means more heat is trapped on the surface, and the Earth is heating up! So by occurring in the correct proportions and amounts, the greenhouse gases in Earth's atmosphere play a key role in maintaining a climate suitable for life.

As I mentioned, climate scientists no longer have any doubt that Earth is presently experiencing a more dramatic increase in greenhouse gas levels in the atmosphere than ever before experienced during human civilization. As a result of that increase, our planet is warming; hence, another term that you've undoubtedly heard, *global warming*. According to the World Meteorological Organization (WMO) of the United Nations, in the past one hundred years, Earth's average temperature has increased by over one degree Fahrenheit, from just under sixty degrees to a little over sixty-one degrees Fahrenheit. Over the same time, we have seen a dramatic increase in greenhouse gases in the atmosphere, in particular a more than 30 percent increase in CO_2 levels (WMO 2011a).

Perhaps a little more than one degree increase doesn't sound like much, and you may ask, "What's the big deal?" Well, part of the problem is that greenhouse gases last a long time in the atmosphere. Many of the gases that we generate today will still be trapping heat decades from now. The increase that we have already seen reflects greenhouse gas emissions going back decades, and today's greenhouse gas output is even greater than it was decades ago. Scientists predict that given the current trajectory of greenhouse gas accumulation, the global average temperature of air near Earth's surface will increase somewhere between 2.5 degrees and 10.5 degrees Fahrenheit by 2100. Furthermore, they say that many land areas, particularly those at high latitudes, will warm even more rapidly than the global average (WMO 2011b).

According to scientists, warming temperatures are linked to many problems and threats to life on Earth as we know it. For example, warming temperatures are causing glaciers to melt at a rate unprecedented in human history. Melting glaciers at the Earth's poles are linked to a host of problems, most notably rising sea levels. And rising sea levels pose many problems, not the least of which is threatening the future of coastal towns and cities (UCS 2009).

Warming temperatures can profoundly alter weather patterns, causing more extreme and unpredictable weather around the globe (NOAA 2011a). More extreme and unpredictable weather likely means more precipitation in areas that have a tendency to be wet, and more droughts in areas that have a tendency to be dry. More extreme weather includes more thunderstorms, hurricanes, and flood events (UCS 2009). Warmer temperatures mean some animal and plant species that are adapted to colder temperatures have to move to new locations or face extinction. Warmer temperatures also lead to the spread of certain diseases. For example, disease-bearing mosquitoes will be able to spread and won't be killed off by seasonal cold temperatures (US EPA 2011b). Unfortunately, the list of problems posed by warming temperatures goes on and on. The term *climate change* refers both to the warming of Earth's surface, air, and water temperatures and to this dizzying array of resulting problems and changes.

It is important to understand that Earth has experienced a number of climate fluctuations in its long-distant past—both dramatic cooling (ice ages) and warming. Indeed, climatic change can be caused by natural factors, such as volcanic activity and shifts in the Earth's rotation and orbit over extremely long time frames. It is also important to understand that when the ancient climatic changes that we know about occurred, they caused profound alteration of the kinds and communities of species that existed at the time—think of the dinosaurs! Scientists widely agree that, unlike those ancient fluctuations, the current climate change is being driven by human activities, in particular the generation of greenhouse gases from our modern way of life. They also agree that the current rate of change is faster and more dramatic than has ever occurred in the span of human history (US EPA 2010b).

Otherwise known as CO_2, carbon dioxide is one of the naturally occurring greenhouse gases. Humans and other animals emit CO_2 with every exhalation. Even plants naturally release it into the atmosphere. Plants also take CO_2 in through their leaves in order to survive. CO_2 is also generated when things naturally decompose. However, it turns out that many of the activities so commonplace in our modern life—from driving vehicles, to making electricity, running factories, extracting raw materials for goods and services, and cutting down forests for agriculture and development—generate *a lot* of CO_2. In fact, the greatest current source of human-caused CO_2 emissions in our atmosphere is the process that underlies all the above activities: the burning of fossil fuels (US EPA 2011a).

Fossil Fuels

Fossil fuels—coal, petroleum, and gas—have come to be the key drivers for the majority of human activity, industry, and productivity today. Petroleum—refined into gas and oil—runs our vehicles. Natural gas and coal are fossil fuels used to heat most of our homes, schools, and buildings, power our factories, and generate the majority of our electricity. Fossil fuels are also used to make plastics and fertilizers and to grow food crops. Fossil fuel–derived ingredients are often present in many everyday items such as ink, cleaning products, tires, heart valves, and deodorants (IER 2011). In short, fossil fuels are central to modern living.

Fossil fuels earned their name because they come from ancient plants and animals that died and were buried and fossilized deep in the Earth millions of years ago. Because these plants and animals were made of carbon (as are the bodies of all living things), we release that carbon in the form of carbon dioxide into the atmosphere when we burn these fuels. Fossil fuels are also associated with other significant environmental problems. Because they are buried deep underground, the process of extracting them is expensive and can be very environmentally damaging. In the case of oil, it must be pumped from deep within the Earth and frequently from under the ocean floor. Sometimes the equipment fails or leaks, creating environmental catastrophes. The process for obtaining coal is equally problematic. Coal is often mined by removing huge amounts of rock and natural land areas in order to expose it, which significantly disrupts natural areas, not to mention the fact that the extraction process itself requires fossil fuels.

The connection between fossil fuels and climate change is an extremely important one. It is the reason that the topics of climate change and energy are commonly grouped together, as in this book. It's true that *energy* is a broad concept defined as the ability to do work or cause change. Examples of energy are all around us, in every movement we make or change that occurs. But the energy that's implied when spoken in the same breath with climate change is specifically fossil fuel energy—the predominant source of power in our world today, and the major human-caused source of increasing CO_2 and other greenhouse gases in our atmosphere.

something, anything. More and more people are becoming aware of the significance of fossil fuels. When we burn them, use the energy created by them, or buy something made of or by them, we are responsible for adding carbon to the atmosphere. Many people have begun to think about how to reduce their *carbon footprint*—the amount of CO_2 added to the atmosphere as a result of their activities and consumption habits. (In chapter 3, I introduced the concept of environmental footprint. The carbon footprint concept is similar, but refers specifically to carbon generation.) It is possible to estimate, or calculate, the pounds of carbon released into the atmosphere from routine daily activities and consumption. For example, a nonprofit called the Minnesota Energy Challenge estimates that the average Minnesota family generates about fifty-one thousand pounds of CO_2 annually through its recreational habits, electricity usage, vehicle use, and consumption of other resources (Minnesota Energy Challenge 2012).

Is Climate Change for Real?

All of this information may make sense to you, but you might still be wondering, "How can we really be certain that the climate is changing?" After all, we know that weather extremes and changing temperatures are nothing new for this planet, right? Maybe you've even heard someone gripe on a bitterly cold day, "So much for global warming!" But remember that climate change refers to *long-term trends*, not the day-to-day phenomenon of weather. Again, this distinction is incredibly important. Scientists have actually measured changes in climate going back hundreds of thousands of years. They have studied CO_2 bubbles trapped in ancient ice and ocean floor sediments, and their data show unmistakably that the rate of accumulation of CO_2 and other greenhouse gases in our atmosphere has increased significantly in the past century and that acceleration correlates with the increase in human generation of greenhouse gases (Riebeek 2006).

As you think about the magnitude and the urgency of this issue, there's a natural urge to want to do

What You Can Do

In appendix H, Additional Resources, I have listed websites and resources that can help you calculate your carbon footprint. On one hand, utilizing one of these resources can be a bit unsettling. There is no way to eliminate our carbon emissions entirely, nor is that the goal. On the other hand, these resources point out that small steps can make a big difference in reducing the amount of carbon one person is responsible for releasing. For example, reducing one's weekly vehicle driving time or turning the thermostat down by just a few degrees can add up to big changes. Imagine what would happen if every family in your program tried to make a few changes to reduce their carbon footprint! If one family generates more than fifty-one thousand pounds of carbon per year, consider the impact of several families making changes!

There are also great resources available to help you think about ways to make our homes and buildings more energy efficient. The *Go Green Rating Scale* and *Go Green Rating Scale Handbook*, both by Phil Boise, can serve as great resources for educators. These manuals offer many ideas and suggestions for conserving energy and reducing fossil fuel consumption at your site.

More broadly speaking, there are numerous developments in the field of renewable energy. Also called alternative (or perpetual) energy, this type of energy comes from sources that are easily replenished, grow back, or will never go away, such as solar or wind power. These energy sources have the potential to produce energy with substantially fewer carbon emissions. The field of renewable energy is growing fast and holds great promise for the future of our planet, not to mention the economic benefit of the communities, nations, and corporations that develop it.

TEACHING ABOUT CLIMATE CHANGE AND ENERGY

So what *can* we do in early childhood to lay the foundation of engagement and curiosity about the natural world, which will later lead to an understanding of climate and related issues? Keeping in mind that you don't want to overwhelm or frighten children, a great starting point is to explore the topic of weather. Though weather and climate are not the same, they're clearly related, and learning about weather can be a great entry point to prepare children for understanding global climate and later taking action to protect it. Weather is also such a natural and perfect topic for the early childhood classroom. Many days in the classroom begin with discussions of the weather during circle time. Children eagerly report on their choices for jackets or hats in response to the temperature outside. They sing songs about whether the sky is sunny or dark and stormy. Arriving at school during the first snowfall of the season, children wear bright smiles and rosy cheeks. Umbrellas and rain gear take center stage during spring rains, and children shriek with surprise (and sometimes delight!) when a loud clap of thunder interrupts playtime in the classroom. Weather can be a source of inspiration for art, storytelling, and dramatic play.

Although the causes of weather are complex and mostly beyond the scope of the early childhood classroom, observing, experiencing, and measuring weather are natural activities for the early childhood classroom. Weather presents limitless opportunities for developing scientific-thinking skills. Even though no one can prove or disprove climate change on the basis of daily weather, you can make observations that ultimately lead to understanding climate change. For example, many people have anecdotally and more formally reported changes in weather patterns and associated natural phenomena over many years, such as earlier spring temperatures and ice-out dates (the day when the ice melts from bodies of water), longer growing seasons, and shifting animal and plant populations. *Phenology* is the study of the timing of natural events in relationship to seasonal change; for example, the opening of buds and thawing of the ground in springtime. Furthermore, it is true that because of climate change, we have and will continue to see changes in these patterns. Phenological observations can help us track, understand, and predict the impact of climate change on different environments. Even more important for the early childhood educator, observing the timing of natural events can be a great activity for young children that can help them fine-tune their observation and critical-thinking skills for more sophisticated observations in the future.

Of course, the best way to teach about weather is to spend lots of time outdoors in all kinds of weather. This will provide children with lots of authentic experiences with different kinds of weather—sunny, hot, rainy, cool, and overcast. Venture outside on a rainy day for some splashing and playing in puddles. Your class may collect water from rain gauges and fill buckets with mud from the soggy ground. Children will take away much more from these experiences than they would from simply hearing a weather story and creating "a rainy day" scene with tempera paint.

Remember to create opportunities for play and joy. Fill your days with lots of time outside. Use the activities that follow to create opportunities for exploration and investigation. If you lay the foundation for a love of nature, critical thinking and scientific inquiry will develop naturally with time. Simply put, there is nothing else that will lay a stronger foundation for a lifetime of environmental stewardship than helping children connect emotionally to the natural world.

Sunshine Sculptures

The sun is critical to life on Earth. Most people have an intuitive understanding about this but rarely have a chance to put it into words. In this activity, children are encouraged to identify what they know about the sun and its role in life on Earth, and they have a chance to creatively make a sculpture of the sun using tissue paper and balloons. This is a great activity to do outside on a sunny day!

Activity Goals

→ To explore ideas about the sun and its role on Earth

→ To creatively express one's understanding of the sun

National Science Education Standards

Physical science: light, heat, electricity, and magnetism

Materials and Supplies

☐ Party balloons, one per child

☐ Torn squares of tissue paper in shades of orange, yellow, and red

☐ Shallow trays

☐ Glue

☐ Water

☐ Paintbrushes

☐ String

☐ Tape

☐ A thumbtack, for adult use only

Procedure

1. Prior to the activity, blow up and tie the balloons. Mix equal amounts of glue and water and pour the mixture into the trays.

2. Invite the children to think about the sun and all it does for life on Earth. Discuss their ideas about why the sun is special. Talk about how it provides heat, which warms the planet and makes it hospitable for life, and how plants use its energy to make food, which in turn supports all life on Earth.

3. Invite the children to make suns of their own to take home.

4. Give each child a balloon and have the children hold their balloons by the knotted end.

5. Using the paintbrushes, children can coat the balloons with the glue mixture and press the squares of tissue paper onto the balloons, overlapping the squares. They'll need five or six layers of glue and paper to make the finished sun sturdy. They should repeat this process until the balloon is covered.

6. When all balloons are covered in tissue, use string to hang them from the knotted end and allow them to dry overnight.

7. The next day, when the balloons are fully dry, insert a thumb tack through the tissue paper to pop the balloons.

TIPS

 If you conduct this activity outdoors, remind children not to look directly at the sun.

- For children who are reluctant to cover their hands in glue, enlist the help of children who are more comfortable to help press the tissue paper onto the balloons. Provide tubs of water so children can wash their hands as needed.

- Glue the midpoint of a length of ribbon to the top of each sun sculpture and tie the ends together so the children can hang them.

- Allow the children to experiment and find what works best for them. Some children will find it easier to put glue on one section of the balloon at a time, while others will want to cover the entire balloon in glue and then layer on the tissue. (A messier approach, but it's perfectly okay!)

CONNECTIONS

Encourage the children to write (or dictate) a story or poem about the sun. They can describe things the sun does, say what they love about the sun, or tell a story of a sunny day.

Have children decorate the dried suns with gold, red, or orange glitter glue for extra sparkle.

Explain that many cultures celebrate the sun. In Argentina, there is a National Day of the Sun in February, while in Greenland, there are celebrations to honor the return of the sun after a long, dark winter. Other traditions celebrate the sun as well. Have children research different traditions and celebrations related to the sun, and your class can plan your own Sun Festival.

If you wish to make lanterns with the children, cover only the bottom three-fourths of the balloons with tissue (leaving an uncovered area at the top or knotted end). After removing the popped balloon, use a hole-punch to make two holes on either side of the lantern. Thread a generous amount of floral wire through the holes. Use enough wire so that when you twist the free ends together, you create a long loop or handle. Insert a small votive candle. A small amount of sand will hold the candle steady, or you may glue a small glass candleholder into the bottom of the lantern.

Before lighting the candles, discuss fire- and candle-safety rules with the children. Remind them not to touch the flame. Supervise the children closely while candles are lit.

Shadow Tracing

Shadows happen when an object blocks the path of the sun's light. Children love playing with their shadows. In this activity, children will play a simple game to learn how shadows are formed and how they change.

Activity Goals

→ To have fun exploring shadow and light

→ To practice tracing and drawing lines

National Science Education Standards

Earth and space science: properties of earth materials, objects in the sky, and changes in earth and sky

Materials and Supplies

☐ A sunny day

☐ Sidewalk chalk

☐ Open pavement, such as a sidewalk, closed parking lot, or blocked driveway

Procedure

1. Talk with the children about the sun and shadows. Ask if they have ideas about how shadows are formed.

2. Invite the children to find a partner or pair the children and give each pair a piece of sidewalk chalk. Partners should take turns tracing around their partner's shadow. They can make funny poses, hold toys, or stand however they want to make a shadow.

3. As the shadows are completed, talk with the children about the shapes and sizes.

4. Return to the area later and ask children to try to "get back in" to the shadow outlines they made, by standing where they were earlier. This will be challenging! The sun's position will have changed.

TIPS

 Be sure that children do not look directly at the sun when doing this activity.

• Younger children may need an adult to trace their shadows; use your knowledge of the children in your program to determine the best way to implement this activity.

CONNECTIONS

Provide measuring tape or yardsticks and invite children to measure the outlines and compare the sizes of their shadows. You could also create a sundial: Mark a spot on the pavement so the children always stand in the same place when tracing their shadows. Record the time next to the shadow. An hour later, stand on the spot and record the time again, tracing the shadow again. Return throughout the day and notice how the shadow outline changes over time.

Taking the Temperature

AGES 3+

How can we understand the sun's effect on places and things? Most children intuitively understand the concepts of shade and sun, but this activity helps them think about the difference between them by making temperature observations in areas where the sun shines and areas where the sun is blocked. In this activity, you and the children will make predictions together about the sun's heat. Then you'll venture outdoors on a sunny day to check your predictions and learn firsthand the variations in temperature in different areas and on different surfaces.

Activity Goals

→ To experience differences in temperature

→ To become familiar with the direct effects of sunlight and shade

National Science Education Standards

Physical science: properties of objects and materials; light, heat, electricity, and magnetism

Earth and space science: properties of earth materials

Materials and Supplies

☐ Chart paper and markers

Procedure

1. Explain to the children that you want to learn more about the sun's effect on things around your site. Tell them you want to learn what effect the sun has on plants, sidewalks, trees, and other things. Invite the children to think about the areas they have access to outside, including the playground, the building itself, the sidewalks, the parking lot, and so on. Ask them which things they think might feel warm and which might feel cool.

2. Record their ideas—and any of your own ideas—in two columns (warm and cool) on the chart paper.

3. Review the list and talk about why they think some things will be warm and others cool.

4. Take the group outside and feel the different surfaces. Use hands, arms, and even cheeks to check the warmth or coolness of all the places they suggested.

5. Be sure to feel warm areas (such as a sidewalk that's had sun shining on it for hours) and cool areas (the shaded side of your building or underneath a slide on the playground) to compare the difference.

6. Return to your list of observations. Ask the children to describe why certain areas and objects were warmer than others and what kept certain areas cool.

TIPS

- Repeat this activity in different seasons so that children experience differences in temperature during all of the seasons.

- Repeat this activity at different times of the day.

CONNECTIONS

Invite the children to set out several thermometers around the play yard, as well as inside, to measure the difference in temperature in various places. Alternately, take the children outside several times to feel the temperature differences. Then have them predict the temperature and the differences before setting out the thermometers. Repeat these activities in different seasons and at different times of the day.

Melting Ice

In this activity, children are encouraged to try melting ice in a variety of settings and situations and to compare the effect of different temperatures on ice. They will learn that heat melts ice and that some colors absorb more heat than others. This experience will help them build connections related to temperature variations in cities, rural areas, and other parts of the world.

Activity Goals

→ To learn about temperature variation and melting ice

National Science Education Standards

Earth and space science: properties of earth materials

Materials and Supplies

☐ Ice cubes, one for each child

☐ Small trays, one for each child (empty, clean microwave food trays work great)

Procedure

1. Ask the children if they'd like to have an "ice melting race."

2. Tell them that they will each be given one ice cube on a tray, and they can place it anywhere they want to see if they can make it melt. Be sure not to tell them where to put their ice cubes. The fun of this activity is in discovering!

3. Allow time for the children to look around, feel different areas, and discuss together their ideas for where to put their ice cubes.

4. Give one ice cube on a tray to each child and have children place their trays where they want.

5. As a class, visit each child's ice cube several different times and notice the different rates at which they are melting.

6. When all the cubes have melted, discuss the different locations and other factors that played a role in how quickly the ice melted.

TIPS

- Use this activity as a complement to the Taking the Temperature activity on page 173; remind the children to think about which areas were warm and which were cool.

- Plan some outdoor playtime while waiting for the ice to melt, and allow the children to check on their ice cubes. The ice will take awhile to melt, even on a hot day.

- Do this activity during different times of the year, and make notes about how long it takes the ice cubes to melt during the different seasons.

CONNECTIONS

Expand the activity by watching to see which puddle of melted ice evaporates first—was it the same one that melted first?

Give each child several ice cubes to place in various locations and invite them to record their comparative data in a science journal.

Color Connections

Dark colors absorb heat and light, whereas light colors reflect heat and light. In this activity, children will use thermometers to measure temperature differences for different colors. Understanding the effect that color can have on temperature can help children later understand why some parts of the Earth are warmer than others. This activity will also help children understand that dressing in darker colors will keep them warmer and lighter colors will keep them cooler.

Activity Goals

→ To use thermometers and compare how dark and light colors effect the temperature of water

→ To experience the effect of an object's color on its temperature

National Science Education Standards

Physical science: light, heat, electricity, and magnetism

Materials and Supplies

☐ Three clear containers filled two-thirds full with water

☐ Black paper

☐ White paper

☐ A thermometer

☐ Tape

☐ Chart paper and a marker

Procedure

1. With the children, use the thermometer to measure the temperature of each container of water and record the temperature on the chart paper.

2. Tape white paper to the side of one container, tape black paper to the side of another container, and leave the third container as is.

3. Place each container in a sunny spot, arranging the wrapped containers so that the sun shines directly on the uncovered side and easily passes through to the water.

4. After thirty to sixty minutes, return to the containers and measure the temperature in each container.

5. Record and compare the results.

TIPS

 Empty glass jars work well, but use caution with glass.

• Provide pictures of different types of homes and buildings. For example, homes on some islands in Greece (where it is hot and very sunny) are all white to better reflect the sun's heat. Many homes in North America have black or dark gray shingles on the rooftops. Explore how the color of one's roof or home can affect its temperature.

• Have children fill the containers with water ahead of time to help prepare for this activity.

CONNECTIONS

Ask the children what they noticed about the temperature differences and why they think the temperatures were different for each container. Have them explain what the activity can teach them about dressing for warm or cool weather.

Colorful Puddles

This activity offers children firsthand experience with the way heat affects different colors. You'll provide them with different colored ice cubes, and they will compare the rates at which they melt. They will see that darker colors respond more quickly to heat and melt faster.

> ## Activity Goals
> → To experience how darker colors respond to heat
>
> ## National Science Education Standards
> *Earth and space science:* properties of earth materials

Materials and Supplies

☐ Ice cube trays

☐ various colors of tempera paint

☐ Water

☐ A sunny location, such as a sidewalk, closed parking lot, or blocked driveway

☐ Timer or stopwatch

☐ Chart paper and a marker

Procedure

1. Prior to the activity, mix each color of paint with water to thin it out, then pour the water into ice cube trays. Also pour plain water into another set of ice cube trays. Freeze to make ice cubes.

2. Ask the children if they think the color of something affects how warm or cool it will be in the sun and why they think so.

3. Ask for ideas on how they could test this idea.

4. Tell them that you have some ice cubes of different colors, and that they can place them in a sunny location and measure how quickly the different colors melt.

5. Place the ice cubes in a sunny outdoor location.

6. Start the timer and ask the children to keep an eye on the ice cubes and let you know when one melts.

7. Record the time it takes for each color of ice cube to melt.

8. Compare the results and discuss what happened. Ask the children to describe why the darker colored ice cubes melted more quickly than the plain ice cubes. (Because they retained more heat.)

TIPS

- It will take time for the ice cubes to melt, even in direct sunlight. Plan a fun activity, such as a nature walk, to pass the time while the ice melts.

CONNECTIONS

Invite the children to think of other ways to experiment with how color affects melting rate. Whenever possible, implement their ideas and compare results.

Have children melt the ice cubes on paper and observe how the colors blend together. Have them set the paper on trays and tilt or prop up the trays just slightly, or have them first crumple the paper and then flatten it so the ice melts into the pattern of the creases.

Ask children to discuss why cities tend to have warmer temperatures than outlying areas. (There is more asphalt and cement, which retain more heat than grassy or natural areas.) Invite children to create a container that would slow the melting of their ice cubes.

Cloudy Days

AGES
5+

Most children, when prompted, will draw a cloud as a puffy bubble. However, there is great variation among cloud shapes, sizes, and textures. This activity offers children a way to express themselves and look at clouds. They will paint outdoors—a new experience for many children—and be encouraged to paint the clouds that they see.

Activity Goals

→ To experience painting outdoors

→ To look closely at clouds

National Science Education Standards

Earth and space science: properties of earth materials, objects in the sky, changes in earth and sky

Materials and Supplies

☐ A partly cloudy day

☐ Black or dark blue paper

☐ White watercolor paint and brushes

☐ Small containers, such as empty applesauce containers or yogurt containers, filled with water

Procedure

1. Ask children to find a spot outside where they will be comfortable and can see the clouds clearly.

2. Encourage the children to watch the clouds for a while, noticing their sizes, shapes, colors, and other details. Invite the children to share their observations.

3. Provide each child with a few sheets of paper, a paintbrush, and access to paint and a container of water.

4. Have the children paint the clouds they see.

5. Allow plenty of time for the paintings to dry before bringing them inside.

TIPS

- Do this activity with children old enough to paint without assistance.

- Keep in mind that watercolor paint can be diluted or thickened more easily than tempera paint, which makes it perfect for painting clouds.

- Don't be afraid to do this activity outdoors in the rain. Just make sure the children are in a sheltered location so their paintings don't get too wet from the rain!

CONNECTIONS

Repeat this activity several times over the course of a month. Make a study of different kinds of clouds. Use this activity as a way to refine the children's observation skills. Have the children describe their observations of the clouds, such as the shapes and textures, and explain the process of painting them.

Venture out during different types of weather and at different times of the day. Children will look forward to these times and enjoy mixing paint colors to find just the right shade to match the gray clouds of a September sky or the pinkish clouds of early morning.

Look for some of the great cloud-themed children's books out there (fiction and nonfiction). Some of them even incorporate teaching on the most basic cloud types and the differences between them.

Share some of the basic cloud types by name:

Cirrus: white and feathery clouds, also some of the highest in the sky

Cumulus: puffy, cotton-ball type clouds

Stratus: flat, wide clouds

Nimbus: dark, gray rain clouds

Cumulonimbus: towering billowy thunderstorm clouds

Raindrop Rainbows

This activity offers children a fun way to create something beautiful from rain. Young children's nervousness about rainstorms might be quelled when they know that rain is helping them make a beautiful picture. This activity requires a rainy day. If done on more than one occasion, it will help children develop an awareness of the different types of rainstorms (drizzle, sprinkling, downpour, and so on).

Activity Goals

→ To create a fun and colorful piece of art made by rain

→ To develop positive feelings about rainstorms

National Science Education Standards

Earth and space science: properties of earth materials

Materials and Supplies

☐ Tissue paper or leftover crepe paper of many different colors (not white)

☐ Heavy white paper, such as poster board, one piece per child

☐ Binder clips or clothespins

Procedure

1. Pass out the paper and allow children to choose a sheet of tissue paper or strip of crepe paper. Ask them to secure the tissue paper to their sheet of white paper using the binder clips or clothespins. They may wish to use more than one color of paper or to use a variety of sheets of crepe paper to make designs.

2. During a rainstorm, place the papers outside and allow rain to fall onto the tissue. It won't take long for the tissue paper to get wet and the color to seep through to the white paper.

3. Bring the papers inside and invite the children to remove the tissue paper to expose the beautiful pattern of raindrops.

TIPS

• Use one sheet of tissue paper at a time. Children can remove the wet tissue paper and replace it with a different color as many times as they like. Just caution them that the raindrop prints may smear.

CONNECTIONS

Create colorful gift wrap using this technique, or invite the children to use this colored paper to decorate covers for journals, placemats, or other personal items.

Use heavy cardstock for this activity. When the children have decorated it to their liking, cut the paper into postcard-size pieces, and invite the children to draw, write, or dictate a message to someone they love. Then mail the postcards together.

Observing Weather

Scientists who observe and predict weather constantly look at different kinds of data, such as temperature, humidity, precipitation, wind direction, and wind speed. Using these and even more kinds of data, scientists form their understanding and make their predictions about weather. In this activity, children will think about how collecting different types of information can help them form a big-picture idea of weather.

Activity Goals

→ To have fun learning about weather

National Science Education Standards

Earth and space science: objects in the sky, changes in earth and sky

Materials and Supplies

☐ Outdoor thermometer

☐ Chart paper and a marker

☐ Weather tools from the Make a Compass activity on page 180, Rain Gauges activity on page 134, or Wind Ribbons activity on page 151

Procedure

1. Ask the children what kinds of things they like to know about the day's weather (the temperature, the chance of rain, the chance of snow, and so on). Discuss their ideas.

2. Ask them why it is good to know about the weather (it helps us plan our activities, it helps us decide how to dress, and so on) and discuss their answers.

3. Ask them which parts of the weather we measure (rain, wind direction, and so on) and record their ideas.

4. Ask the children what kinds of tools they can use to measure the factors they are most interested in.

5. Place the thermometer and any other weather tools you have made in the schoolyard. You may want to put them all in the same general area or place them in different areas.

6. Develop a chart to use as a group to record your weather observations. Include columns for the different things the children are measuring, such as temperature, wind direction, and rain.

7. Make a point of reading the weather tools every day. Ask the children to report on their observations and to describe how they know what the temperature is, if it has rained, and which direction the wind is blowing.

TIPS

- Allow the children time to decorate the chart. They may wish to draw pictures on the chart or to use cut-up images of different weather phenomena from magazines as decorations.

- Use simple weather tools made in the activities named above, or purchase more complex, household-grade weather instruments.

- Be sure to place the tools in a location the children will be able to visit daily. It may be best to place them where you can see them clearly from inside the classroom.

CONNECTIONS

Start a class weather chart at the beginning of the year. Record data daily and make observations about your results.

Invite children to write a story about their favorite kind of weather. To get them started, ask them what they like to do outside in this weather and why it is their favorite.

Make a Compass

It's important to be accurate in your description of why shadows change. Although we often say the sun is rising or setting, the Earth is really moving around the sun, which creates the appearance of the sun moving in an arc across the sky. In this activity, children will use their shadows to create a simple compass. A compass offers a great way to learn about the four directions, to find your way using a compass, and to have fun learning about Earth's magnetic poles.

Activity Goals

→ To measure one's shadow and see how it changes throughout the course of a day

→ To find the four directions

National Science Education Standards

Earth and space science: objects in the sky

Materials and Supplies

☐ A wooden dowel or stick, about eighteen inches long

☐ A shovel

☐ Four fist-size stones

☐ A flat area in direct sunlight

☐ Chalk

Procedure

1. Prior to the activity, dig a hole about six inches deep and place the wooden dowel in it, so that twelve inches are above ground. Fill in the hole with the soil you dug out and pack down the soil so the dowel is secure.

2. Visit the stick in the morning with the children, and see where the shadow is cast.

3. Place one stone at the very end of the shadow.

4. Later in the afternoon, observe the shadow again. The shadow should be roughly the same length, but on a different side of the stick.

5. Place another stone at the end of this shadow.

6. Ask a child to place her right foot on the side of the compass with the stone you put down in the morning, and her left foot on the side with the stone you put down in the afternoon. This child's body now faces south.

7. Place a stone in front of this child to mark south. Using chalk, write an "S" on this stone.

8. Place another stone directly behind this child to mark north. Write an "N" on this stone with the chalk.

TIPS

• Be sure that there is a relatively straight line between the stones.

• Keep in mind that each child will probably want to make a compass. If you have the space, great! Remember that for this exercise to work, it must take place in an area of direct sunlight.

• If you can't place a dowel or stick in the ground, do this activity in a closed parking lot. Simply use a traffic cone or t-ball stand in place of the dowel.

• See the other activities related to shadows, including Shadow Tracing on page 172.

CONNECTIONS

Ask the children to describe the process of the sun's apparent motion across the sky both before and after doing this activity. Have them describe and write down the process of creating the compass.

Circle of Energy

Electricity is one form of energy that we use and depend upon every day. We use it to power our lights, computers, televisions, refrigerators, and many other things. The way electrical currents travel is complex. This simple activity makes a game of imagining energy traveling through a cord to power a lamp. This activity is fun to do outside, but it can also be done indoors.

Activity Goals

→ To become familiar with the idea of electricity and energy

National Science Education Standards

Earth and space science: properties of earth materials

Science and technology: abilities of technological design

Science in personal and social perspectives: types of resources

Materials and Supplies

☐ A flashlight

Procedure

1. Explain that to make electrical appliances work, electricity must travel from a receptacle (outlet) through the cord to the object.

2. Tell the children that they are going to act out this process.

3. Ask all but one of the children to join hands in a line and tell them they are the electrical cord. The one child not in the line is the electrical receptacle. This child should stand an arm's distance from one end of the line.

4. Give the child at the other end of the line the flashlight and explain that she is going to pretend to be a lamp. Tell the child holding the flashlight to turn it on when the child next to her in line squeezes her hand.

5. When everyone is ready, join the hand of the first child in line (without the flashlight) to the hand of the child acting as the receptacle and announce, "Plugging in!"

6. Instruct the children to gently squeeze the hand of the child next in line to represent the electricity traveling up the cord to the lamp.

7. Instruct the last child reached to turn on the flashlight to represent the lamp being on.

8. Repeat the game many times, so every child has a chance to turn on the flashlight.

TIPS

- Use this activity to wake up the class in the morning or late afternoon. Imagine that you're all sharing energy to help each other have fun!

- If children have trouble squeezing hands one at a time, provide them with a soft ball to pass from one child to the next as the "energy" travels.

CONNECTIONS

Use this activity as a shared story activity. Have each child tell part of a story until she squeezes the hand of the next child, and so on, until all the children in the circle have had a turn.

Have children experiment with electrical circuits by having one child be the lightbulb at the end of the two parallel lines (holding hands with both lines), and one child be the receptacle at the other end. The receptacle takes one hand from each line, but squeezes only one side. The children then squeeze hands going around the line, keeping the lightbulb lit.

Lightbulb Treasure Hunt

AGES
3+

In this activity, children will count the number of lightbulbs in their classroom. This is not something many people are aware of, or ever pay attention to, but it's helpful to know. It builds an awareness for children and teachers alike of how many lightbulbs are used on any given day. When they are older, children will make the connection that the number of lightbulbs used directly affects the amount of energy used.

Activity Goals

→ To count the number of lightbulbs in the classroom

→ To become aware of how many lights are used in a given day

National Science Education Standards

Science in personal and social perspectives: types of resources

Materials and Supplies

☐ An indoor space with lightbulbs in use

☐ Paper on a clipboard and pen

Procedure

1. Ask the children if they have any idea how many lights the building uses in a day. Allow time for children to guess. Record the guesses, if you like.

2. Ask the children where they see lightbulbs in the classroom and where else lightbulbs might be. Discuss ways that they can find the answers.

3. As a group, travel throughout the classrooms and other areas, recording the number of lightbulbs—on or off—in each room. Remember the tiny lightbulbs on appliances, such as coffee pots and toasters, and on office equipment, such as computers or copy machines.

4. If you wish, include the lightbulbs outside the building as well.

5. Return to the classroom and tally up the number of lightbulbs. See if the actual number is close to the children's guesses.

TIPS

• Make this activity extra special by taking children to areas of the school where they do not normally have access, such as staff areas, the kitchen, and offices.

CONNECTIONS

Have children make separate counts for lightbulbs turned on and lightbulbs turned off. Ask the children why they think there are so many lightbulbs, how many were switched on, and if there are any areas that don't need lightbulbs. Discuss the many reasons we need light in our homes and schools and how we can help remind people to turn the lights off when they are finished in a room.

Energy Everywhere

Energy is the force that makes something move, work, or grow. It comes from different sources, and there are many examples of energy in our daily lives. In this activity the children will be encouraged to find examples of energy in their surroundings.

Activity Goals

→ To explore the concept of energy and what it means

→ To identify the many sources—and uses—of energy in our lives

National Science Education Standards

Physical science: light, heat, electricity, and magnetism

Life science: characteristics of organisms

Materials and Supplies

☐ Illustrations or photographs from magazines or books depicting plants, cars, people, animals—anything that uses energy

☐ Chart paper and a marker

Procedure

1. Discuss the meaning of the word *energy*, as defined in the introductory paragraph.

2. Pass out the pictures or make them available to the children to look at and discuss. Ask the children to describe what's happening in the pictures and how they can see that energy is being used.

3. Look at the pictures together and discuss the following ideas: Plants get energy from the sun to grow. People get energy from food so our bodies can move and work. Cars get energy from burning gasoline. Computers get energy from electricity that comes through the socket in the wall.

4. Invite the children to count different examples of energy in the classroom. Some examples might include food energy powering children's bodies, electrical energy for the lights and machines, batteries—another form of electrical energy—that make toys or machines work. If there are plants in the room, there is solar energy helping them grow. If there are cars passing outside, gasoline is burning inside a car's engine, helping the car move.

5. Tally or chart the different forms of energy inside and outside the room.

TIPS

• Stick to just one form of energy at a time to help clarify the concept; then return another day to the activity, and introduce a new form of energy. This activity will be more meaningful for younger children if done over time, since the concept of energy can be difficult for younger children to grasp.

• Work together to build a classroom list of all the different forms of energy.

CONNECTIONS

Invite the children to organize and classify the different examples of energy using criteria they develop.

Have the children draw pictures of all the different forms of energy they discovered. Create an Energy Book with all the pictures bound together with ribbon or yarn.

Invite children to create a story about how energy travels from one place to another, or have them choose their favorite example of energy and write (or dictate) a story about how that energy will be used.

Invite children to think about *how* the electrical energy gets to their school. Take a walk around the building and look for the electrical lines carrying electrical energy to the school.

CHAPTER 8

Indoor Environments and Children's Health

Caring for our environment is fundamental to caring for our own health. To neglect or harm our environment is to jeopardize our own wellness. However, it can be easy to overlook the fact that our environment includes *all* the places where we spend our time: the natural areas outside as well as our indoor spaces, where some of us spend the majority of our time. It is important that we become attuned to factors, such as toxic chemicals in everyday household supplies and materials, that may adversely impact our health. It is also essential that we do our best to make our indoor environments as *healthy* as possible. Doing so is good for our well-being as adults, and it is particularly good for the children in our care. As we know, children are small and growing and are uniquely sensitive to their environments. Caring for our indoor environments is also good for the Earth, because many of the indoor pollutants that can harm our health also escape our homes and schools as they run down our drains, are carried out with the garbage, or are emitted into the air.

Environmental Health in Early Childhood

The phrase *environmental health* refers to elements that affect the health of humans, both negatively and positively, such as the effect of air pollution on asthma or secondhand smoke on cancer incidences. Although there are many issues pertaining to indoor environmental health, this chapter focuses on two that I find most concerning in the early childhood environment: chemicals in cleaning products and chemicals in personal care products. As with the other chapters, this introduction is meant as an overview to help raise your awareness in working with young children. While I'm not proposing you teach children about the chemicals or the potential risks of human exposure, which may be upsetting and difficult for them to handle, I do propose that there are many constructive and productive ways to involve children in creating, maintaining, and becoming attuned to a healthy indoor environment. Helping children develop a sense of responsibility for their spaces and their bodies is a fundamental building block for environmental stewardship. In subtle and not-so-subtle ways, children learn that by caring for their indoor environments and their bodies, they care for their outdoor environment as well. This chapter will help you explore how.

Some chemicals, while *benign*—or harmless—in small concentrations, actually stay in the body, building up in fatty tissues. This may be more problematic in children. In fact, because children's metabolisms differ from adults', chemicals may actually stay in their bodies longer and build up more rapidly (US EPA 2008a). The term *body burden* refers to the amount of toxic chemical buildup in the body. In general, we know that children are especially susceptible to the harmful effects of chemicals. Children's bodies are still developing and relative to their size, children breathe more air, drink more water, and eat more food per total body weight compared to adults (US EPA 2012a). Children also go through certain phases of physical development during which exposure to harmful chemicals may have even greater negative effects than it would during other times. These times during children's lives are known as "critical windows" (National Children's Study Interagency Coordinating Committee 2003, 642). Children's developing brains may be more susceptible to harm from environmental toxins as well. Likewise, there are some suspected links between the increase in asthma, developmental issues, and other long-term health effects and exposure to toxic chemicals.

Early childhood educators are often experts in teaching children good practices around health and hygiene, such as hand washing, toothbrushing, and using sunscreen. Undoubtedly, you are well aware of the importance of such practices for children's health. These practices can also contribute toward a more productive and happy environment by reducing colds, stopping the spread of germs, and minimizing discomfort from sunburn.

Exposure to Chemicals in Cleaning Products

Most likely you are already using good practices when it comes to cleaning your site. You clean and sanitize surfaces, including bedding and toys, when required. You know that this is essential for minimizing *pathogens*—microorganisms that cause disease—and reducing the risk of exposure to bacteria and viruses in the early childhood setting. You take pride in a clean environment and the message that it sends. It tells parents that you not only care for their children, but also that you work hard and take measures

to ensure the space where you care for them is clean and healthy. You're probably also aware that there are many positive (though unmeasurable) effects of a clean environment on learning and productivity. Anecdotally, many educators can attest to the fact that when children feel good, they learn better, they cooperate better, and they function better overall. "Feeling good" can mean enjoying a state of good health, or simply feeling physically comfortable and at ease in one's surroundings. During a time when young children are making sense of their world—by ordering and organizing their inner experiences—spending time in a space that is clean and orderly helps them grow and make sense of things (Copple and Bredekamp 2009).

On top of your sense of pride in how you maintain your facility—and your awareness of the many benefits it offers—your child care program may be required by law to clean and sanitize tables, toys, and other objects frequently. In many places, government agencies may also make recommendations in response to seasonal changes or viral outbreaks. These recommendations are important, though they may change from year to year, or even season to season.

It pays to think carefully about the cleaning products we use. Believe it or not, many of our everyday cleaning supplies contain chemicals that may pose risks to human health and the environment. Often the powerful chemicals that are required or suggested for tough jobs contain chemicals that do more than just clean surfaces. For example, if a cleaning product contains bleach, it is legally considered an antimicrobial pesticide because it kills bacteria and viruses. It is also known to irritate eyes, lungs, and mucous membranes. Many of us use products every day that are potentially hazardous to our health, and to the health of the children in our care. Examples of cleaning products that contain potentially hazardous ingredients include aerosol cleaners and degreasers, drain cleaners, window sprays, laundry solutions, bathroom cleaners, floor cleaners, carpet cleaners, dishwashing detergent, and laundry detergent. That might surprise you. These items are commonly available at any supermarket and are intended for use in homes and child care programs, even those with very young children, right? These products *are* intended for the uses stated on the containers. However, if improperly used or used in combination with other products—or through exposure to residue—they may be harmful to children and adults alike.

Unfortunately, we don't and can't know all the different chemicals that are used in cleaning products. Proprietary laws regarding chemical formulations allow manufacturers the freedom to not disclose all of their ingredients. An even bigger problem is that we really don't know the potential or actual effects these chemicals have on human or environmental health. According to the US Environmental Protection Agency, only a small fraction of the more than eighty thousand registered chemicals have undergone complete testing for health effects (US EPA 2012b). For many reasons, studying their effects on the body is very difficult. In addition to other challenges, chemicals may react differently when combined with other chemicals. Many complex factors, such as genetics, environment, and more, might influence how a person's body handles any given chemical. Moreover, scientists cannot knowingly expose people to potentially harmful substances just to study their effects.

We do know that some chemicals can have immediate effects on our bodies. For example, chemical air fresheners common in infant changing areas and bathrooms can irritate eyes and respiratory systems. Chemical air fresheners often come in aerosol cans or plug into the wall, where the resulting heat warms a chemical to release the scent. Many laundry soaps and fabric softeners have a fragrance that can be irritating to mucous membranes. Some scented detergents can cause skin rashes or itchy skin.

Even if you keep all cleaning products out of the reach of children, they can still cause them harm. Even if a child does not use or have direct contact with the container of a cleaning product, there are a number of ways that chemicals can enter the body. These are called *exposure pathways* (US EPA 2011c). The two common exposure pathways for children are ingestion and inhalation.

INGESTION

When you eat or drink something (even accidentally!) you ingest it. Even though children aren't touching the containers, we create the potential for ingestion of chemicals whenever we use cleaning products. All cleaning products leave residue on the surfaces and objects that we clean. If we neglect rinsing surfaces following use of a cleaning product, residue lingers. Even though children aren't using the cleaning products, their hands and bodies may come in contact with both the surfaces and objects we've cleaned and with the lingering residue. Whenever little hands find their way into mouths, children ingest whatever is on those hands.

Cleaning in and near food preparation areas especially creates ingestion opportunities. For example, if you're cleaning a countertop with an aerosol spray and neglect to remove a bowl of fruit you'll be serving for snack later, when you spray the cleaner a fine mist of droplets will cover the countertop and the fruit. *Overspray* is a term that describes the liquid that goes beyond the target area. Similarly, your wet cleaning rag may splash a bit of liquid onto the fruit as you wipe down the countertop. The chemicals stay on the fruit, which children will later eat. From the stomach or intestines, the chemicals can enter the bloodstream. Therefore, the best strategy for minimizing the possibility of accidental ingestion is to remove all food, food serving utensils, dishes, and drinking glasses before spraying any type of cleaner near food preparation and eating areas. Also, be sure to rinse any object or surface thoroughly with a clean cloth and water following use of cleaning products.

Very young children also spend a great deal of time on the floor—sitting, crawling, rolling, or simply lying there—so they face other potentially problematic ingestion opportunities. Spending time on the floor means they are also exposed to soil contaminants (which could include arsenic, lead, and heavy metals) that may be tracked into your building if your visitors don't remove their shoes upon entering the children's area.

INHALATION

Some cleaning products create vapors or fumes in the air. Aerosol sprays generate tiny liquid droplets that linger in the air. These liquid droplets can be so tiny as to go undetected. Any time there are vapors, fumes, or liquid droplets in the air around us, we take them in through our normal breathing. From the nose or mouth, the vapors or chemicals go into the lungs and then into the bloodstream. Always wait until the room is empty of children before spraying cleaning fluids on tabletops. If there is a spill or an accident, remove the children from the room before spraying chemicals onto the spill, and then allow for ample ventilation. If necessary, remove the group to a different classroom (or better yet, go outside!) until the fumes have sufficiently dissipated.

READING LABELS

In its Solid Waste Disposal Act, the US EPA (2002b, 8) created extensive guidelines for determining whether household waste is considered "hazardous." Among the guidelines is the chance that the waste will "pose a substantial present or potential hazard to human health or the environment when improperly treated, stored, transported, disposed of, or otherwise managed." Given this guideline, how can you know if the products you use are considered hazardous? The products will have a *signal word* that indicates the degree of harm that might be caused by handling the product in its originally packaged formulation. Therefore, it's essential that you read labels. "Caution," "Warning," and "Danger" are specific words used to indicate whether and how hazardous a product registered

with either the EPA as a pesticide or the Consumer Product Safety Commission (CPSC) as a cleaner is. Unfortunately, the two agencies use different guidelines for the same terms. "For example, most bleach concentrates labeled by the EPA for disinfecting will have a 'Danger' signal word, based on the potential to cause damage to the skin, eyes, or lungs. Similar products labeled for laundry purposes have a signal word of 'Warning,' based on a different set of CPSC criteria. Note: because laundry bleach does not list percentages of ingredients, it is impossible to determine if it is identical to disinfecting bleach" (Boise 2010a, 63).

Labels will also contain words known as *characteristic words*. What's the difference? Signal words warn us of the potential danger or harmful effect to humans. Characteristic words describe the properties and other hazards of the ingredients. Here is a list of characteristic words (Hennepin County Environmental Services 2009):

- Flammable/combustible: This term indicates that the product can easily catch fire and burn. Paint thinner is a good example.

- Corrosive: The terms "corrosive," "caustic," "acid," "lye," "alkaline," or "causes burns to the skin" mean that the product will burn the skin or eyes. These products can also corrode other materials they come into contact with, such as soft plastics or wood. Examples of this kind of product are abrasive cleansers, rust removers, and drain cleaners.

- Toxic: The terms "poison" or "harmful if swallowed" mean that the product can be harmful or fatal if ingested, inhaled, or absorbed through the skin. Many everyday products, including some soaps, disinfecting solutions, ice melting crystals, and floor cleaners will have this word on their label.

- Reactive: The phrases "do not mix with . . ." or "store separately from other products" mean that the product may react violently or produce harmful fumes or vapors if mixed with other substances. Examples include certain types of disinfectants or similar products containing bleach, ammonia, or lye. It is important to note that when a product label specifies that you not mix it with other products, you must follow those instructions. While mixing products may not necessarily cause an explosion, it may produce very harmful gases.

Knowing how to read a label is very important. It can help you determine not only the appropriate product to use but also the appropriate precautions and preventative measures for safety when using the product.

In many cases the presence of signal words indicates that products also have specific disposal requirements. Because of the chemicals they contain, the plastic containers from household cleaning products can't be discarded in the recycling—even once emptied—and any excess product should *never* be poured down a drain. Those very same chemicals that you use to clean the bathroom may be harmful to water quality and wildlife if poured down the drain. In addition, some chemicals may enter and persist in municipal water supplies. Chemicals thought to have originated from everyday cleaning and personal care products are now widespread in our environment. As with human bodies, the effect these chemicals are having on ecological communities and natural systems is not yet well understood. High levels of certain chemicals can be found in fish and animal tissues, drinking water, and even in ocean water (US EPA 2011c). Without knowing it, we are ingesting these chemicals all the time. They build up in our bodies, and because of the chemicals' tendency to build up in fatty tissues, they have even been found in human breast milk. Though many health professionals and scientific organizations recognize that despite this reality, breastfeeding remains the ideal way to feed babies—it helps form strong attachment bonds between mother and child, and it offers a host of health benefits to both mother and child—it also pays to be aware that chemicals persist in our bodies (Landrigan et al. 2002).

Certain cleaning routines and standards of cleanliness are required by law to meet state licensing requirements; therefore, it may not be possible to remove all toxic chemicals from your environment. For health reasons, state and national standards require a clean facility. These standards are in place to reduce bacteria, viruses, and other germs and to ensure safety and reduce exposure to diseases. No one argues about those benefits! In some cases, however, it is possible to reduce the toxic chemicals used in maintaining a site. Check your local regulations to be sure you understand what kinds of cleaners are required by law, how frequently and in what cases they must be used, and where you have more freedom.

EXPOSURE TO CHEMICALS IN PERSONAL CARE PRODUCTS

Not all personal care products contain harmful chemicals, and not all product formulations are harmful, but as with cleaners, it's worthwhile to take the time to examine our use of personal care products, especially with children, since their growing bodies and brains are more susceptible to harm from chemicals found in those products. Even though the skin is an effective barrier against many substances, some things can and do permeate it. Many of the most common personal care products, such as soaps, lotions, and even sunscreens, can be problematic if you're trying to avoid questionable chemicals or are concerned about possible health effects. For example, disinfecting wipes contain chemicals and should never be used to wash children's hands. The chemical residue may remain on hands and later be ingested or absorbed through the skin. Products that have "antibacterial" or "antimicrobial" on the label contain ingredients that could potentially be absorbed (US FDA 2008). Even commonplace hand sanitizers may pose potential absorption risks.

Some of these chemicals are irritating to the lungs or mucous membranes, while others can be linked to disruptions in the *endocrine system*—the system within the body that regulates hormone production and output. *Hormones* are chemical messengers that affect everything from mood to how the body utilizes minerals and vitamins from foods. Hormones affect the process of cellular growth, and there is a growing body of evidence that links some chemicals to disruption of the endocrine system, especially in children (Landrigan, Garg, and Droller 2003). These chemicals, known as *endocrine disruptors*, are used in numerous personal care products, and their presence is giving many scientists—and anyone concerned with the well-being of children—pause to think. Endocrine disruptors have been linked to early onset of puberty, reproductive difficulties, and low sperm count in males, among other things. Even exposure to endocrine disruptors in utero can have serious effects on infants' growth and social-emotional, behavioral, and higher-functioning development (Engel et al. 2010).

Endocrine disruptors can also be found in drinking water, since many products containing these chemicals are washed down the drain during regular bathing or hand washing. Although current technology allows for many substances to be removed from municipal water supplies during regular processing, many endocrine-disrupting chemicals persist in water supplies, where they enter the bodies of children and adults through consumption and use of water. These chemicals have also been shown to have harmful effects on ecological systems and wildlife (Snyder et al. 2003). This is another illustration of the link between personal health and the health of the environment.

Some chemicals that may be relatively benign on their own can have deleterious effects when combined with other chemicals (Rajapakse, Silva, and Kortenkamp 2002). Many personal care product companies keep certain ingredients and product formulations a secret. This is allowable by law so that product manufacturers can protect trade secrets. But this lack of information doesn't serve the consumer who wants to know specifically what chemicals she may be exposed to through the use of personal care products. Often, the ambiguous term "fragrance," which may encapsulate a long list of ingredients, is listed in the ingredients.

Finally, personal care products have also been shown to emit VOCs (volatile organic compounds), which can irritate mucous membranes and may exacerbate breathing problems. They may even have invisible effects: harmful chemicals may form as by-products when VOCs react with other chemicals present in the air (Steinemann et al. 2011). The ingredient listed on many products simply as "fragrance" may contain any number of chemicals. Even products labeled "unscented" or "natural" may contain a mixture of chemicals (a fragrance, which will be listed in the ingredients!) designed to mask the scent. Be sure to read ingredient lists thoroughly, and avoid products whose lists include the word "fragrance."

The science behind endocrine disrupting chemicals and the effects of personal care products on children's health is growing rapidly. Consult the Additional Resources section at the end of this book for some helpful websites where you can learn more about this group of chemicals. The following pages present information on how you can help protect the children in your care.

What You Can Do

There are lots of small steps you can take to protect children from the risks of hazardous chemicals. Whenever possible, use pump spray products instead of aerosols to minimize overspray. Because they contain *propellants*—gas kept under pressure—aerosols put unnecessary chemicals into indoor air, and the mist produced by a pressurized aerosol can is finer and more easily inhaled than the mist from a pump spray. If you must use an aerosol, spray it into a rag and then wipe down the surface, rather than spraying the entire surface. Also avoid using aerosol or spray-on insect repellent or sunscreen. The overspray from these products can irritate young lungs too.

Done properly, good old hand washing with soap and water is one of the most effective ways to stop the spread of diseases and infections in most environments (CDC 2011a). Concentrate on teaching children these proper techniques. That means rubbing wet, soapy hands together, front and back, as well as between fingers, for at least twenty seconds (remember to turn the water off when doing so!). Then rinse hands thoroughly. Opt for the soap-and-water method for hand washing every time you can. Although hand sanitizers are convenient—they don't require trips to the bathroom or create long waiting lines at the sink, and they do work at killing germs—save them for "in a pinch" situations. In addition to the potentially problematic ingredients, they aren't intended for removing visible grime or dirt from hands.

Thankfully, countless varieties of environmentally friendly cleaning products are available. It is possible to find products and adapt practices that will ensure your program meets necessary standards without jeopardizing the health of the children you care for. Using more environmentally friendly products when possible will help reduce the total amount of harmful chemicals that come into contact with children's vulnerable bodies while also maintaining a very clean, healthy facility.

Green or eco-friendly products have recently increased in popularity, which means they are easy to find in just about every store. Don't forget that, as with anything we buy, it's important to be a very savvy consumer. Some companies market their products as "green" or "all natural" whereas in reality they may be no less harmful than their toxic counterparts! In the United States, there are currently no federal standards or criteria for use of the word "green." Familiarize yourself with the signal words, learn how to read labels, and compare products—it's your job to keep children safe.

THIRD-PARTY CERTIFIERS

Third-party certifiers are another great resource for helping us choose products. Such organizations evaluate products, ingredients, and formulations according to health, safety, or sustainability criteria. Different third-party certifiers use different criteria, so familiarize yourself with the criteria used by each one. The purpose of third-party certification is to provide neutral guidance to consumers. Refer to the *Go Green Rating Scale* by Phil Boise for a list of green-oriented third-party certifiers. Some of them, such as Green Seal, evaluate products specifically used in schools and other settings with young children. For some additional sources for consumer education on green products, see appendix H.

If researching products to determine third-party certification feels like more than you want to take on,

consider this: you may already have some great, effective, and safe cleaning substances on hand in your home or program. Many food-grade materials that you are likely to have can do a fine job of cleaning tables, sinks, and other surfaces. For example, baking soda and water can be mixed into a paste to clean sinks, ovens, and even toilet bowls. Plain old vinegar has some antimicrobial properties and is an effective mold killer. See appendix G for some simple recipes you can use in creating your own environmentally friendly cleaning supplies. Because many of these products are so easy to make and harmless to use, they also make great projects for children.

There are so many products involved in the daily care and maintenance of an early childhood setting. Many are benign, some are not. Check the manufacturer's website or look for resources online. The *Go Green Rating Scale* has an excellent section on toxic cleaning products, should you wish to evaluate your program's overall practices with regard to chemical use. I highly recommend reviewing this resource.

I want to restate that this chapter is not intended to be a comprehensive introduction to the topics of hazardous products or green cleaning. Rather, my hope is to address some of the more common questions and concerns I've come across in my work as a consultant, because so many early care and education settings are embracing the green movement, including the use of cleaning products. As you make choices with regard to cleaning and personal care products, I recommend that you keep in mind above all, the precautionary principle. This principle urges us to opt for the safest possible material or action, whenever possible, if there is the potential of harm to humans or the environment.

What to Teach the Children

Is it necessary to teach children about hazardous cleaning products? No. In fact, I discourage it. Consider this: children aren't buying the cleaning products used at your site or in their homes. The purchasing decisions related to these products do not, nor should they, rest on the children. Expecting children to educate their parents about this important issue is unrealistic and unfair. Furthermore, learning that there might be harmful chemicals on their lunch table or the sink handles can be very unsettling! What I do encourage is that you have fun with the children as you make connections about personal care and the environment. Chances are you already do a lot with the children to teach about germs and proper hygiene. You probably also do many things to engage them in taking responsibility for their classroom at cleanup time, and at other times. These practices and routines actually do a lot to teach children about the value of caring for our environment and taking care of ourselves. The activities that follow will offer you some ideas for playing simple games, learning about health and wellness, and creating safe and effective cleaning products that the children can make and use themselves. These activities will complement your program's use of the *Go Green Rating Scale* and will offer a nice addition to your environmental education curriculum.

Taking care of one's body and immediate surroundings are environmental actions that are inextricably linked. Having a strong and consistent focus on these practices will help children develop a stewardship ethic. Modeling these behaviors will help develop the mindset that all systems and actions are connected. Caring for one helps cultivate the mindset of caring for another. It is also something you can model and communicate through your behavior. You communicate the value of good hygiene when you wash your hands in front of the children. You communicate the importance of caring for the environment when you make the classroom environment the healthiest it can be for all children, especially by choosing to use products that minimize exposure to potentially harmful chemicals when possible. When you choose safer products, you are supporting children's physical health as well as the health of the natural environment. You're also making consumer decisions that support cleaner, greener alternatives for people and the Earth.

Muddy Me

Children love dirt! Some have a higher tolerance for it than others, but overall, most children can't resist getting their hands dirty whenever they have the chance. In this activity, children will have the delicious freedom to get their hands as dirty as possible and then to test out different methods of getting them clean again.

Activity Goals

→ To enjoy the feeling of free play with mud and sand

→ To playfully wash hands and experiment with techniques

National Science Education Standards

Science in personal and social perspectives: personal health

Materials and Supplies

- ☐ Access to mud or wet sand
- ☐ Buckets full of water
- ☐ A bar of soap
- ☐ Liquid soap in a pump dispenser
- ☐ Dry cloth towels
- ☐ Wet cloth towels
- ☐ Dry paper towels
- ☐ Wet paper towels
- ☐ Hand sanitizer
- ☐ Premoistened towelettes
- ☐ Chart paper and a marker

Procedure

1. Ask the children how many times each day they are told to wash their hands.

2. Ask them to explain why this is so and why it is important to have clean hands. Invite them to describe times when they need to clean their hands. Allow time for discussion.

3. Ask them what gets their hands clean. Challenge them to think of all the ways they can wash their hands. Elicit a variety of responses and record their ideas.

4. Tell them that today they're going to get their hands really dirty and see what works best for getting them clean again.

5. Allow them time to play in the mud and get their hands dirty.

6. When the children are ready, invite them to wash or clean their hands however they like and to report on the result. Ask them if they can see any dirt on their hands and if their hands smell clean.

7. Invite interested children to repeat the activity.

TIPS

- Provide smocks or a change of clothes so children will not worry about getting their clothes dirty. Provide gloves for children to wear or scraps of fabric to dirty instead of their hands. Some children will not be comfortable with this activity if they don't want to get their hands dirty or they're worried about their clothing getting messy.

- Do this activity outside on the grass to make cleanup a breeze!

CONNECTIONS

Work with the children to compare the results of all the different methods. Ask children to describe which method worked the best and why. Create a chart or graph depicting the results.

Invite the children to create a mural of muddy handprints on a bedsheet or long piece of paper.

Hand Washing Is Beautiful

No one disputes the value of regular hand washing, especially in the early childhood setting. But with the hustle and bustle of everyday life, we often forget to do a thorough job. In this activity, the children will create signs reminding people to wash their hands.

Activity Goals

→ To express one's self creatively

National Science Education Standards

Science in personal and social perspectives: personal health

Materials and Supplies

☐ Art supplies, such as paint, markers, glue, glitter, and other sparkly items

☐ Paper

☐ Chart paper and a marker

Procedure

1. Ask the children what kind of reminder they could make to help people remember to wash their hands regularly. Record their responses.

2. Ask the children if they think a sign would need to have words or just pictures. (Any response is okay.)

3. Provide the children with paper and access to a variety of art materials and let them create signs.

4. Allow the children to take the signs home or post them prominently in hand-washing locations throughout your facility.

TIPS

• Offer to transcribe what the younger children dictate for their signs.

• If possible, laminate the signs or cover them in clear sheet protectors to keep them from getting wet.

• If you use a song to teach children how long to wash their hands (for example, some use "Twinkle, Twinkle, Little Star" to track the amount of time children need to spend washing their hands), encourage the children to include illustrations of the song as a reminder.

CONNECTIONS

If there are nonnative English speakers in your classroom, have them create signs in their native language as well. Invite families to come in and help with the spelling or writing if you aren't comfortable writing in that language.

Sharing Germs

AGES 3+

Although children are constantly being told to wash their hands to prevent the spread of germs, few of them really understand how germs spread. This activity offers a concrete example of how easily germs can be spread from person to person.

Activity Goals

→ To have fun playing a game with glitter

→ To become familiar with the concept of how germs spread

National Science Education Standards

Science in personal and social perspectives: personal health

Materials and Supplies

☐ Three or four shaker jars, each filled with a different color of glitter

Procedure

1. Invite the children to share why they think hand washing is important.

2. Tell them that germs are so tiny they are impossible to see, but they stick to our skin and spread easily.

3. Ask the children if any of them have traveled, if they like to travel, and the different ways people can travel. Allow time for discussion.

4. Tell them you'd like to play a game to learn how germs travel.

5. Remind the children that you are not using real germs—you'll be using glitter (pretend germs) to learn how germs travel.

6. Have the children open their hands, and then shake some glitter onto their hands. You want a good amount of glitter, but not too much. The glitter will stick to their hands due to sweat and warmth.

7. Ask them to look at their hands and remember the color of the glitter.

8. When all the children have glitter on their hands, engage them in some everyday activities, such as dramatic play or finger plays. Invite the children to pass a ball back and forth and to hold hands during a song.

9. After some time playing, invite the children to stop and look at their hands. Ask them how many colors of glitter they now have on their hands.

10. Explain how the "germs" have traveled from person to person, and that many are left behind on objects as well.

11. Have the children wash their hands thoroughly with soap and water to remove the glitter.

TIPS

• Do this activity outdoors to minimize cleanup.

• If there are children who don't want glitter on their hands, have them choose a color of glitter and then follow its movement from child to child.

CONNECTIONS

Sprinkle just one child's hands with glitter, and have her shake hands with one other child or touch a table. Invite the other children to touch the table or shake hands with the second child. This illustrates the point that it only takes one person to spread germs!

Laundry Day

In this activity, children have the opportunity to compare squares of fabric washed in soap with those not washed in soap and to try cleaning the fabric using different methods, supplies, and techniques. This activity will help children make the connection that soap and water are necessary for thorough cleaning.

Activity Goals

→ To enjoy getting fabric as dirty as possible, and then washing the fabric

→ To compare the effects of soap and water versus just water in cleaning fabric

National Science Education Standards

Physical science: properties of objects and materials

Science in personal and social perspectives: personal health

Materials and Supplies

☐ Five-inch squares of fabric, one per child (old sheets work well)

☐ Permanent marker, for adult use

☐ Several trays or buckets of mud, sand, and dry dirt

☐ Clothesline and clothespins, hung at the children's height

☐ Two plastic tubs per child (or pair of children) filled with water

☐ Nontoxic dish soap or a bar of hand soap

Procedure

1. Prior to the activity, mark half of the fabric squares with an "S" or another symbol to remind the children that these are the pieces to wash with soap. The other half will be washed with water alone.

2. Tell the children that you are curious to learn whether it's really important to use soap when washing. Ask them if they think so and why or why not.

3. Tell them you have an idea about how they can test whether soap actually gets things cleaner than just plain water.

4. Pass out the scraps of fabric and invite the children to get them as dirty as possible. Allow children access to the buckets of mud, sand, and dirt. Let them really have fun getting the fabric dirty.

5. While they are dirtying their fabric scraps, fill two dishpans with water for each child or pair of children.

6. Put nontoxic dish soap or hand soap in one tub, and leave the other one filled with plain water.

7. Invite the children to wash their fabric squares and hang them to dry on the clothesline.

8. Ask them if the soapy water or plain water got the fabric the cleanest and why. Discuss whether the soap really makes a difference in cleaning the fabric.

TIPS

• Hang the clothesline before beginning this activity.

• Do this activity where children will have access to dirt.

• Explore different methods for cleaning the fabric. Children may scrub, soak the fabric, or rub it with their hands to clean it.

• Let the children work on the task they most enjoy if possible. Some children will love the cleaning portion of this activity. Others will gravitate more toward the dirtying part.

CONNECTIONS

 Have children paint designs on their fabric using powdered drink mix, cold coffee, or mud.

Soap Sculpture

Children love sculpting and molding figures with dough. In this activity, the children make modeling dough out of nontoxic detergent flakes and then have fun molding and shaping the dough. This activity reinforces the value of nontoxic soaps, as most chemical soaps are much too harsh for handling by children.

Activity Goals

→ To sculpt with a fun, creative, and nontoxic new medium

National Science Education Standards

Science in personal and social perspectives: personal health

Materials and Supplies

☐ Four cups of white, nontoxic laundry detergent flakes or grated bar soap or glycerin soap (Note: be sure soap is nontoxic and chemical free)

☐ Four tablespoons of water

☐ A large bowl

Procedure

1. Pour detergent into a large bowl.

2. Add water gradually while mixing and kneading with your hands.

3. When the soap forms a ball and holds its shape, divide it into portions for the children to use for sculpting. Explain to the children that when soap is made to be gentle on our skin, it's okay to use it for other fun projects besides cleaning. Tell them that you are making a new kind of clay that can be sculpted and molded.

4. Be sure the children wash their hands with soap and water when they are finished.

TIPS

- Adjust the amount of water as needed; the consistency should be like thick peanut butter.

- Invite some children to help mix the soap dough.

- Be sure to have lots of water and clean towels available.

- Add natural ingredients, such as rose petals, lavender, or dried herbs, to make scented dough.

- Grate wax crayons and add them to the dry soap flakes before adding water. This will result in a confetti effect (and it's a great way to reuse broken crayon pieces!).

 The detergent is nontoxic, but it will sting if it's rubbed in eyes.

CONNECTIONS

Invite children to dissolve the soap sculptures in a small saucer of water. Before placing the sculptures in water, ask the children to estimate how long it will take for the sculptures to dissolve. Alternately, send the sculptures home for use in the bathtub!

Soap Making

AGES
5+

Making homemade soap is simple and easy. There are numerous recipes available online; however, many of them call for lye, which is a very caustic substance. In the early childhood classroom, you can make lovely homemade soaps by melting plain glycerin soap bars and letting the children add natural ingredients.

Activity Goals

→ To complete a fun and easy project, making a product children will use

→ To create soaps using natural materials

National Science Education Standards

Physical science: properties of objects and materials

Science in personal and social perspectives: personal health

Materials and Supplies

☐ Two average-size bars of glycerin soap (purchase at a health foods store or specialty craft store)

☐ Double boiler and spoon

☐ Hot plate or place to heat water (for adult use)

☐ A variety of pleasantly scented natural materials, such as pine needles, rose petals, lavender, grasses, or oatmeal

☐ Essential oils of your choice, such as lemon, pine, mint, or eucalyptus

☐ Small plastic food storage containers, such as clean, empty yogurt or single-serving applesauce containers

☐ Oven mitts (for handling the soap-filled containers)

Procedure

1. Prior to making soap, talk with the children about how soap is made and what various soaps smell like. Discuss which natural materials and oils to include in the soap you will make together.

2. When you are ready to make the soap, carefully heat the glycerin soap in a double boiler. Stir constantly.

3. When the soap is a liquid, add the natural materials the children have gathered.

4. Add up to five drops of essential oil to the mixture.

5. Pour the mixture into plastic storage containers and let it cool. This will take fifteen minutes to several hours, depending on the size of the containers.

6. When the soap is cool, simply pop it out of the container and enjoy!

TIPS

Use extreme caution when doing this activity with children. Melted glycerin is very hot and will burn skin!

Be sure to read the contents and any precautionary information about the oils you choose. Some essential oils are not suitable for use on skin.

Use with care. Although this soap and the added ingredients are nontoxic, they will sting eyes.

- Invite the children to gather natural materials from your school grounds, or purchase them if preferred.

- Grate the soap beforehand or use a cheese plane to help it melt faster.

- Purchase soap colorants at craft stores or online to add color to your soaps.

- If necessary, cut away the plastic container to remove the soap.

CONNECTIONS

If the children have used a variety of different natural materials, have them write and decorate recipe cards for the soaps. The cards should include the approximate quantities of each natural material as well as the other ingredients used.

Make Bubble Bath

AGES
4+

Children of all ages love bubble baths. This simple recipe requires no heating and can easily be customized with scented oils. The bubble bath contains all-natural ingredients and will be lots of fun for children to make. You can also add this solution to the water table for instant fun! This activity can easily be implemented outside.

Activity Goals

→ To experience a fun and exciting way of making nontoxic bath bubbles

→ To have fun exploring measurement

National Science Education Standards

Physical science: properties of objects and materials

Science in personal and social perspectives: personal health

Materials and Supplies

☐ Measuring cups and spoons

☐ A large plastic bowl

☐ A permanent marker

☐ Stirring spoons

☐ Small containers with lids that will hold at least one cup of bubble bath

☐ A large container with lid

For every two containers of bubbles, include the following:

☐ 1 cup of olive oil

☐ ½ cup of liquid soap—not antibacterial (dishwashing soap)

☐ ¼ cup of honey

☐ ½ teaspoon of natural colorant

☐ 1 tablespoon of peppermint fragrance or extract

Procedure

1. Invite the children to work with you in small groups to make some fun, homemade bubble bath.

2. Explain that some of the bubbles will be used in the water table, and they may also take a small container home.

3. Have children measure the recommended quantities of ingredients and pour them into the bowl.

4. Allow the children to take turns stirring the ingredients so they are well mixed.

5. Use the permanent marker to write the child's name and "Bath Bubbles" on a small container. Fill the children's containers and add any remaining bubble bath to the larger container for classroom use; secure the lids.

6. When you're ready to use the bubble solution, pour a small amount into your water table as you add water. Invite the children to stir vigorously with their hands, and enjoy!

TIPS

• Purchase natural colorants for soap making at craft supply stores or online.

• If the containers have a small opening, use a funnel when pouring the bubble bath from the bowl.

✋ *Use care when handling. Although all the ingredients in this recipe are natural and nontoxic, this soap will sting if it gets in eyes.*

(continues on next page)

CONNECTIONS

Ask the children why each ingredient was added to the soap and where they think the bubbles come from. Add the bubble solution to the water table without swirling and stirring, then ask the children if there are as many bubbles and why they think there aren't.

Using the above recipe as a starting point, ask the children to determine how much of each ingredient is needed to make a quantity for the entire class.

Make Cleaning Spray

Cleaning can be great fun for children, as long as the soap and other cleaning products are nontoxic. In this activity, children will use a simple nontoxic recipe for an effective natural cleanser that can be used on everything from countertops to floors. Making their own cleaning solution can help children feel more invested and motivated during the cleaning activities.

Activity Goals

→ To feel responsible and helpful

→ To enjoy mixing and measuring

National Science Education Standards

Physical science: properties of objects and materials

Science in personal and social perspectives: personal health

Materials and Supplies

☐ Empty, clean thirty-two ounce spray bottles, one per child

 Do not use any spray bottle that once held chemicals of any kind.

☐ Pitchers of water, or access to water from a hose or faucet

☐ White vinegar

☐ Nontoxic liquid dish soap

☐ Essential oils, if desired, such as lemon, mint, or eucalyptus

☐ Half-cup measuring cups

☐ One-tablespoon measuring spoons

☐ Funnels

☐ A permanent marker

Procedure

1. Work with one small group of children at a time. Explain that you will be making a cleaning solution that is safe and easy to use, and that they can help clean their classroom and their own houses with this special soap.

2. Provide each child with a spray bottle.

3. Have children take turns using the measuring cup to measure vinegar and then using the funnel to pour the vinegar into their spray bottle.

4. If the child wants to add a scent, have him add a few drops of essential oil.

5. Next, have the children add water so that the liquid reaches almost to the top of the bottle.

6. Last, instruct each child to measure and add one tablespoon of liquid dish soap.

7. Secure the lids onto the bottles and use a permanent marker to write the child's name and "Cleaning Spray" as well as a list of the ingredients on the bottle.

8. Have the children shake their bottles, and tell them they are ready to clean.

TIPS

• Make pouring easier by providing the children with funnels.

• Find essential oils at natural foods stores or online.

• Provide safety goggles if you have them, and encourage children to wash their hands thoroughly after this activity. Vinegar is nontoxic, but it will sting if it gets into eyes.

• Use a permanent marker to write the recipe for this cleaner on the bottle. That way, parents will always know what's inside and can replenish their supply when they run out.

 Always clearly label cleaning products with the contents.

(continues on next page)

CONNECTIONS

 Have the children research the ingredients that are needed for this cleanser. Ask them to describe why each ingredient is used or what purpose it serves. Invite the children to mix up a few test batches of the cleaner but omit certain ingredients. Have them compare the results.

Refer to appendix G for more nontoxic cleaning recipes to make and use.

Cleaning Station

Most children love to play house in the dramatic play area, so why not provide real cleaning tools? Children love to be responsible for their surroundings and, when shown how to properly use tools, can help maintain a clean classroom. This activity encourages children to clean their classroom, building a stewardship habit.

Activity Goals

→ To clean and contribute to the care of the classroom

→ To have fun using real cleaning supplies

National Science Education Standards

Physical science: properties of objects and materials

Science in personal and social perspectives: personal health

Materials and Supplies

☐ Cleaning supplies in child-appropriate sizes, including mops, buckets, washcloths, sponges, cleaning cloths, brooms, dustpans, hand brooms, and spray bottles filled with water

Procedure

1. With the children, choose an area of the classroom for the cleaning station.

2. Carefully arrange the cleaning supplies to make them accessible to children when they want to use them.

3. Invite the children to take part in classroom maintenance by cleaning furniture, wiping down tables and chairs, and sweeping and mopping the floor.

TIPS

• Use plain water in the spray bottle to eliminate the risk of injury.

• If you wish to use real cleansers, see the recipe for nontoxic cleaner in the Make Cleaning Spray activity and provide that to the children. Use your best judgment with regard to its accessibility.

• Know that sometimes when children help with cleaning, it creates a bit of a mess. This is normal and natural. Be patient, and remember how important it is that the children have the opportunity to help keep their classroom environment clean and healthy.

• Provide real mops, brooms, and other supplies, rather than toys. Child-size cleaning supplies can be purchased at some toy shops and online. A good source is Montessori supply catalogs.

CONNECTIONS

Provide books and read stories from other cultures about cleaning and caring for one's home. Look at how homes and schools are depicted. Discuss the differences and similarities. Throughout the world, people care for their homes and schools in different ways. If you can, find pictures of boys and girls cleaning and taking care of their homes.

Mitten Wash

Children feel silly and have a great time when they can wear mittens or socks on their hands and use them to help clean up. Doing so can help them to see the amount of dust and other particles found on many surfaces. Seeing the immediate result of their efforts can really motivate children to take care of their classroom.

Activity Goals

→ To have fun cleaning

→ To participate in taking care of the environment and surroundings

National Science Education Standards

Science in personal and social perspectives: personal health

Materials and Supplies

☐ Light-colored mittens or old socks, one pair per child

Procedure

1. Pass out the mittens or socks to the children and invite them to help you clean the classroom!

2. Explain that an important part of cleaning is getting rid of all the dust and tiny particles that settle on surfaces, such as tabletops and shelves, and that also float in the air, making us cough or sneeze. Tell the children that they will use the mittens and socks to clean up these tiny particles and make the classroom a healthier place to be.

3. Let them use their mitten- or sock-covered hands to wipe down surfaces such as tables, shelves, or windowsills.

4. Ask the children to report on which area of the room was the dustiest and why they think that is. Discuss this with them.

TIPS

- Keep in mind that it's not necessary to use cleaning solution or even water. Cotton tube socks work great as dust cloths, and the children will be surprised to see how much dust they can collect!

- Ask families to donate old, clean socks that are still in good condition.

- If your program operates only on weekdays, try this activity on a Monday. Usually there will be a bit more dust if the building has been empty for a few days.

CONNECTIONS

Decorate the socks with fabric paints. Each child can have her own set of dust cloths complete with initials, the child's name, or illustrations of the child's own design.

Under adult supervision, send the children out in teams to use the socks to dust other rooms in the building. When all rooms have been dusted, compare the results. Have children record which rooms were dustiest and explain why this might be so. Do this activity at different times of the year and on days when the windows have been open, and compare the results.

Floor Cleaning Boogie

Cleaning the floors can be a fun activity when done to music! Children love the silliness of having washcloths taped to their feet and will dance around like crazy if given the chance. This activity helps them be active participants in the care and upkeep of their environment and requires no harsh cleansers. Remind them that small particles of dust or dirt often settle on the floor. These tiny particles can be difficult to see until they are wiped up with a rag. Using their feet as dust mops, children will be surprised to discover how much they can pick up.

Activity Goals

→ To be part of the class community

→ To help clean and care for the classroom

National Science Education Standards

Science in personal and social perspectives: personal health

Materials and Supplies

☐ Washcloths or scraps of old dish towels, two per child

☐ Masking tape

☐ Fun and lively music

☐ Large, uncarpeted area

Procedure

1. Explain to the children that they are going to clean the floor with their feet!

2. Tape one washcloth to the bottom of each shoe—it's best to secure the tape across the top of the shoe, so the washcloth stays on.

3. Turn on fun music and encourage the children to spread out around the room. They can slide around under tables, in corners, behind shelves, and so on until they decide the floor is clean.

4. Ask the children to tell you how they know the floor is clean.

TIPS

• Clear away the furniture before doing this activity to prevent injury from bumping into furniture.

• Remember that you don't need to get the washcloths wet when doing this activity, although the children would likely enjoy that too!

• If the children are able, have them tape the washcloths to their own shoes to save time.

• Place some washcloths on your feet and get moving! The children will really love it if you get involved!

CONNECTIONS

 Make up a song together about cleaning the floor. Sing it as a class while you clean.

 Have the children "skate around" and then use hand lenses to examine the material that has been collected on the washcloths. Ask them where this dust and grime would wind up if they hadn't cleaned the floor.

Puppets from Pictures

Children love books! Many teachers have realized that a great way to expand their collection is to shop for used children's books at thrift or reuse stores. Unfortunately, some old books found in secondhand stores smell of mildew or dampness. This poses a potential problem to children's health, as mildew and mold can irritate young lungs. Do not use books that smell strongly of mold or mildew in this activity. Instead use worn-out books that need a new life; these may have a slightly musty scent. In this activity, these worn-out books will get new life when children cut out pictures of animals and people to create puppets, which they will also enjoy using.

Activity Goals

→ To make simple toys using characters and animals

National Science Education Standards

Physical science: properties of objects and materials

Life science: characteristics of organisms, life cycles of organisms (if science extension is used)

Materials and Supplies

☐ Children's scissors, one for each child

☐ Glue sticks

☐ Craft sticks

☐ A variety of old children's books with sturdy pages, at least one per child

Procedure

1. Show children the books and explain that they are old and a bit musty, but that you'd like to see the books used to make children happy.

2. Tell the children that they should always ask an adult before cutting a book, but that these books are so old and smelly that you can't keep them on your shelves.

3. Invite the children to choose pictures from the books and cut them out to create puppets that they can use for their own stories.

4. Allow plenty of time for the children to work, and provide assistance as needed.

5. Once the pictures have been cut, instruct the children to glue them to craft sticks and then place them in a safe spot to dry.

6. Once the glue has dried, invite the children to use their new characters to put on puppet shows.

TIPS

- Invite children to cut scenery out of books too! Large images can be glued to cardboard to make sturdy "stages" for the puppet shows.

- Designate a special bin or basket for the "books for cutting," so children do not cut other books.

- Once the children have cut out all their pictures, recycle as much as you can of the leftover book material. Pages can be cut out and recycled with other paper, and covers can be placed in cardboard recycling in some areas.

CONNECTIONS

Invite children to choose images that go along with a certain theme, such as insects or plants. Alternately, challenge them to find images of animals at all different life stages (for example, eggs, chicks, and hens).

Cut letters and words from the books and create signs to designate children's desks or cubbies with the children's names. Create labels for other objects around the room.

Work with the children to write scripts, create scenery, and perform a full-length puppet show.

Sunny Days, Sunny Skin

This simple activity shows children the effects that the sun can have on apple slices. After leaving apple slices in the sun for several hours to a full day, children will see the drying effect of the sun. Children can repeat the activity, coating the apple slices with sunscreen to compare the effects. Plan to do this activity two times over the course of two sunny days and compare the effects.

Activity Goals

→ To explore what happens when apples are left in the sun too long

National Science Education Standards

Physical science: properties of objects and materials

Science in personal and social perspectives: personal health

Materials and Supplies

☐ Several wire clothes hangers

☐ Several apples, cut into ring slices

☐ Nontoxic sunscreen

☐ Access to a tree branch or hook outdoors in the sun

☐ Ribbon or string, optional

☐ Chart paper and a marker

Procedure

1. Tell the children you want to know what happens when something is left in the sun too long. Ask if they, or someone they know, have ever been sunburned. Allow time for the children to share their stories of people being sunburned.

2. Tell the children that you are going to hang slices of apples outside and see how the sunshine affects them. Ask them what they think will happen.

3. Have the children hang the apple rings on the wire hangers and place them outside. Depending on your slices, you may need to tear or cut them in order to attach them to the wire hangers. You can also tie them to the hangers with ribbon or string.

4. Record the children's observations and descriptions of the apple slices.

5. Check on them after a few hours. Ask the children to describe what has happened. Record the children's observations and descriptions.

6. Talk about the fact that apples contain a lot of water. Ask them to describe what happens to water in the sun's heat. Explain that even though apples are very different from our bodies, our bodies also contain a lot of water.

7. Ask the children how they might be affected by being in a lot of sunlight.

8. Repeat the experiment on another day; this time, talk about the sunscreen products that we put on our skin when we're going out in the sun. Explain that sunscreen helps protect our skin from sunburn, and that it also helps prevent our skin from drying out like the apple slices did.

9. Invite the children to coat apple slices in sunscreen and hang them outside in the same manner as they hung the apples without sunscreen.

10. Check on them after a few hours. Ask the children to describe how these apple slices look compared with the ones they hung outside that didn't have sunscreen.

11. Reflect on the activity with the children: Discuss the effects of sunscreen on the apple slices and how the sunscreen kept the apples from losing moisture. Sunscreen is important for preventing sunburns, but it also adds moisture to skin and coats our skin so that it doesn't dry out so quickly in the sun.

TIPS

- Before doing this activity, talk about evaporation and do one of the activities on that subject in chapter 7.

CONNECTIONS

Repeat this activity using different kinds of fruit, and ask the children to describe the differences. Alternately, leave the apple slices outside for several days, and have the children record daily observations and sketch the progression of the apple slices drying.

Invite the children to use the apple slices without sunscreen on them to make an outdoor collage, or have them string the slices on a rope or length of yarn to make a garland. Hang the garland from a tree and allow it to dry fully, and then watch the birds or squirrels enjoy it.

CHAPTER 9

Greening Your Program

Perhaps you've picked up this book simply to get some new ideas for incorporating nature and the environment into your work with young children. Great! I hope it will be helpful. As I stated in chapter 1, this book is also intended to be a resource for those of you wishing to incorporate a more fundamental environmental perspective into your programming, operations, or mission. In this chapter, I offer some ideas and activities to help administrators or program leaders take steps in that journey. Although most people would agree that caring for our environment is valuable and important, it can be challenging to make changes, even small ones, in the way we do things. In trying to change established practices, even in the best of circumstances you may encounter barriers in terms of finances, logistics, or staff or parental acceptance. The key is to be deliberate, thoughtful, and honest in your communications and in your planning. I hope that the discussion that follows can offer some insights and guidance to support your success in raising the level of environmental awareness at your program.

by reviewing your current practices. Undoubtedly, you can find areas where your practices already coincide with those of environmental education. For example, maybe you already use both sides of a piece of paper before throwing it away, or you reuse items in other ways. Perhaps children drink from reusable water bottles or cups instead of disposable paper cups at snacktime. Do the children in your program spend time outside, in nature, on a regular basis? It is important to congratulate yourself on the environmentally friendly actions you already take, perhaps without ever having named or established an interest in the environment. As you reflect on these actions, you might be surprised when you realize how much you are already doing!

There are so many steps that you can take—some large, some small—that will help your program go green. In the following sections, you'll find suggestions for evaluating your current practices, including staff and families in your efforts, and even reaching out to the community to build partnerships and utilize the many resources available to you.

Establish Your Starting Point and Pat Yourself on the Back

If you're just beginning to think about what you can do to green your program, I encourage you to start

BE CLEAR ABOUT YOUR EDUCATIONAL PHILOSOPHY

As teachers expand the curriculum to include an emphasis on environmental education, be sure everyone—staff and families—understands the underlying philosophy: the goal for early childhood environmental education is to provide children with many opportunities to explore and experience nature, not to fill them with facts and information about issues. If necessary, explain that the value of this approach is in laying the foundation for children to become responsible stewards of our Earth. Review chapter 1 if needed. Build your resource library with books suggested in the Additional Resources section. Remember, frequent, joyful experiences outdoors lead to feelings of stewardship and a desire to care for the Earth as children grow older.

KNOW YOUR TEAM

It's important to meet people wherever they are in their journey. Before you make any detailed plans or commitments, survey your staff's level of interest in different environmental topics, and seek out their feedback about challenges or ideas for success. There is a staff questionnaire in appendix C that you may reproduce freely. You can circulate copies at staff meetings or invite staff members to complete them anonymously. Staff members can note the topics of most interest to them, any concerns they may have, and ideas for how to make the program successful. They can also identify any special talents, strengths, or knowledge they may have. For example, maybe you have a teacher who loves to take photographs and document classroom activities. Enlist her help in spreading the word to families through newsletters and other promotional materials. Maybe there's a teacher who loves to write who can help identify and apply for grants to further your green efforts. Perhaps there's a teacher who loves to garden and would enjoy the opportunity to get the children involved in a schoolyard garden.

Tapping into the strengths and talents of your staff members can contribute greatly to your program's success. They will more than likely appreciate being supported in their areas of interest and be pleased to have the opportunity to share their unique talents. This will result in more buy-in and commitment from staff. The questionnaire also provides an opportunity for staff to list any concerns or confusion

they may have about environmental education topics or activities. In having your staff fill out this questionnaire, you may learn that your staff members are ready to try something new. Perhaps stepping up your program's focus on environmental awareness and action will provide staff with a perfect opportunity to update their teaching approach and educational outcomes!

On the other hand, you may learn that members of your staff are new to environmental information, confused, or nervous about not knowing all the answers. Maybe they feel time pressures already and are worried about yet another demand on their time. Whatever the reason for frustration, allow them a space and some time to vent their concerns. Often people feel their frustration is alleviated when they simply feel heard. You can have a meeting in which staff can voice their concerns, you could ask them to respond on paper in the questionnaires you distribute, or you can set up an anonymous comment box for them to write down their frustrations. Be sensitive to their concerns. Support staff wherever they are on the journey. Perhaps they're unsure of the value of environmental education, eco-friendly practices, or increased time outdoors. Maybe they are curious but reluctant to embrace change to a program they've known and loved for years. Wherever your staff members are on the spectrum, welcome them and accept them.

As with any new venture, there will likely be some "reluctant dragons" among your staff who are skeptical, cynical, or just plain not interested. This is to be expected. Even though most people agree that environmental education is important because they recognize the developmental benefits of exposure to the outdoors, the environmental health benefits for both children and staff, or the positive impact that an environmental education program will have on your budget, some of your staff may not agree or may not understand how it fits into the big picture of the program. If this is the case, there are a number of strategies you can employ to help bring them around. For example, maybe after a coworker sees the financial benefit of reusing materials, she'll be more likely to embrace the idea of going green. Likewise, perhaps she'll feel better about teaching about the environment when she realizes that the children are benefitting from the increased time outdoors. Regardless of the ways in which your coworkers ease in to environmental education, continue to show your support and encouragement. I'm confident that they will eventually recognize the value of it in the early childhood setting. When they see the smiles and joy in the faces of the children and parents who are exposed to these activities and lessons, they'll hopefully begin to soften just a bit and become more open to environmental education.

Ultimately, be prepared to move slowly if your staff shows resistance or apathy. Continue to gently point out the benefits to all involved and share your enthusiasm. Above all, continue to stand behind your commitment to environmental education. It's important for the Earth and for families and children, and it may be important for your program's bottom line.

HAVE A CONVERSATION

Depending on the level of knowledge and interest already present in your staff—or when new staff members join your team—you may need to start at a very basic level by thoughtfully sharing with others why you're thinking about these issues. Perhaps you're driven by concern for the health and well-being of the children in your care. You may have children in your program with allergies or sensitivities, for whom use of nontoxic products is helpful or necessary. Perhaps you can speak about a local concern such as a neighboring stream becoming excessively contaminated or the local landfill reaching its capacity. If you can, focus on your most immediate and local concerns as a starting point. Remember that adults, just like the children with whom you work, tend to care most about what they know best.

Don't forget to point out the positive environmental actions you're already taking at your program. Take the time to compile that list and then share it freely. There are undoubtedly green measures you're already engaged in that people may not explicitly recognize or name as such. Also, keep in mind the crucial point that many environmentally friendly behaviors can also be financially beneficial. For example, using both sides of the paper before recycling it gives your program twice as much paper for the same cost! Reusing items, such as empty yogurt containers for paint cups or egg cartons for sorting trays, is a positive step for the environment that saves your program money too. Provide staff with clear examples of how a particular environmentally friendly practice may save your program money in the long run. Chances are that once they discover the financial benefits of going green at work, they'll start to make changes in their personal habits as well!

KEEP IT POSITIVE

On the one hand, adults can handle learning deeply troublesome facts, and it's fair to say that more adults need to know about the very real threats—such as climate change and air and water pollution—facing our planet. The sense of urgency with regard to these problems is stronger than ever before in our planet's history. Perhaps knowledge might be the catalyst some adults need to make changes. On the other hand, adults, just like children, respond best to positive communication and tend to tune out judgments, lectures, or preaching. Although the type of positive statements you would make to adults is obviously different from what you would say to children, the point is the same. We all feel better when we know we are doing something positive. We respond better to positive feedback than we do to guilt or fear. Recognizing your staff and coworkers for reducing waste in the classroom will garner much more positive results than shaming or making them feel guilty about the plastic bags they put in the trash. Responding to positive behaviors with praise and feedback is much more effective at creating change than drawing attention to negative behaviors.

IDENTIFY YOUR LEADERS

The more people invested in a common vision, the better. I highly recommend creating a "green team" for your site. This team might include you as well as a few interested and enthusiastic teachers and parents. Ideally, identify one lead person who will serve as the team's coordinator. If you've begun using the *Go Green Rating Scale*, you may have already taken this step. Since you're reading this book, that person might be you, or perhaps you have a good idea of the person who might best fill that role. Keep in mind that the path to going green can be focused on your educational efforts with children, on the environmental impacts of your operations, or on both. It may be beneficial to identify two people: a teacher who can provide leadership in the educational arena, and an administrator who can provide leadership in the operations arena. Your green leaders may be responsible for a variety of jobs: maintaining records, applying for grants, overseeing materials and program supplies, communicating with families and other staff, planning lessons, organizing training, and more. As you develop a plan, the assortment of possible jobs will become clearer. The tasks will depend on your program, your goals, and your plans for implementation. It is very important that the green coordinator(s) receive the support that they need. This may include time in their schedule for program development and research, a budget for supplies, or support from administrative staff.

NORMALIZE ENVIRONMENTAL BEHAVIORS

Studies show that when people see their friends, coworkers, and neighbors engaging in environmental behaviors, they are encouraged to try them as well. Remember to "walk the talk" and be consistent with your environmental actions and your commitment to environmental education. When you lead this way, it puts friendly pressure on others to do the same. It is important to expose the children and families with whom you work to a consistent display of your agreed-upon values. As most early care and education professionals know, it is important to be consistent, sincere, and genuine with young children. They know when you are being otherwise! If one teacher recycles but others don't, it sends a confusing message about the importance of this action. Likewise, when teachers lead activities about water conservation but are wasteful and careless in their use of this resource, it communicates a subtle message of inconsistency.

PICK UP THE *GO GREEN RATING SCALE* (IF YOU HAVEN'T DONE SO ALREADY)

As I described in chapter 1, the *Go Green Rating Scale* by Phil Boise (2010a) is a valuable tool that can help you assess the environmental impacts of your program and facility. It will guide you step by step through your assessment as well as recommend changes you can make to improve your score, including such things as developing an environmental purchasing plan for your site and evaluating your site's water quality. It also contains information on how some environmental actions, such as auditing your program's water use, can benefit your site financially. There is also a *Go Green Rating Scale Handbook* by Phil Boise (2010b), which provides additional background information and details about the issues highlighted in the *Go Green Rating Scale* and specific information on how to improve your scores. The *Go Green Rating Scale Handbook* also contains numerous sample parent letters, which are great resources for you in your efforts to involve and educate parents and families in greening your child care program. The *Go Green Rating Scale* and the *Go Green Rating Scale Handbook* are organized according to some of the most commonly discussed environmental concerns, such as food, water, and air. With a fairly quick glance, you can gain perspective on the most critical areas that could be assessed at your site. Some of you working with the *Go Green Rating Scale* may be in a position to systematically work through the entire book. For most, however, it is probably a good—and more realistic—idea to identify two or three topic areas as a starting point.

As a team, you and your staff can discuss which areas to prioritize, given your individual program needs and circumstances. Use the reproducible questionnaire in appendix C to get feedback from your staff on their interests and ideas. Keep in mind that some people find it easier to share honest comments on paper than in person. Choosing a few interest areas initially is helpful in

- providing variety for staff that may have interest in different areas.

- limiting your topic areas so you and other educators can provide depth to the content and activities rather than just highlighting a topic and never revisiting it.

- enabling your program to make changes and integrate curriculum at the same time, rather than doing one at the expense of another due to limited resources. This approach works especially well when both this book and the *Go Green Rating Scale* are employed side by side.

- helping families understand the changes that you're making within your program. If you're taking steps to be more environmentally aware as a program, and the children are engaged in environmental activities as well, you'll find the level of support, understanding, and interest among families may increase.

REVIEW YOUR CALENDAR

Some topics lend themselves to certain seasons; for example, you may choose to focus on organic food and gardening during the spring and summer months. In other cases, annual events or festivals at your site may be the perfect opportunity to highlight other topics; for example, initiate waste-free lunches on Earth Day in April. After you've reviewed your program's calendar, determine what makes the most sense in terms of connecting topic areas to seasons, holidays, or events.

DETERMINE YOUR RESOURCES

Do you have any additional funds for greening your program? There are many environmental grants available that focus on early childhood. It can take a bit of legwork to find them, but it may well be worth it. Since websites and funders change frequently, I've elected not to include specific sites or names of funding organizations in this book; however, an Internet search for "environmental grants for early childhood programs" or "green grants" will likely generate a large number of potential funding opportunities. Do you have a parent willing to volunteer to write a grant or a staff person who's a great writer who would be willing to try? Reach out to the local community. Start with

your local government, public works, or parks department. Tell them of your plans and ask for suggestions or ideas for funding and partnerships. Ask families to provide materials for activities with the children, and consider reaching out to local organizations for donations or to loan equipment for bigger projects.

ENCOURAGE FAMILY INVOLVEMENT

Families are often the key to any program's success. Use parent education nights and other outreach opportunities to provide families with tools and resources for building on their children's learning. Provide news from the classroom on a regular basis, and assign activities to parents such as sample questions to ask their children, suggestions for reflecting on the day's activities, or ideas for getting outside and enjoying nature as a family.

As you move forward in planning your program's green efforts, you may wish to evaluate the ways your program currently encourages family involvement. Perhaps there are new ways families can get involved. Adult family members can be tapped as volunteers or chaperones for outdoor experiences and field trips or as an extra set of hands when you're doing art projects or making journals. Many programs exchange child care hours for volunteer time, whether administrative or providing classroom support. Some programs even require parents to volunteer a certain number of hours each season. For those parents who are simply too busy or unavailable, there are always a few who are able to help out. Family involvement helps build community and supports children's early education too. It shows children that families value education and help each other. Many parents would love the opportunity to help out in a new and fun way. If you're in need of additional help, never underestimate the value of parents.

COORDINATE GREENING EFFORTS WITH EDUCATIONAL ACTIVITIES

It makes sense to undertake educational activities in the same areas that you are choosing to prioritize in greening your program. If you're launching a new or expanded recycling effort, choose an activity to highlight this with your children; likewise if you're focusing on reducing water waste or energy usage. After you've identified some overall changes and goals for your program, it makes sense to coordinate those with your educational curriculum. For example, if you and your staff have decided to reduce waste and increase recycling, why not turn to chapter 2 and plan a few months' worth of classroom activities that support those goals as well. The topic will be at the forefront of everyone's mind, parents included. You'll be sending a clear, consistent message about your environmental values to everyone involved in your program: the teachers, parents, and children alike.

SUPPORT STAFF IN SPENDING TIME IN NATURE

Once staff members realize that they are helping children move toward becoming environmentally literate, it might make the new ideas for nature exploration that you are proposing easier to handle. Remind staff that environmental education and nature play are a natural fit for early childhood and have many benefits for children. Regular, consistent time outdoors is good for children's brains, bodies, and emotional development. Experiences in the natural world help children develop scientific-thinking skills and many other learning domains. Each activity in this book is designed to address a few learning domains and disciplines. Remind staff that these lessons aren't just about the environment; they are also building literacy skills, scientific and aesthetic understanding, gross-motor skills, and more.

CONSIDER YOUR MISSION

At some point, it may be helpful to revisit your program's mission statement or vision. Does it say anything about the environment or the natural world? Consider developing a vision for your environmental education plans. While this may seem lofty, it can be very important. A vision statement can influence and guide behaviors in powerful ways. Work together with staff and your parent advisory group, if you have one, to develop a vision for a green program that identifies the program's environmental values. If you aren't yet sure what those values are, consider the interest areas

you've been drawn to as you thumb through this book or the *Go Green Rating Scale*. What topics are most exciting to you and to others with whom you work? Your vision statement will be a helpful reminder of your motivation and outcomes. Consider this example of a vision statement: "The Oak Meadow Preschool strives to include environmental education to support children's environmental health and literacy by providing numerous meaningful opportunities for children to learn about the natural environment in a developmentally appropriate way. We seek to demonstrate an environmental ethic through conservation, care, and wise use of our air, water, and energy resources in all that we do." Again, a vision statement will be a helpful reminder of your shared values for your staff and the greater community.

BE REALISTIC AND CELEBRATE SMALL STEPS

Some people need time to get accustomed to new ways of thinking and acting. Opening the window of awareness even a tiny crack can lead to bigger shifts down the road. Remember that your teammates will all be at different places on the spectrum with regard to environmental education. Welcome them with open arms, and enjoy the journey together.

Following is a list of activity ideas you can use as you move forward in greening your program. In a manner similar to the organization of this book and the *Go Green Rating Scale*, the list is organized by topic area. The structure and presentation of these activities is somewhat different from those in the other chapters. These activities do not have activity goals, nor do they include detailed procedures or materials lists. I've tried to simply give ideas, with some steps to take to make them happen. The overall nature of these activities will vary widely depending on such things as your program's size, ages of children served, location, community partners, and other factors. Think of them as stepping stones—a starting point. See an idea you like? Consider how to make it work given your unique situation. Present the idea to staff and families, and brainstorm together how to make it happen. I wish you the best of luck in your efforts!

Host Spring and Fall Cleanups

Despite our best intentions, school grounds often become cluttered with litter, which blows in from nearby roads, falls out of lunch boxes and pockets, or seemingly arrives out of nowhere. Reducing the amount of trash on your school grounds can lift spirits, which can help everyone feel better about your site. It can also help children and staff be more attentive to litter in general as they move about their lives.

STEPS TO TAKE

Enlist families and friends of the school to come on a Saturday or on a spring or fall evening. Provide, or invite people to bring from home, gloves, garbage bags, and extendable trash grabber tools. Venture throughout the school grounds, play areas, and parking lots picking up trash and sorting out recyclables. Be sure to include your custodial staff in planning the event, or simply let them know it's happening so they can be prepared. Consider expanding your efforts to a nearby park or nature area if feasible.

Reduce Food Waste

As anyone who works with young children can attest, lots of food gets left uneaten during snacktime and lunchtime. Many schools and child care settings have found that by simply having outdoor play happen before lunch instead of afterward, food waste is dramatically reduced. Children no longer feel rushed to gobble up their food so they can get outside. They are also hungrier after outdoor playtime. And, of course, the time outdoors offers many other benefits as well.

STEPS TO TAKE

Try offering outdoor time before lunch for a few days. Compare, if possible, the amount of food waste generated on those days versus days with outdoor time after lunch.

Encourage Reuse

Reusing materials is one of the simplest ways to bring less stuff into our lives and programs. As I mention in chapter 2, simply becoming more conscious of our buying habits is an important first step. It's also helpful to buy the highest quality products we can afford so that the things we buy last longer. In early care and education, there are many options for encouraging staff, families, and children to reuse. I present a few ideas here, but I encourage you to think about the possibilities for your program and go wherever your creativity takes you.

STEPS TO TAKE

Reuse paper. Use both sides of paper before recycling it. Start a box to collect sheets of paper that have been used on one side, and you'll soon have plenty on hand for writing and drawing projects. Start a scrap box for bits of construction and other decorative paper, and you'll soon have an endless supply of craft and art materials.

Reuse books. Start a "birthday books" tradition whereby children donate a special book of their own to the class library instead of bringing in sugary birthday treats or other food items. Children will love selecting a book from home to share with friends and will feel great seeing their favorite books on the shelves each day. This offers the added benefit of shifting the focus away from the ever-popular, but not-so-healthy, sugary treats.

Reuse doodads. As I describe in chapter 3, doodads are quirky objects or random parts that have outlived their original purpose, are too good to throw away, but cannot be recycled. Think marker lids, extra puzzle pieces, the plastic core from tape dispensers, or game tokens with no homes. The Create a Doodad Center activity on page 53 focuses on engaging children creatively and constructively in organizing and utilizing doodads in the classroom. There is also a parent letter in appendix D that you can use to help launch a doodad drive with the families in your program.

Reuse dishes and utensils. If health, safety, and logistics permit, use reusable dishes and utensils. You can visit a local thrift store or invite families to send a set of reusable dishes, utensils, and a cup to school with their child. If your site does not have a dish-washing service, you could send the items home each day to be washed and returned the next day. If this feels too difficult for you, simplify it by just asking for a cup from home. Ask parents to label anything brought from home so that only their child will use it. Or, if possible, recruit a parent volunteer to be in charge of taking home reusable items, washing them, and returning them the next day.

Reuse bags, mugs, and water bottles. Bring in a set of reusable shopping bags for those last-minute trips to the dollar store or grocery store. Ask staff to bring in reusable mugs. Ask staff and children to bring in reusable water bottles that are clearly labeled with the owner's name.

Encourage Reuse at Home

Often families are interested in reducing their consumption habits but are unsure about how to proceed. The following ideas will provide families with great ways to help your program and reduce their own consumption at the same time.

STEPS TO TAKE

Consider hosting a clothing swap. Invite families to bring in used (but still usable) winter gear, rain boots and coats, or costumes. Families can also be invited to select something to take home. If you need to raise funds, consider asking for a small cash donation for participation. If appropriate, leftover clothing can be

put to use at your program (think spare clothes for children following muddy outdoor explorations), or they can be donated to a local charity.

Start a toy library. Invite families to donate used toys that are still in good condition to your site. Participating families can check out toys for a period of time and then return them to the library. It's a great way to help kids experience different toys they may be coveting without having to buy them. And parents may find out which toys the child truly plays with and which aren't that great after all.

Consider a multifamily garage sale. Besides being a great way to promote reuse, an event like this could also be a fundraiser for your program. Invite families to bring in their gently used toys, books, and clothing, then have a sale for the general public. Any leftover items can be donated to a local charity.

Start an E-Newsletter

Newsletters are a great way to share events and happenings at the program and to provide families with important information on safety, health updates, field trip plans, and more. Many programs offer newsletters to families, and some send them home with children on a weekly basis. Thus the paper often winds up in the recycling bin at home. By switching to an electronic version, you can reduce trash and save your program money on paper.

STEPS TO TAKE

Be sure to communicate your plans and motivation for this change a few weeks ahead of time so all families know. Most families have access to computers, but you should continue to print just enough paper copies for those who don't. You could also post a copy prominently at your entrance, so parents can read it if they arrive a few minutes early for pickup. If possible, make a computer available to parents in the lobby or entrance of your school for them to use while they wait for their child. Enlist computer-savvy parent volunteers—or school-age children, if they attend your program—to help you in this effort; engage them in developing and sharing the newsletter after teachers submit their regular news items and updates.

Encourage Organic

As I discuss in chapter 4, chemicals applied to food crops can enter the environment and can remain on the foods after they've been picked and processed. Because we don't know all the chemicals used in food production, nor have they all been tested for human health effects, it makes sense to choose organic when and to the extent you can.

STEPS TO TAKE

Provide ideas. Suggest specific reasonably priced organic foods that parents can bring in for snacks or special birthday treats. Alternately, create a wish list to share with families that includes organic foods or minimally processed foods.

Collect a special fee. Do you ask families for a supply or materials fee? Consider asking families to pay a bit extra so that you can purchase organic fruits and vegetables for snacktime.

Know the "dirty dozen." Many families want to purchase organic foods but are restricted by the higher price. As a strategy for making organic choices fit within the family budget, encourage families to consider choosing organic for just one or two fresh fruits that they regularly buy. The nonprofit Environmental Working Group publishes the Dirty Dozen, a list of the top twelve fruits and vegetables that are typically most chemical-laden at www.ewg.org/foodnews. This list can be a helpful resource for those families who stick to a budget, by helping them prioritize their food-buying choices.

Provide support. Use your e-newsletter to offer educational tips and suggestions for families regarding organic food, health, and the environment. Offer suggestions for healthy lunches and snacks, and ask families to share favorite recipes for healthy snacks.

Explore Local CSAs

Community-Supported Agriculture programs (known as CSAs) are local farms that offer memberships to people in the community. In exchange for purchasing a membership, you receive freshly picked (often organic) produce (and in some cases even fruits, cheeses, and meats!) delivered to a site near you. Dues and programs vary from region to region. Most CSA farms also host family events and get-togethers, such as strawberry picking and fall harvest festivals. CSAs are gaining popularity across the nation as people embrace a healthier lifestyle and try to eat more locally grown foods. The added benefit is supporting local farmers!

STEPS TO TAKE

Become a CSA pickup site. To find a CSA farm near you, search the internet for "Community Supported Agriculture" followed by the name of your county. Some areas have more CSAs than others. If you have a lot of families who might be interested, you could become a CSA pickup site, where the boxes of produce would be delivered and families could pick them up.

Explore other options. If there aren't CSAs in your area, speak with local farmers or visit farmers markets to inquire about how you can help share locally grown food with your families, and help the farmers too.

Start Your Own Garden

Perhaps you are fortunate enough to have access to a garden plot at your site. Maybe you have space, but no established garden. Even if your site includes mostly pavement, you can still grow vegetables and flowers with the children in your program. Large pots, barrels, or other containers such as raised beds can make classroom gardens a reality for you.

STEPS TO TAKE

Enlist some helpful parents to construct flowerboxes or planters, and you can grow enough vegetables for the children to snack on throughout the year. Ask around to find out which parents might be willing to build garden beds or containers. Solicit donations of soil and plants from parents or the community (try garden stores, hardware stores, and even grocery stores). Once you have the containers and supplies, have a Family Garden Day where families and children can help fill the containers and plant vegetables.

Provide a sign-up sheet so families can volunteer to come back and water, weed, and care for the plants.

Manage Rainwater at Your Site

There are a number of things you can do—some small, others large—to manage rainwater and improve water quality at your facility.

STEPS TO TAKE

Install a rain barrel. A rain barrel is simple to install and can serve as a water supply for your plants. Rain barrels can be purchased online or at most large home and garden stores. Many cities sell rain barrels at a reduced price through Public Works departments. They can be installed under a rain gutter, and most models have a spigot to make it easy to obtain and use the rainwater.

✋ **Water collected in rain barrels should not be used for irrigating vegetables or for play in water tables. Since it landed on your building's roof and has been through the gutter, it may contain chemicals or pollutants that are not suitable for eating, drinking, or playing. This water can, however, be used for watering flowering plants or lawns, for watering trees and shrubs on your grounds, or for filling bird baths.**

Establish a rain garden. A rain garden is a garden intentionally designed to absorb excess rain or snowmelt in a given landscape, thereby slowing the flow of water into the local sewer system. A rain garden is planted near a source of runoff, such as a downspout, or in a depression or low-lying area in the landscape. It is also planted with a specific assortment of plants that have deep roots and are especially good at taking up water deep underground. The particular species of plants recommended for a rain garden depends on the region in which you live. A rain garden can also be a great teaching tool: the children can learn about biology, colors and textures, animals and insects, and

more. Look to your local watershed organization or state natural resources or waterways department for assistance, grants, and help planning a rain garden. Often a watershed organization or other local water stewardship organization in your area will be able to provide assistance with curriculum development as well as guest speakers.

Consider replacing some pavement. Can you spare even a small area of pavement? Perhaps there is an old patch of sidewalk or corner of your parking lot in rough shape. Replacing impervious surface (hard surfaces that do not absorb water) with gardens or other green space will improve water quality by reducing the amount of runoff from your site. Often, local conservation organizations or city public works departments offer grants for projects such as these.

Encourage Water Conservation at Home

Chapter 5 provides a lot of information about the importance of protecting and conserving water. Although most families appreciate the need to conserve water, few really know how, and fewer still realize that seemingly small actions really do make a difference!

STEPS TO TAKE

Share information with families. In your program's e-newsletter, consider letting families know about some simple steps they can take to reduce water consumption at home. On average, the largest uses of household water are for bathing and showering and for flushing toilets. Installing low-flow showerheads and toilets can save hundreds of gallons of water per year per household. Other ideas for conservation at home include turning off faucets when brushing teeth and washing hands.

Make water the topic of a family education night. Have the children demonstrate some of their knowledge and activities, or organize some activities that parents and children can do together. While you're at it, you can share resources about water quality and water conservation with parents. Family education nights are also great ways to recruit volunteers for cleanup events (see page 217) and other projects to benefit your program.

Reach out to water quality organizations in your area. Many of them will provide guest speakers or teaching materials on loan or for very little cost. Water quality organizations include state natural resource or wildlife departments, city or county public works departments, parks and recreation organizations, or governmental agencies known as watershed districts.

Host a Community Shoreline Cleanup

If your facility is located near a body of water—such as a river, lake, or even a pond—gather families together for a special shoreline cleanup. It is important (and a great partnership opportunity) to coordinate and communicate with your local public works or parks department. Often, they will provide cleanup materials (such as trash bags and gloves) and collect the filled trash bags at the end of the day!

STEPS TO TAKE

Promote the activity for weeks ahead of time. Remind families to bring gloves and large trash bags, and have extras on hand for those who forget. Send groups out to collect trash found along the shoreline and near the water. This will help wildlife and improve water quality too. Don't forget to separate the recyclables as you collect! Have fun! Consider awarding prizes, such as for the biggest item, the strangest item, or the most mysterious item. This is a great event to have on or around Earth Day (April 22) or on National Day of Service (September 11). Remind adults to monitor their children at all times near water, and not to pick up anything sharp or rusty. Children will love to share tales of the items they collected, and it's a great way to get families involved.

> ### AIR IS ALL AROUND US

Celebrate Wind!

Family festivals are great fun and a wonderful way to generate interest in and celebrate your accomplishments. Consider having a themed festival around wind and air to promote your environmental efforts and education.

STEPS TO TAKE

Host a wind festival. Do you have access to a large open space, such as a playing field or large meadow? Invite families to attend a wind festival at your site on a Saturday or a warm spring evening to play in the wind. Children and their parents can work together to make kites or wind chimes, and decorate a tree or flagpole with ribbons that will dance in the breeze.

Plan a kite festival. Invite families to bring their own kites, or spend time in class making kites for the festival. You can use rice paper, plastic grocery bags, ribbons, crepe paper, and thin fabric for making kites. Kite festivals are colorful and exciting, and they are especially welcome in the wintertime!

Establish a No-Idle Zone

Idling vehicles dump carbon dioxide and other pollutants into the air and contribute to climate change. These emissions can irritate the lungs of young children in your program. In some states, idling vehicles is illegal.

STEPS TO TAKE

Encourage families not to idle their vehicles when picking up or waiting for children. Gently remind them that when they leave their cars idling, they are polluting the air that the children breathe. Vehicle exhaust is harmful to our health, especially for children, the elderly, and those with asthma. You may also want to remind them that they are wasting gas and money. Idling for ten seconds uses more gasoline than turning off and restarting a car's engine. Provide facts about why idling is harmful to children in your e-newsletter, and make signs for the pickup area outside your school reminding families not to idle their cars. This will eliminate the need for direct confrontation. To reduce the amount of time parents need to wait, make sure children are ready to go when their parents arrive. Check out the EPA's Anti-Idling Toolkit listed in the Additional Resources section under Air.

Lower Your Energy Use

An energy audit determines where a building is leaking air and losing energy. You'll discover things such as how your heating and cooling systems work, how efficient your insulation is, and other helpful information. It is a great way to learn more about your building's use of energy and how to improve practices to be more efficient.

STEPS TO TAKE

Determine a few simple things on your own. For example, if you have a refrigerator or freezer, place a dollar bill in the door as you close it, and try to pull it out. If the fridge seals properly and tightly, you won't be able to remove the bill without effort. If it slips right out, it's time for a new seal, because cold air will escape through a leaky seal just as easily as that dollar. Unscrew the covers on your electrical outlets. Do you see a gaping hole? If so, you're losing heat through that hole. Warm air will escape through the hole and up through the ceiling and roof of your building.

Conduct an energy audit. Contact your local utility company to see if they offer audits. Alternately, local nonprofit organizations specializing in energy use or an energy contractor may be able to help. There are also web-based audits, such as the Home Energy Saver available at http://hes.lbl.gov/hes/db/zip.shtml.

Enlist families. Host a work day and ask families to make small improvements to your building, such as installing weather stripping or caulking leaky openings.

Buy smart. When replacing appliances or office equipment, choose Energy Star certified items, which are more efficient than their noncertified counterparts. The US EPA started this program to help consumers make more informed choices when purchasing common office and home appliances. The program rates items based on their energy efficiency. Certified items are more energy efficient than their counterparts and often save the consumer money in the long run. Find out more at www.energystar.gov.

A NOTE ABOUT COMPACT FLUORESCENT LIGHTBULBS (CFLS)

As more and more sites are becoming aware of the need to conserve energy, compact fluorescent lightbulbs have become very popular. While they do save energy, and will result in long-term savings for your site, CFLs contain small amounts of mercury and, therefore, proper disposal is absolutely necessary when the bulbs burn out. Further, in the event of breakage, special care must be taken to carefully clean up the spill using techniques that ensure the mercury is contained. The choice to use CFLs offers benefits but also carries with it significant responsibility.

Host a Bike- or Walk-to-School Week

Many schools and early childhood programs are encouraging families to walk, bike, or take alternative transportation. Even carpooling reduces the amount of fossil fuel emissions. While it is difficult to quantify exactly how much carbon emissions are reduced—that number depends on average miles traveled one-way, number of families in your program, and more—families will be glad to have the chance to try alternative transportation and get out of their cars for a change.

STEPS TO TAKE

Ensure that you have bike racks or adequate parking areas for bikes. Provide families with local bike maps and enlist experienced bike commuters to help plan safe routes to school. You may wish to have a "walking school bus," meaning all families meet at a central location and walk to school together. This is a great way to build community, get to know the families, and reduce carbon dioxide emissions all at the same time. Also, be sure to check out the Safe Routes to School program at www.saferoutesinfo.org. You can promote alternative ways to travel to your program through family events and ongoing support.

Switch to Nontoxic Cleaners and Personal Care Products

Most likely, you're already engaging the children in routines and activities related to personal hygiene, such as hand washing and toothbrushing. These habits relate to environmental education because they involve chemicals and their interactions with the human body. The choices you make with regard to cleaning and personal care products can have an effect on the environment, and on children's health too. Choosing nontoxic products is better for the Earth, and better for children's health!

STEPS TO TAKE

Evaluate the cleaning products you have on hand. Utilize the *Go Green Rating Scale* section 3 for background information and guidance in doing this. Are your cleaning products benign or harmful? (Most will likely be somewhere in between!) Where are the harsh chemicals found? Consider nontoxic substitutions, such as food-grade materials, including baking soda and vinegar.

Become familiar with signal words. See chapter 8 for a discussion of these words. It's very important to understand these words, read labels before using any products, and then follow the directions on the label.

Start small. Try replacing all antibacterial soap (which contains some potentially hazardous chemicals) with nontoxic soap. Also, replace aerosol air fresheners in your bathroom with a vase of fresh flowers or herbs instead. Use plain or homemade vinegar instead of harsh chemicals to clean surfaces. Just be sure the mixtures you make are clearly labeled with the purpose, ingredients, directions, and the person's name who made the mixture. Always label bottles with their contents.

Share Information with Families

There are many resources available to help people understand the issues and choices surrounding cleaning and personal care products. For example, an excellent resource is the nonprofit Environmental Working Group (EWG) dedicated to researching the environmental health of common products and activities. EWG maintains a website (www.ewg.org/skindeep) that provides evaluations for more than sixty-nine thousand personal care products, from sunscreen to toothpaste and everything in between. Products are rated according to the amount and kinds of chemicals present in the products. How much is known or unknown about the chemicals also is indicated.

STEPS TO TAKE

Share the EWG Skin Deep website and information about it with families in your program. Include a link in your e-newsletter. Encourage families to research the products they use every day. Better still, you could make it easier for families by visiting the website yourself and creating a list of a variety of safe brands of sunscreen and bug repellents for children. Post the list prominently at your site and share it in an e-newsletter. Keep in mind that EWG's ratings of products can and do change as more studies are done or information is made known.

Reflection

In the early years, there is so much happening inside a child's mind and heart. Each child is making connections and having emotional experiences that are laying the groundwork for a lifetime of feeling safe, secure, and joyful in the world and of caring for our Earth. By engaging in the activities in this book, you've played a major role in supporting that development, and that is a great gift. When we work with children, every day we see that true learning comes when there is a positive emotional experience followed by ample time for reflecting on and processing the experience. Now it's important for you to take time to reflect on your efforts.

Maybe you have worked your way through this book cover to cover or have simply selected a few activities to try environmental education in your program. Perhaps you have the *Go Green Rating Scale* and are using it to retool your program, or maybe not. In any case, you've made a difference in helping children develop a love for the Earth, and that is to be celebrated. Any action, no matter how large or small, whether visible or not, makes a difference.

It may be helpful at this point to sit down and evaluate your use of this book. Think about the children in your program. Which activities did they most enjoy? Why? What would you like to have spent more time on? Did any of the children's interests or discoveries surprise you? Were you able to let go of the desire to teach specific content or topical information about environmental issues and instead offer children playful, open-ended opportunities for exploration? Did your process of discovery take you in any new directions? What kinds of experiences did the children respond to most? Above all, did you get outside with the children more than you did before you picked up this book?

Finally, think about the future of your environmental efforts. What would you still like to do? Do you have new ideas for activities or topics you'd like to explore further? Are there ways to connect the existing activities in this book to other disciplines or experiences? It's my hope that this book has provided you with resources you'll continue to use as you explore the environment together. Get together with your staff and coworkers. Reassemble your green team. Did you create a checklist in the beginning, when you were just getting your green program started? Pull it out and read it over. What successes can you share? Which areas were particularly challenging? Why? How has this book helped your staff work together? Just as teachers differentiate education for children in the classroom, did you differentiate the activities, practices, or approaches based on your team's interest level, commitment, or new ideas? It's a good bet you've done a lot more than you knew was possible. And maybe you realized just how much you were already doing to support environmental learning without knowing it! Consider what you might like to do in the future. What worked well, and why? Were you able to engage families as much as you'd hoped?

I welcome any comments about this book, suggestions for additional activities or future topic areas, or feedback on the activities included here. Please feel free to contact me at patty@smallwondersmn.com or visit my website, www.smallwondersmn.com. You can also find my site by looking up the book's page on the Redleaf Press website, www.redleafpress.org.

. Above all, I hope you have embraced the practice of environmental education through active, playful experience outdoors. The joy and wonder you've fostered in young children will surely be the fertile ground for years of continued discovery and exploration. That discovery and exploration will ultimately lead to a greener Earth because you have helped create a generation of children who are in love with the natural world and have an innate sense of how the environment works and the important role they play in its keeping. *Thank you!*

National Science Education Standards: Content Standards, Grades K–4

UNIFYING CONCEPTS AND PROCESSES

- Systems, order, and organization
- Evidence, models, and explanation
- Change, constancy, and measurement
- Evolution and equilibrium
- Form and function

SCIENCE AS INQUIRY

- Abilities necessary to do scientific inquiry
- Understandings about scientific inquiry

PHYSICAL SCIENCE

- Properties of objects and materials
- Position and motion of objects
- Light, heat, electricity, and magnetism

LIFE SCIENCE

- Characteristics of organisms
- Life cycles of organisms
- Organisms and environments

EARTH AND SPACE SCIENCE

- Properties of earth materials
- Objects in the sky
- Changes in earth and sky

SCIENCE AND TECHNOLOGY

- Abilities to distinguish between natural objects and objects made by humans
- Abilities of technological design
- Understanding about science and technology

SCIENCE IN PERSONAL AND SOCIAL PERSPECTIVES

- Personal health
- Characteristics and changes in populations
- Types of resources
- Changes in environments
- Science and technology in local challenges

HISTORY AND NATURE OF SCIENCE

- Science as a human endeavor

For a complete description of each content standard, see www.nap.edu/openbook.php?record_id=4962.

Using Children's Literature for Environmental Education

Children's literature can be a wonderful source of inspiration for your environmental explorations with children. Although nonfiction works can clearly introduce children to environmental topics, I've found that fiction can also be extremely helpful in infusing curriculum with science and helping inspire questions for further exploration. In fact, for a number of reasons, I actually prefer fiction over nonfiction for inspiring science concepts. Many nonfiction children's books tend to teach vocabulary for its own sake, often out of the context of the children's lives. In this way, they lack real-world application or relevance for young children. Nonfiction books may require a fundamental or beginning-level knowledge of science concepts in order to be understood. And some young children have a hard time getting excited or interested in them.

The story format, on the other hand, is great for sustaining the interest of most children. Children love to follow a plot and learn what will happen to the characters in a story. Stories help them to draw conclusions and make connections between the natural world and their own personal world. They look to create context and meaning, and stories help them do so. I've found that nature stories are especially appealing to children. Children are drawn to nature and animals. They are interested in animals' lives and stories, and often, when the animal is a character, stories can have a therapeutic or comforting effect, as with the popular *The Kissing Hand* by Audrey Penn. Children may be able to identify with animal characters in ways they are unable to with human characters. Nature is a world not created or controlled by adults and can be a welcome place to visit, if even in a story.

Of course, fiction books and children's literature are not intended to be science texts, nor should they be expected to present factual information or portray their subjects with the realism one would expect from nonfiction stories. Don't rely on literature to provide children with facts; instead, rely on literature as a source of inspiration, curiosity, and wonder. Use story time with children as a jumping-off point for introducing environmental concepts.

Excellent children's books on environmental topics can be found in abundance. As much as I'd love to specifically recommend some of my favorites, I know my recommendations might be obsolete as soon as the ink dried on this page because new books are coming out all the time. Therefore, I'd like to make some simple suggestions to guide you in choosing books that will evoke positive feelings and curiosity about the natural world.

As much as possible, look for books that approach environmental topics with sensitivity and grace. As with classroom activities, it is far better to choose those that inspire wonder and curiosity, rather than despair and fear. Some children's books dealing with environmental issues can actually draw on fear and despair. This may be overt or it may be subtle. Read a book several times yourself, and consider the message being sent to children. Is it one of fear, shame, or punishment? What role do children have in the story? In one popular story, children are urged to recycle; when they don't, the world is completely overtaken by garbage and the children lose their home.

Some children's books present a bleak or dismal picture of nature. It might appear depressing, sinister, or barren. Be cautious about using books that present a barren or depressing view of nature. Consider the impression that children take from the story. Also, be aware of how animals are portrayed in stories, and avoid books that villainize certain species or portray them as cruel or less than intelligent. These kinds of stories perpetuate myths or misinformation about some animals.

After you read a book to children, share it with them. If possible, make numerous copies available so children can work in groups to page through the book, discussing and making observations. Ask them questions to spark their thinking, such as "What questions do you have about this book/this owl/this tree?" Challenge children to create new endings or change the stories altogether. Challenge them to find out more about the subjects in the story, or about the plot itself. Follow the children's interests and be open to finding the possible connection to a particular nature or science exploration. Let their questions and interests drive your ideas for projects and activities in the classroom.

Another great way that you can use children's literature to enhance learning is by reading books that are related to a theme of exploration in the classroom. For example, choose water stories as you do a unit on water. Make the books available to the children and obtain multiple copies if possible, so children can look together and share observations with each other. Then be sure to record their questions and descriptions. Use their questions to guide your activities and choose your materials. Consider the book a starting point for your further exploration.

Confidential Staff Questionnaire

We have identified a need and desire to embrace environmental topics as part of our program's overall mission. We would like to implement more environmental activities and we need your help!

We would really appreciate your input on this as we move forward with these efforts. Please take the time to consider the following questions, and answer as honestly as you can. Your answers will be kept confidential.

1. Which environmental or green topics are of most interest or concern to you? Please check all the following that apply:

   - ☐ recycling/waste reduction
   - ☐ food and gardening
   - ☐ water quality
   - ☐ air quality
   - ☐ nontoxic cleaners
   - ☐ energy conservation
   - ☐ children spending time in nature

2. Any comments you can share about the topics you selected?

   _____

   _____

   _____

3. In thinking about ways to improve the environmental friendliness of our program, which areas do you think we should prioritize? Please number the following areas from 1 to 6 in order of priority, with 1 being the most important and 6 being the least important.

   _____ recycling/waste reduction
   _____ food and gardening
   _____ water quality
   _____ air quality
   _____ nontoxic cleaners
   _____ energy conservation

4. Any comments you can share about your choice of priorities?

   _____

   _____

   _____

5. Do you have any specific ideas for programs or activities we might implement that would make our center more environmentally friendly?

   _____

   _____

   _____

6. Do you have any special talents or interests that you would be willing to share that could help improve the environmental friendliness of our program? (For example, grant writing, gardening, or researching environmental topics.)

   _____

   _____

7. Do you have any other ideas, suggestions, comments or concerns regarding environmental issues and the operation and administration of our program?

   _____

   _____

   _____

From *Early Childhood Activities for a Greener Earth* by Patty Born Selly, © 2012. Published by Redleaf Press, www.redleafpress.org.
This page may be reproduced for classroom use only.

Sample Letter to Families for a Doodad Drive

Dear Families,

Over the next few weeks, we are collecting "doodads" (also known as found objects) to be used with supervision in our classrooms for science activities, art activities, and other projects. Doodads are small objects that can be used for other things before being thrown away. Often, a quick cleanup under the couch will turn up a handful of doodads too good to pass up!

Examples of doodads include broken rubber bands, broken toy pieces, rubber tubing, the hard cores from inside tape rolls, paper towel tubes, marker lids, scratched or old CDs, springs, pieces of gears, foam packing peanuts, lids from plastic bottles, broken drinking straws, random buttons . . . you get the idea.

In the interest of safety, please do not bring in any sharp or rusty items, dead batteries, glass items, electric cords, or food items. Any food containers should be washed thoroughly and rinsed well.

The children will be having fun sorting and organizing these items as well as using them for a variety of projects. We will be sure to share our creations with you!

We are collecting doodads not only to get more fun and interesting supplies, but also as part of our effort to go green and encourage the creative reuse of objects that might otherwise be thrown away.

We will have a collection container near the front door so you can deposit doodads when you drop off or pick up your child. The collection container will be there through March 30, so please feel free to bring in your donations at any time before then.

Thank you,

Patty

Sample Letter to Families Sharing Ideas for Waste-Free Lunches

Dear Families,

We're very excited to be reducing the amount of waste we generate at our school. As part of this effort, we would like to encourage you to consider reducing the amount of prepackaged and disposable items you send to school with your child each day. Reducing waste, even just a little, sends a positive message to the children that their families are involved and supportive of what's happening at school. Below is a list of easy and inexpensive suggestions for you to consider when preparing your child's snacks and lunches each day:

- Instead of paper napkins, include a special cloth napkin, which can be washed and reused again and again.

- Provide real silverware instead of plastic utensils. Include a reusable thermos, cup, or bottle for drinking beverages. If possible, avoid juice boxes, pouches, and plastic water bottles designed for single use.

- Check out the many options for reusable containers that are great for packing lunches. For example, you can find colorful, reusable plastic storage boxes that are just right for child-size lunches and are easy for children to open and close on their own. You can also find lunch and snack containers made of nonbreakable glass or stainless steel, or waterproof, washable fabric snack and sandwich pouches, often with fun designs, that children will enjoy finding in their lunch boxes.

- Avoid buying prepackaged items to the extent you can. Prepackaged lunch kits and single-serve items have a lot of packaging, most of which cannot be recycled. They are also quite expensive relative to the amount of food they contain. We encourage you to consider buying food in bulk and preparing lunches at home. Consider packing snacks such as fruit, vegetable sticks, breads, or crackers that don't come prepackaged.

We truly appreciate your support of our program's efforts to minimize waste and go green!

Sincerely,

Patty

Starting and Maintaining a Compost Pile

Compost is a dark brown dirt-like material, odorless and rich in nutrients, that is created when food and other natural waste materials decompose. Microorganisms in soil (including bacteria and fungi as well as insects and worms) digest and break down waste materials, converting them into this rich substance that you can spread on your garden. Compost is great for gardens and lawns. It provides essential nutrients that plants need to grow. It improves the soil's structure, helping soil to have the right amount of moisture and air. And it increases soil's biodiversity. It's so valuable for gardeners that it's called "black gold!"

Backyard composting can be a great project to do with children. It's easy, fascinating, and can cost little to nothing, and it's a wonderful addition to any school garden. Children grow more mindful about food waste when they know it will be composted. They pay more attention to how much food is left on their plates at lunchtime, and they feel good knowing the leftovers will be put to use. Composting helps children see firsthand the way nature recycles. Leftover food scraps become garden fertilizer, which helps flowers and vegetables grow. Composting can save you money as well. If you have gardens or container plants, you are likely purchasing fertilizers or enrichments to enhance your soil. Backyard composting produces this for free. Compost is also good for the environment. If food waste doesn't go into a compost pile, it will go into the trash.

Starting Your Compost Pile

A compost pile is typically contained in a bin or structure of some kind. This can be as simple as a circle of chicken wire on a grassy corner of your parking lot or as high-tech as a store-bought barrel that you can tumble with a crank. Be sure to review your city's ordinances first; some cities require compost piles to be completely contained and enclosed. For the beginner, I'd recommend a standard, store-bought composter that looks like a large barrel with a removable lid. Though the lid is not essential, it can help deter animals, such as raccoons and rodents, that would be interested in raiding your pile. This standard type is relatively inexpensive, and you may even be able to buy one at a wholesale price or receive a subsidy through your city or county environmental management or solid waste department.

The most important consideration when selecting a compost bin is ease of use. Once you have a compost pile going, you (and the children in your program) will need to stir it often, using long-handled shovels or pitchforks. If you choose a bin with a cover, ensure that it can be easily removed and replaced. Try to choose a bin or system that the children will be able to reach comfortably. Nothing's more frustrating for a young child than wanting to help but being "too small" to do so!

Once you've selected a container for your compost pile, choose a location. For ideal results, your compost pile should be situated on the grass or soil so critters in the soil can access it. You'll also want your pile to be in a readily accessible place so you and the children will use it often. Most people prefer to have it in or very near their garden so it is easy to make use of the compost once it's ready. Ideally, start your pile in a sunny spot, because the sun's heat will help speed the decomposition process. Natural waste materials will still turn into compost in the shade, but it will take longer than it does in the sun. Likewise, the process of decomposition still happens in areas where the winters are long and cold; it just happens more slowly. Your pile also needs water, and if there's not enough regular rainfall, you'll need to add water to it. If possible, locate your pile where you can easily access it with a hose or watering cans.

Making Compost!

You'll want to follow a basic recipe as you build your pile. It's typical and helpful to think about the key composting ingredients in two categories: greens and browns. *Greens* are wet materials such as food scraps, eggshells, coffee grounds, tea leaves, and fresh grass clippings. (You can even add weeds to your pile, although you probably want to avoid adding weed seeds, as they may survive in the compost and sprout later wherever you spread your compost.) Green materials will add nitrogen and other nutrients to the compost as they break down. This is important, because nitrogen and other nutrients are essential for the flowers and vegetables on which you'll later spread the compost. *Browns* are dry materials such as dried leaves and grass, straw, newspaper, construction paper, shredded cardboard, or paper towels. These materials add carbon to the mix, and carbon provides energy to the microorganisms doing the work of decomposition. These colors are used to describe the materials because in general, though definitely not always, many of the items are green or brown. But don't get stuck on the terms. You can certainly put items of many colors, such as orange peels, banana peels, and colored construction paper, into your pile. It is important to have a good balance of browns and greens, because it is that mix which creates heat in the pile, and that heat means that decomposition is happening.

Some sources recommend an equal balance between greens and browns, others say you should aim for a mix of one-third greens to two-thirds browns. You don't need to measure your materials, but do pay attention to the condition of your pile and fine-tune as necessary. If you add too many greens, your pile will become wet and may even take on an ammonia-like odor. If you add too many browns, your pile will decompose slowly. Don't give up! Just keep adjusting

the ratio of ingredients. Keep a bag of grass clippings and one of dry leaves near your pile to adjust the balance, if needed. Although animal products such as meat and cheese do decompose, they take much longer than plant-derived products and often have a smell or are more likely to attract scavenging animals during the process of decomposition. For that reason, most people recommend keeping animal products out of backyard compost piles.

In addition to waste materials, your pile needs oxygen. That's where the stirring comes in. You'll need to stir your compost regularly with a pitchfork or shovel. Simply scoop up shovelfuls, mixing them around as best you can. Some people recommend stirring each time you add food waste or other materials to the pile. Mixing or stirring the compost adds air and helps stimulate activity in the pile, speeding the process of decomposition. Keep in mind that once your pile gets built up, it can be a bit heavy and challenging to stir. Although children will want to be involved fully and feel invested and excited by the process of making compost, it's also up to you to make sure it gets tended appropriately. Be sure to take your turn stirring the pile once the children have finished.

Compost also needs a certain amount of moisture. Your pile should be somewhat damp (think of a damp sponge) but not excessively wet. A very wet pile will not decompose quickly. If your pile is too wet, or soggy, adding brown ingredients can help. Keep tabs on whether your pile is getting regular rain, and if not, add a little water (with a watering can or hose) to dampen the pile slightly when you are adding your waste materials.

If your compost pile doesn't seem to be working the way you expect it to, consult a reference online or consult a book to troubleshoot what you need to do. Most likely, a simple adjustment of the balance between greens and browns or a thorough stirring will do the trick. Also, if your pile seems to be attracting fruit flies or insects, remember to cover all food when you dump it in. Drop in your food scraps, turn your pile, and add a layer of dry leaves and grass clippings (kept handy!) to cover them.

Maintaining your compost pile can be fun, interesting, and offer great learning opportunities for children. Add materials often and mix the pile frequently. Keep a small covered container in the classroom for your food scraps. During recess or at the end of the day, make a trip to the compost bin together or send one or two children out to add the day's scraps to the pile and mix it well. This routine can be pleasant, and the children will look forward to tending the pile each day. Stirring and mixing the pile is a great way for children to warm up in the wintertime!

Once your pile is up and running, you should see the results of your efforts in a few weeks to months, depending on how warm or cold it is outside, how frequently you add materials and mix the pile, and how much sun and rain the pile gets. Although composting is easy, it works best when you give it attention. Be patient and stick with it! That black gold is worth the wait.

Using the Compost!

Once you've generated some compost, you can go to work enriching the soil in your garden and container plants! Mix it in with potting soil when you start indoor container plants, or layer compost on top of the soil in containers or outdoor garden beds. In the garden, worms and other critters will "turn over" the compost and incorporate it into the top layer of soil in no time. If you like, you can dig compost into the soil as you're digging your garden. Scoop some compost into the soil as you dig, and mix it as you turn over shovelfuls of dirt.

Although composting is quite straightforward and fairly foolproof, it is not uncommon to have specific questions arise as you plan or maintain your compost pile. Unfortunately, this context does not allow me to address specific questions. There are many great resources on composting, in print form as well as on the web. See the Additional Resources section at the end of this book for some recommendations. County extension agencies, solid waste offices, and environmental departments are also good places to go for local resources. If your state has a master gardener program, this is also a great resource for help with your composting project. They can answer questions, provide helpful suggestions, and often can provide ready-made bins for you at little or no cost. Many programs will even send a speaker to your site to demonstrate and provide an educational program about composting!

With a little work, some energetic and helpful children, and some food scraps, you can be on your way to creating rich, healthy compost for your garden or planting containers. Even though it may seem daunting at first, composting is actually easy and quite enjoyable. It is worth the effort you put in to get your pile started: just roll up your sleeves, gather up your food waste, and get started!

Recipe for Good Compost

- *Brown ingredients (dry leaves, shredded paper, straw, newspaper, paper towels)*
- *Green ingredients (food scraps, coffee grounds, egg shells, fresh grass clippings, and fresh weeds)*
- *Water*
- *Air*

Add ingredients frequently. Each time you add ingredients, stir well. Water enough to make your pile moist but not soggy.

Recipes for Nontoxic Cleaning Solutions

Many everyday materials and household supplies can be employed to create nontoxic homemade cleaners that are safer for children and better for the environment. The following recipes are easy to make and use materials that may be mixed and handled by children, making them perfect for classroom projects or family night activities. Remember to label every bottle or container with its contents.

 All of these products are harmful if swallowed.

- Washing soda is not the same as baking soda and should not be used in place of baking soda. Washing soda is usually sold with cleaners and soaps.

All-Purpose Cleaner

¼ cup white vinegar

3½ cups hot water

20 drops essential oil, such as mint, lavender, or tea tree

¼ cup liquid dish soap

In a 32-ounce spray bottle, thoroughly mix the vinegar and water. Add essential oil, if desired, then add dish soap last.

Carpet Spot Remover

Blot stain immediately. Sprinkle with baking soda or cornstarch and let dry.

Wash with club soda, and vacuum.

- Eucalyptus, peppermint, and tea tree oils can be found at natural foods stores. Each contributes to cleaning and will cover the vinegar smell in many of these products.

These oils should not come into direct contact with skin. Use no more than necessary when mixing solutions. Use extra caution when working with children.

Floor Cleaner

⅛ cup liquid soap

¼ to ½ cup white vinegar or lemon juice

½ cup herbal tea (peppermint has some antibacterial properties) or several drops essential oil

Combine ingredients in a bucket with 3 gallons of warm water, and swirl until sudsy. After washing, rinse with a mixture of 1 cup of vinegar in 3 gallons of cool water.

Window Cleaner

¼ cup white vinegar

½ teaspoon liquid soap or detergent

2 cups water

Combine the ingredients in a spray bottle, and shake to blend.

Wood Cleaner

¼ cup white vinegar

¼ cup water

½ teaspoon liquid soap

A few drops olive oil

Combine the ingredients in a bowl, saturate sponge with the mixture, squeeze out the excess, and wash surfaces. The smell of vinegar will dissipate after a few hours.

Wood-Floor Cleaner

Use ½ cup vinegar per gallon of water. Wipe dry.

Bacteria, Mold, and Germs Eliminator

A 5-percent solution of vinegar (the concentration available in stores) is effective for eliminating some types of harmful bacteria, mold, and germs—although this will not pass muster with state and federal regulations for disinfecting and sanitizing. Keep a spray bottle of vinegar in your bathrooms and kitchen.

Soft Scrubber for Sinks or Countertops

½ cup baking soda

Enough liquid soap or detergent to make frosting-like consistency

5 to 10 drops antibacterial essential oil (peppermint, tea tree, or eucalyptus)

Place baking soda in bowl and slowly pour in liquid soap, stirring continuously. Add essential oil. Scoop mixture onto sponge, wash surface, and rinse. For a stronger disinfecting effect, wipe surface with vinegar afterward.

Unclog and Deodorize Drains

Sprinkle a generous amount of baking soda in and around drain opening. Follow with a cup of white vinegar. Repeat if needed, and flush with very hot water.

When mixing these products together, you may wish to provide safety goggles for the children. While all the ingredients are natural and nontoxic, some—such as soaps and vinegar—can sting if they get into eyes. Use your best judgment.

Additional Resources

Websites

There are many excellent online resources that provide information and children's activities related to the broader environmental topics in this book. It is impossible to create a static list of the best or most useful websites, simply because individual needs and interests vary. Also, websites and organizations come and go. Keeping that in mind, I offer you a short list of some of my favorite web-based resources in addition to those cited in the reference list. I encourage you to check these out as well as the ones cited in the reference list, and remember that a search for broad terms such as "environmental activities families" will often yield hundreds of great websites for your perusal.

CHAPTER 2: EXPLORING NATURE

www.allianceforchildhood.org
The Alliance for Childhood "promotes policies and practices that support children's healthy development, love of learning, and joy in living." This site provides research and information on national policy related to children and childhood.

www.childrenandnature.org
Children and Nature Network is an organization dedicated to connecting children of all ages with nature. Its website has loads of research on the benefits of nature for children and maintains a list of state-by-state grassroots efforts to connect children and nature through family nature clubs, programs, partnerships, and more.

www.neefusa.org
The National Environmental Education Foundation offers ideas and guidelines for those who work with children and are interested in environmental health and its role in children's health. The website also includes grant and fundraising ideas, news and research related to environmental education, and links to other environmental education organizations.

www.playday.org.uk
Playday is a national day of play in the United Kingdom. This website offers resources, research, and ideas for organizing play events anywhere you live.

www.plt.org
Project Learning Tree provides lots of great activities and other resources for educators. Project Learning Tree also has training events throughout North America. This curriculum is based on natural resources and environmental education. The curriculum and resources are for K–12 educators as well as early childhood educators.

www.projectwild.org
Project WILD is an environmental education and conservation education program with curricula and other resources, including service-learning projects and early childhood resources for educators.

www.smallwondersmn.com
Small Wonders MN is my website, where I maintain a blog on children and nature.

CHAPTER 3: THE THREE RS: REDUCE, REUSE, RECYCLE

www.composting101.com
Composting 101 offers a composting guide for the home gardener. This site also has lots of technical information on composting, bin ideas, how-to guides, a troubleshooting section, and links to other sites.

http://earth911.com

Earth 911 has information about how and what you may recycle. Simply type the name of an object in the "search" field and you will get a list of locations for recycling that object. This website also offers facts and statistics related to recycling, craft ideas, current events related to recycling and reuse, green news, and even videos of recycling and manufacturing.

www.epa.gov/osw/education/toolkit.htm

The United States Environmental Protection Agency's Tools to Reduce Waste in Schools web page offers many ideas, downloadable resources, and activities.

www.greeneducationfoundation.org

The Green Education Foundation provides tools and resources for all things green in schools, including a Green Energy Challenge for schools, curriculum ideas, activities, teacher training, and downloadable posters and handouts.

www.newdream.org

The Center for a New American Dream website helps redefine our consumer culture. You will find blogs, news related to consumer issues, tools, and resources for families and communities seeking to simplify and reduce their environmental footprint. Be sure to check out the section on kids and consumerism.

CHAPTER 4: THE FOOD WE EAT

www.calrecycle.ca.gov/Education/curriculum /worms

The California Department of Resources Recycling and Recovery Worm Guide is an online guide to everything related to worm composting. You'll find a special section for school worm composting programs as well as resources on recycling and other green initiatives.

http://compost.css.cornell.edu/worms/basics .html

The Cornell Waste Management Institute provides a simple online reference for worm composting in schools.

www.ewg.org

The Environmental Working Group is a consumer organization that maintains a huge body of research on food and health, current events, and policy issues related to food and chemicals.

www.fns.usda.gov/cnd/F2S/Default.htm

The United States Department of Agriculture has numerous resources on school garden programs, Farm-to-School programs, and healthy eating programs. You'll also find tips on locating a farm-to-school program in your area.

www.kidsgardening.org

Kids Gardening is a popular resource with lots of information and planning resources for families, schoolyard gardens, and other gardening projects. This website also provides fundraising resources and ideas, lists of potential grant opportunities, and ideas to assist programs in embarking on healthy eating campaigns.

www.meatlessmonday.com

The website of Meatless Monday is a campaign to eat meat-free meals just one day per week. This site has loads of recipes, research, and news on health and food.

CHAPTER 5: WATER, WATER, EVERYWHERE

www.epa.gov/WaterSense

The Environmental Protection Agency website has water-related facts and figures, resources on water and water education, and a special section for educators with children's activities and projects.

www.projectwet.org

Project Wet is a national environmental education curriculum and resources website with a focus on water education.

www.waterfootprint.org

Water Footprint is a website that helps you calculate the total water cost of your consumer habits, much like the carbon footprint or environmental footprint. This website also provides access to research and reports related to water and water issues.

CHAPTER 6: AIR IS ALL AROUND US

www.airnow.gov
AIRNow is a website for the Air Quality Index (AQI). You can learn more about how the AQI works and find toolkits and other resources for educators. This site also offers videos about air and pollution.

www.atsdr.cdc.gov/general/theair.html
The Agency for Toxic Substances and Disease Registry offers technical information on air and air toxins, sources of pollution, an A–Z index of specific pollutants, and educational resources.

http://epa.gov/cleanschoolbus/antiidling.htm
The Environmental Protection Agency National Idle-Reduction Campaign website offers information on the health consequences of vehicle idling, educational materials you can print and distribute, toolkits, and other resources especially for school settings.

CHAPTER 7: WEATHER, CLIMATE, AND ENERGY

www.MNEnergychallenge.org
The Minnesota Energy Challenge has an online carbon footprint calculator and lists many steps for reducing fossil fuel consumption. This website also offers lots of simple things individuals can do to reduce their carbon footprint.

www.epa.gov/climatechange/emissions/ind _calculator.html
The US EPA provides a step-by-step guide to calculate your household emissions.

www.footprintnetwork.org/en/index.php/GFN /page/calculators
The Global Footprint Network is a nonprofit organization that offers information on sustainability as well as carbon footprint quizzes and calculators. This website also provides blogs, sustainability-related reports, and newsletters.

www.willstegerfoundation.org
The Will Steger Foundation and educational organization was founded by polar explorer Will Steger.

This website, created for educators, offers curricula, research, training opportunities, information about expeditions, and opportunities for children to participate in virtual expeditions.

CHAPTER 8: INDOOR ENVIRONMENTS AND CHILDREN'S HEALTH

www.ewg.org/skindeep
The Environmental Working Group's Skin Deep cosmetics database provides information about specific products and ingredients and their relative safety and environmental impact. See the section devoted to children's products.

www.greenerchoices.org
The Consumer Reports website helps consumers understand green labeling and make informed consumer choices.

www.greenseal.org
The Green Seal program is an organization that has developed sustainability standards and certifies cleaning and other products.

www.healthychild.org
Healthy Child, Healthy World is a website dedicated to children's environmental health. This site provides research, current events, and policy updates with regard to children's health issues.

http://hpd.nlm.nih.gov/about.htm
The National Institutes of Health maintains the Household Products Database, where you can search by brand, ingredient, or product name for many common household products, including cosmetics and cleaners.

www.ourstolenfuture.org
This website expands on the content from *Our Stolen Future* by Theo Colborn, Dianne Dumanoski, and John Peterson Myers. On the site, you will find links to recent research about endocrine disruption and related public policy issues.

Books

Campbell, Stu. 1998. *Let It Rot! The Gardener's Guide to Composting*. 3rd ed. Pownal, VT: Storey Communications.

Carson, Rachel. 1998. *A Sense of Wonder*. New York: HarperCollins.

Chaillé, Christine. 2008. *Constructivism across the Curriculum in Early Childhood Classrooms: Big Ideas as Inspiration*. Boston: Allyn and Bacon.

Chalufour, Ingrid, and Karen Worth. 2003. *Discovering Nature with Young Children*. St. Paul, MN: Redleaf Press.

———. 2005. *Exploring Water with Young Children*. St. Paul, MN: Redleaf Press.

Colborn, Theo, Dianne Dumanoski, and John Peterson Myers. 1997. *Our Stolen Future: Are We Threatening Our Fertility, Intelligence, and Survival?* New York: Plume.

Essa, Eva, and Melissa Burnham, eds. 2009. *Informing Our Practice: Useful Research on Young Children's Development*. Washington, DC: National Association for the Education of Young Children.

Garrett, Linda, and Hannah Thomas. 2005. *Small Wonders: Nature Education for Young Children*. Woodstock, VT: Vermont Institute of Natural Science.

Grant, Tim, and Gail Littlejohn, eds. 2005. *Teaching Green: The Elementary Years*. Gabriola, BC: New Society Publishers.

Harlan, Jean, and Mary Rivkin. 2012. *Science Experiences for the Early Childhood Years: An Integrated Affective Approach*. 10th ed. Boston: Pearson.

Hennepin County Environmental Services. 2011. *Environmental Education Toolkit for Early Childhood and Family Education*. Minneapolis, MN: Hennepin County.

Jenkinson, Sally. 2001. *The Genius of Play: Celebrating the Spirit of Childhood*. Gloucestershire, UK: Hawthorn Press.

Kalich, Karrie, Dottie Bauer, and Deirdre McPartlin. 2009. *Early Sprouts: Cultivating Healthy Food Choices in Young Children*. St. Paul, MN: Redleaf Press.

Lingelbach, Jenepher, and Lisa Purcell, eds. 2000. *Hands-On Nature: Information and Activities for Exploring the Environment with Children*. Woodstock, VT: Vermont Institute of Natural Science.

Louv, Richard. 2008. *Last Child in the Woods: Saving Our Children from Nature-Deficit Disorder*. Rev. ed. Chapel Hill, NC: Algonquin Books.

Lovejoy, Sharon. 1999. *Roots, Shoots, Buckets and Boots: Gardening Together with Children*. New York: Workman Publishing.

McNair, Sharon, ed. 2006. *Start Young! Early Childhood Science Activities*. Arlington, VA: National Science Teachers Association Press.

Mooney, Carol Garhart. 2000. *Theories of Childhood: An Introduction to Dewey, Montessori, Erikson, Piaget, and Vygotsky*. St. Paul: Redleaf Press.

Nhat Hanh, Thich. 2011. *Planting Seeds: Practicing Mindfulness with Children*. Berkeley: Parallax Press.

Oltman, Marcie, ed. 2002. *Natural Wonders: A Guide to Early Childhood for Environmental Educators*. Minnesota Early Childhood Environmental Education Consortium. www.seek.state.mn.us/publications/naturalwonders.pdf.

Rivkin, Mary S. 1995. *The Great Outdoors: Restoring Children's Right to Play Outside*. Washington, DC: National Association for the Education of Young Children.

Sobel, David. 2008. *Childhood and Nature: Design Principles for Educators*. Portland, ME: Stenhouse Publishers.

Topal, Cathy Weisman, and Lella Gandini. 1999. *Beautiful Stuff! Learning with Found Materials*. Worcester, MA: Davis Publications.

Worth, Karen, and Sharon Grollman. 2003. *Worms, Shadows, and Whirlpools: Science in the Early Childhood Classroom*. Portsmouth, NH: Heinemann.

Glossary

absorb: to take up by chemical or physical action

adhere: to stick to a surface or substance

air pollution: a damaging substance introduced into the atmosphere; can be human-caused, naturally occurring, or both; may consist of particles, vapor, or gas

air pressure: the force exerted by the weight of particles of air

anemometer: a device used for measuring wind speed

antibacterial: a substance that kills or slows down the growth of bacteria

antimicrobial: a substance that kills or slows down the growth of microorganisms

atom: the smallest unit of an element that can exist alone or in a combination; commonly considered to be the building blocks of matter

atmosphere: the layers of gases surrounding the Earth; protects Earth's life by absorbing the sun's ultraviolet radiation and by regulating the surface temperature on Earth

aquatic: relating to, living in, or taking place in water

benign: harmless

biodegrade: to break down and be absorbed into the ecosystem over time

body burden: a buildup of harmful chemicals in our bodies; can have negative health effects

buoyancy: the tendency of an object to float when submerged in a liquid

carbon dioxide: a colorless, odorless gas that occurs naturally and is also produced through combustion of fossil fuels; comprises a small but important part of air; is one of the greenhouse gases that regulates the Earth's surface temperature

carbon footprint: a measure of the impact of consumption activities or behaviors on the environment; based on the amount of carbon produced in order to support those activities, behaviors, or consumption

carbon monoxide: an odorless, colorless gas that is toxic to humans and other animals at high concentrations; occurs naturally and is also produced through combustion of fossil fuels

characteristic words: words that describe individual traits of a substance or chemical

climate: the average of weather conditions of a place or region over a period of years to decades; based on temperature, wind velocity, and precipitation

climate change: the slow variations of climate characteristics (changes in the average) over time due to natural processes or human activities; usually refers to the portion of change attributed to human activity that alters the composition of the atmosphere

coal: a combustible rock that can be used as fuel; composed mostly of carbon

compost: organic matter that has decomposed and is reused as fertilizer

compound: a substance made up of two or more different chemically bonded elements

condensation: the change of water from its gas form to its liquid form

constructivism: the idea that knowledge and meaning are constructed as a result of interaction with one's environment; the idea that learning is an active process of constructing or building meaning

contaminant: a substance present in an environment where it doesn't belong or is present at levels that may be harmful

conventionally grown food: crops that are not certified organic; typically indicates foods that are grown with chemical fertilizers and pesticides

decompose: to break down, decay, or rot

density: a substance's mass per unit volume; often confused with weight; can be thought of as the amount of weight for the amount of space it takes up

dichotomous key: a key for identifying an organism based on a series of either-or choices about its characteristics

ecosystem: a community of organisms and their environment

electricity: a form of energy resulting from the presence and flow of electric charge

emission: something given off into the air, such as a greenhouse gas

endocrine system: a system of glands in the body that send hormones into the bloodstream; regulates growth and development

energy: the ability of a physical system to do work; usable power

environmental footprint: the amount of land, water, and other natural resources required to support one's daily life and consumption habits

environmental literacy: awareness, knowledge, skills, and attitudes about environmental considerations and their effect on daily decisions about consumption, lifestyle, career, and civics

erosion: a wearing away of the surface of the Earth by agents such as water, wind, and waves

evaporation: the change of water from its liquid form to its gas form

exposure pathways: the ways in which a hazardous substance might enter a body; for example, inhalation, ingestion, and direct contact

formaldehyde: a colorless, pungent, irritating gas primarily used as a disinfectant and preservative

fossil fuel: a fuel composed of materials that originate from within the Earth and contain fossils or other organic matter deposited millions of years ago

glacier: a large body of ice that slowly moves and flows

global warming: the rising of the average temperature of the Earth's atmosphere and oceans

greenhouse gas: a gas in the atmosphere that traps heat; acts to maintain Earth's temperature so it is suitable for life; currently accumulating to such a degree that the Earth's temperature is rising

groundwater: the water within the Earth that supplies wells and springs

hormones: chemical messengers that affect everything from mood to how the body utilizes minerals and vitamins from foods

household hazardous waste: household products that contain harmful ingredients, such as paints, cleaners, oils, and batteries

impervious: a material or surface that does not allow water or liquid to pass through it

incinerator: a furnace for destroying waste by burning it

indoor air pollution: indoor air containing pollutants that can damage one's health; causes include pollen, mold, dander, smoke, and gas

infiltrate: to permeate or become part of something

landfill: a disposal area where garbage is piled up and eventually covered with dirt and topsoil

leach: to drain away from soil, ash, or similar material by the action of percolating liquid, especially rainwater

life cycle: a period involving all different stages in the life of a species of plants or animals

methane: a colorless, odorless gas found widely in nature; the primary component of natural gas, and a powerful greenhouse gas; the majority estimated to be produced by human activities, including fossil fuel production and distribution, raising livestock, and landfills; occurs as a result of natural processes, including decomposition

microorganism: a living thing too small to be seen by the naked eye

molecule: a group of atoms that is held together by chemical bonds

mucous membrane: the lining of a body passage or cavity that communicates with the exterior

nervous system: the body system made up of the brain, spinal cord, and nerves that receives and interprets signals from the outside world and sends impulses throughout the body

neurotoxin: a poisonous compound that acts on the nervous system

organic: natural and related to living things; in agriculture, organic products are grown without synthetic pesticides and chemical fertilizers

overspray: airborne spray that is accidentally applied to an unintended area

particle pollution: a complex mixture of microscopic solids and liquid droplets suspended in air made up of a number of components, including acids, organic chemicals, metals, and soil or dust particles; particles can affect the heart and lungs and cause serious health effects if inhaled

particulate: a tiny bit of solid matter

pathogens: microorganisms, such as viruses and bacteria, that cause disease (also known as germs)

phenology: the study of seasonal changes in the natural world, covering plant and animal life cycles, weather, and climate

pollen: a fine dust made up of tiny grains from a seed plant

pollutant: a material that causes pollution of air, water, or soil

precipitation: the water that falls from the atmosphere when gaseous water condenses into liquid; includes rain, sleet, snow, and hail

propellant: a gas kept under pressure in a bottle or can for expelling the contents when the pressure is released, as in an aerosol spray can

runoff: the water that flows over the Earth's surface when precipitation cannot be immediately absorbed into the ground

signal words: the words found on labels that describe how toxic the product is; "danger," "warning," and "caution" are common signal words

smog: a thick, discolored fog containing large quantities of soot, ash, and gas pollutants; responsible for many breathing issues and respiratory illness

storm water: the water from precipitation (rain and melted snow) that runs off of surfaces, such as rooftops and paved streets, and can pick up pollutants along the way

synthetic: produced artificially by chemical synthesis

toxic: harmful or poisonous

transpiration: the loss of water vapor from parts of plants; part of the water cycle

troposphere: the lowest part of the Earth's atmosphere

vermicomposting: producing compost using worms

volatile organic compound (VOC): an organic compound from which large numbers of molecules evaporate from the liquid or solid form of the compound and enter the surrounding air; many VOCs can be harmful to human health and the environment

water cycle: the continuous movement of water on, above, and below the Earth's surface; for example, liquid water on the Earth evaporates into the air, where it condenses back into liquid and falls to Earth as precipitation

watershed: the area of land where all of the water that is under it or drains off of it goes into the same place

water vapor: water in gas form

weather: the temperature, wind velocity, and precipitation occurring at one place at a specific time; varies dramatically from day to day and from year to year

References

AAP (American Academy of Pediatrics). 2011a. "About Childhood Obesity." Accessed November 21. www.aap.org/obesity/about.html.

———. 2011b. "National Center for Medical Home Implementation: Obesity and Medical Home." Accessed November 21. www.medicalhomeinfo .org/about/newsletter/spotlight_issues/obesity .aspx.

AMAP (Arctic Monitoring and Assessment Programme). 2011. *Arctic Pollution 2011*. Oslo, Norway: AMAP.

Bloom, Barbara, Robin Cohen, and Gulnur Freeman. 2011. *Summary Health Statistics for US Children: National Health Interview Survey, 2010*. Vital and Health Statistics 10 (250). Hyattville, MD: National Center for Health Statistics.

Boise, Phil. 2010a. *Go Green Rating Scale for Early Childhood Settings*. St. Paul, MN: Redleaf Press.

———. 2010b. *Go Green Rating Scale for Early Childhood Settings Handbook: Improving Your Score*. St. Paul, MN: Redleaf Press.

CalRecycle. 2010. "'Give Green' by Decking the Halls with Less Waste This Year!" Last modified December 1. www.calrecycle.ca.gov/PublicEd /Holidays.

CDC (Centers for Disease Control and Prevention). 2011a. "Celebrate Global Handwashing Day October 15th!" Last updated October 14. www .cdc.gov/features/handwashing.

———. 2011b. "Diabetes Public Health Resource: Children and Diabetes—More Information." Last modified May 20. www.cdc.gov/diabetes /projects/cda2.htm.

Center for Climate Change Communication. 2012. "Frequently Asked Questions about Climate Change." George Mason University. Accessed February 7. www.climatechangecommunication .org/resources_faq.cfm.

Chawla, Louise. 2006. "Learning to Love the Natural World Enough to Protect It." *Barn* 2:57–78.

Cioci, Madalyn, and Tim Farnan. 2010. *Digging Deep through School Trash: A Waste Composition Analysis of Trash, Recycling, and Organic Material Discarded at Public Schools in Minnesota*. St. Paul, MN: Minnesota Pollution Control Agency. www.pca.state.mn.us/index.php/view-document .html?gid=14235.

Copple, Carol, and Sue Bredekamp, eds. 2009. *Developmentally Appropriate Practice in Early Childhood Programs Serving Children from Birth through Age 8*. 3rd ed. Washington, DC: National Association for the Education of Young Children.

Elkind, David. 2005. "The Changing World of Toys and Toy Play." *Exchange*, no. 116: 11–12.

Engel, Stephanie M., Amir Miodovnik, Richard L. Canfield, Chenbo Zhu, Manori J. Silva, Antonia M. Calafat, and Mary S. Wolff. 2010. "Prenatal Phthalate Exposure Is Associated with Childhood Behavior and Executive Functioning." *Environmental Health Perspectives* 118 (4): 565–71. http://dx.doi.org/10.1289/ehp.0901470.

Environment Canada. 2010. "Technical Document for Batch Waste Incineration." Last modified April 22. www.ec.gc.ca/gdd-mw/default.asp?lang =En&n=8A09EA04-1.

Faber Taylor, Andrea, and Frances E. Kuo. 2006. "Is Contact with Nature Important for Healthy Child Development? State of the Evidence." In *Children and Their Environments*, edited by Christopher Spencer and Mark Blades, 124–40. Cambridge: Cambridge University Press.

FAO (Food and Agriculture Organization of the United Nations). 2003. "Securing Food for a Growing World Population." In *Water for People, Water for Life*, edited by United Nations Educational, Scientific, and Cultural Organization (UNESCO) and the United Nations World Water Assessment Programme (WWAP), 189–223.

http://webworld.unesco.org/water/wwap/wwdr/table_contents.shtml.

———. 2006. "Livestock a Major Threat to Environment: Remedies Urgently Needed." Last modified November. www.fao.org/newsroom/en/news/2006/1000448/index.html.

———. 2011. "The Role of Livestock in Climate Change." Accessed November 21. www.fao.org/agriculture/lead/themes0/climate/en.

Global Footprint Network. 2011. "World Footprint." Last modified July 2. www.footprintnetwork.org/en/index.php/gfn/page/world_footprint.

Hennepin County Environmental Services. 2009. "How to Identify Hazardous Products—Read the Label." Fact sheet, February. www.co.hennepin.mn.us/files/HennepinUS/Environmental%20Services/HHW/Toxicity%20reduction/Toxicity%20Reduction%20Static%20Files/Read%20the%20label0509.pdf.

Hill, Holly. 2008. "Food Miles: Background and Marketing." National Center for Appropriate Technology, National Sustainable Agriculture Research Service. Last modified July 8, 2011. https://attra.ncat.org/attra-pub/viewhtml.php?id=281.

IARC (International Agency for Research on Cancer). 2004. "IARC Classifies Formaldehyde as Carcinogenic to Humans." Press release, June 15. www.iarc.fr/en/media-centre/pr/2004/pr153.html.

IER (Institute for Energy Research). 2011. "Fossil Fuels." Accessed November 21. www.instituteforenergyresearch.org/energy-overview/fossil-fuels.

IPCC (Intergovernmental Panel on Climate Change). 2012. "Organization." Accessed February 7. www.ipcc.ch/organization/organization.shtml#.TzFc5l1v2Ch.

Kellert, Stephen R. 2005. *Building for Life: Designing and Understanding the Human-Nature Connection.* Washington, DC: Island Press.

Landrigan, Philip J., Anjali Garg, and Daniel B. J. Droller. 2003. "Assessing the Effects of Endocrine Disruptors in the National Children's Study." *Environmental Health Perspectives* 111 (13): 1678–82. www.ncbi.nlm.nih.gov/pmc/articles/PMC1241693/pdf/ehp0111-001678.pdf.

Landrigan, Philip J., Babasaheb Sonawane, Donald Mattison, Michael McCally, and Anjali Garg. 2002. "Chemical Contaminants in Breast Milk and Their Impacts on Children's Health: An Overview." *Environmental Health Perspectives* 110 (6): A313–15. www.ncbi.nlm.nih.gov/pmc/articles/PMC1240884.

Lappé, Anna. 2010. *Diet for a Hot Planet: The Climate Crisis at the End of Your Fork and What You Can Do about It.* New York: Bloomsbury.

Leikauf, George D. 2002. "Hazardous Air Pollutants and Asthma." *Environmental Health Perspectives* 110 (4): 505–26.

LUMC (Louisiana Universities Marine Consortium). 2011. "Annual Shelfwide Cruise: July 25–August 6, 2011: Press Release." www.gulfhypoxia.net/Research/Shelfwide%20Cruises/2011/PressRelease2011.pdf.

MDH (Minnesota Department of Health). 2010. "Volatile Organic Compounds (VOCs) in Your Home." Fact sheet, April. www.health.state.mn.us/divs/eh/indoorair/voc/vocfactsheet.pdf.

Minnesota Energy Challenge. 2012. "About the Challenge." Accessed January 23. www.mnenergychallenge.org/About-the-Challenge/Challenge-FAQs.aspx.

Mintzer, Erica S., and Craig Osteen. 1997. "New Uniform Standards for Pesticide Residues in Food." *FoodReview* 20 (1): 18–26. www.ers.usda.gov/publications/foodreview/jan1997/jan97c.pdf.

Mississippi River Gulf of Mexico Watershed Nutrient Task Force. 2012. "The Mississippi-Atchafalaya River Basin (MARB)." United States Environmental Protection Agency Office of Wetlands, Oceans, and Watersheds. Accessed January 13. www.epa.gov/owow_keep/msbasin/marb.htm.

NAAEE (North American Association for Environmental Education). 2010. *Early Childhood Environmental Education Programs: Guidelines for Excellence.* Washington, DC: NAAEE.

National Children's Study Interagency Coordinating Committee. 2003. "The National Children's Study of Environmental Effects on Child Health and Development." *Environmental Health Perspectives* 111 (4): 642–46. www.ncbi.nlm.nih.gov /pmc/articles/PMC1241458/pdf/ehp0111 -000642.pdf.

National Research Council. 1996. *National Science Education Standards.* National Academy of Sciences. Washington, DC: National Academies Press.

NIEHS (National Institute of Environmental Health Sciences). 2008. "Residential Traffic and Children's Respiratory Health." *Environmental Health Perspectives* 116 (9): 1274–79. doi: 10.1289 /ehp.10735.

———. 2012. "Pesticides." Accessed January 23. www.niehs.nih.gov/health/topics/agents /pesticides/index.cfm.

NOAA (National Oceanic and Atmospheric Administration). 2011a. "Global Climate Change Indicators." Last modified November 3. www.ncdc .noaa.gov/indicators.

———. 2011b. "Marine Debris: De-mystifying the 'Great Pacific Garbage Patch.'" NOAA Marine Debris Program. Last modified August 4. http:// marinedebris.noaa.gov/info/patch.html#5.

Ogden, Cynthia L., Margaret D. Carroll, Lester R. Curtin, Molly M. Lamb, and Katherine M. Flegal. 2010. "Prevalence of High Body Mass Index in US Children and Adolescents, 2007–2008." *Journal of American Medical Association* 303 (3): 242–49. doi: 10.1001/jama.2009.2012.

Pollan, Michael. 2008. *In Defense of Food: An Eater's Manifesto.* New York: Penguin.

Protano, Carmela, and Matteo Vitali. 2011. "The New Danger of Thirdhand Smoke: Why Passive Smoking Does Not Stop at Secondhand Smoke." Correspondence section. *Environmental Health Perspectives* 119 (10): 422.

Rajapakse, Nissanka, Elizabete Silva, and Andreas Kortenkamp. 2002. "Combining Xenoestrogens at Levels below Individual No-Observed-Effect Concentrations Dramatically Enhances Steroid Hormone Action." *Environmental Health Perspectives* 110 (9): 917–21. www.ncbi.nlm.nih.gov /pmc/articles/PMC1240992/pdf/ehp0110 -000917.pdf.

Riebeek, Hollie. 2006. "Explaining Rapid Climate Change: Tales from the Ice." In *Paleoclimatology: Explaining the Evidence.* National Aeronautics and Space Administration (NASA). http:// earthobservatory.nasa.gov/Features /Paleoclimatology_IceCores.

SEHN (Science and Environmental Health Network). 1998. "Precautionary Principle." Wingspread Conference on the Precautionary Principle, January 26. www.sehn.org/precaution.htm.

Snyder, Shane A., Paul Westerhoff, Yeomin Yoon, and David L. Sedlak. 2003. "Pharmaceuticals, Personal Care Products, and Endocrine Disruptors in Water: Implications for the Water Industry." *Environmental Engineering Science* 20 (5): 449–69. www.liebertonline.com/doi /pdfplus/10.1089/109287503768335931.

Sobel, David. 1996. *Beyond Ecophobia.* Great Barrington, MA: The Orion Society.

Steinemann, Anne C., Ian C. MacGregor, Sydney M. Gordon, Lisa G. Gallagher, Amy L. Davis, Daniel S. Ribeiro, and Lance A. Wallace. 2011. "Fragranced Consumer Products: Chemicals Emitted, Ingredients Unlisted." *Environmental Impact Assessment Review* 31 (3): 328–33.

Swinburn, Boyd A., Gary Sacks, Kevin D. Hall, Klim McPherson, Diane T. Finegood, Marjory L. Moody, and Steven L. Gortmaker. 2011. "The Global Obesity Pandemic: Shaped by Global Drivers and Local Environments." *The Lancet* 378 (9793): 804–14.

UCS (Union of Concerned Scientists). 2007. *How to Avoid Dangerous Climate Change: A Target for U.S. Emissions Reductions.* Cambridge, MA: UCS. www.ucsusa.org/assets/documents/global _warming/emissions-target-report.pdf.

———. 2008. "So-Called 'Clean Coal' Technology Offers Promise along with Considerable Risks, New Report Finds." Press release, October 15.

———. 2009. *Climate Change in the United States: The Prohibitive Costs of Inaction.* Cambridge, MA: UCS. www.ucsusa.org/assets/documents /global_warming/climate-costs-of-inaction.pdf.

———. 2012. "Coal vs. Wind." Accessed January 20. www.ucsusa.org/clean_energy/coalvswind /c01.html.

UN (United Nations). 2012. "Water for Life." Accessed January 23. www.un.org /waterforlifedecade/scarcity.shtml.

UNESCO (United Nations Educational, Scientific, and Cultural Organization). 1975. *The Belgrade Charter: A Global Framework for Environmental Education.* Paris, France: UNESCO. http://portal .unesco.org/education/en/file_download.php /47f146a292d047189d9b3ea7651a2b98The +Belgrade+Charter.pdf.

Urban Mining. 2011. "Holiday Trash: Tips to Reduce, Recycle and Make Your Holiday Greener." Last modified December 23. http://urbanmining .org/2011/12/23/holiday-trash-tips-reduce -recycle-make-holiday-greener.

USDA (United States Department of Agriculture). 2012. "National Organics Program: Rulemaking Actions and Notices." Last modified February 14. www.ams.usda.gov/AMSv1.0/nop.

USDA and US HHS (United States Department of Agriculture and United States Department of Health and Human Services). 2010. *Dietary Guidelines for Americans, 2010.* 7th ed. Washington, DC: US Government Printing Office. www .cnpp.usda.gov/Publications/DietaryGuidelines /2010/PolicyDoc/PolicyDoc.pdf.

USDA NRCS (United States Department of Agriculture Natural Resources Conservation Service). 1998a. "Soil Quality Resource Concerns: Pesticides." Information sheet, January. http://soils .usda.gov/sqi/publications/files/Pesticides.pdf.

———. 1998b. "Soil Quality Resource Concerns: Soil Biodiversity." Information sheet, January. http://soils.usda.gov/sqi/publications/files /biodivers.pdf.

———. 2010. "Farming in the 21st Century: A Practical Approach to Improve Soil Health." September. www.mo.nrcs.usda.gov/technical/soils/out /21st_century_soil_health_tech_doc.pdf.

———. 2012. "Soil Organic Matter." Accessed January 11. http://soils.usda.gov/sqi/concepts/soil _organic_matter/som.html.

US EPA (United States Environmental Protection Agency). 2002a. "Children Are at Greater Risks from Pesticide Exposure." Last modified February 16, 2011. www.epa.gov/pesticides /factsheets/kidpesticide.htm.

———. 2002b. Solid Waste Disposal Act. 42 U.S.C. 6901. http://epw.senate.gov/rcra.pdf.

———. 2003. *America's Children and the Environment: Measures of Contaminants, Body Burdens, and Illnesses.* 2nd ed. Washington, DC: US EPA. www .epa.gov/ace/publications/ace_2003.pdf.

———. 2005. "Emission Facts: Average Carbon Dioxide Emissions Resulting from Gasoline and Diesel Fuel." www.etieco.com/content-files/EPA %20emissions%20calc%20420f05001.pdf.

———. 2007. "What Is Acid Rain?" Last modified June 8. http://epa.gov/acidrain/what/index.html.

———. 2008a. "Child-Specific Exposure Factors Handbook (Final Report) 2008." http://cfpub .epa.gov/ncea/cfm/recordisplay.cfm?deid =199243#Download.

———. 2008b. *Municipal Solid Waste Generation, Recycling, and Disposal in the United States: Facts and Figures for 2008.* Washington, DC: US EPA. www.epa.gov/epawaste/nonhaz/municipal/pubs /msw2008data.pdf.

———. 2009. *Municipal Solid Waste Generation, Recycling, and Disposal in the United States: Facts and Figures for 2009.* Washington, DC: US EPA. www.epa.gov/osw/nonhaz/municipal/pubs /msw2009-fs.pdf.

———. 2010a. *Municipal Solid Waste in the United States: 2009 Facts and Figures.* Washington, DC: US EPA. www.epa.gov/wastes/nonhaz/municipal /pubs/msw2009rpt.pdf.

———. 2010b. "Transportation and Climate." Last modified September 14. www.epa.gov/otaq /climate/basicinfo.htm.

———. 2011a. "Climate Change—Climate Economics." Last modified September 21. www.epa.gov /climatechange/economics/international.html.

———. 2011b. "Climate Change—Health and Environmental Effects: Climate-Sensitive Diseases." Last modified November 29. http://epa.gov /climatechange/effects/health.html#climate.

———. 2011c. "Exposure Pathways." Last modified January 27. www.epa.gov/osweroe1/content /hazsubs/pathways.htm.

———. 2011d. "Methane: Sources and Emissions." Last modified April 18. www.epa.gov/methane/sources.html.

———. 2011e. "Paper Recycling: Basic Information Details." Last modified November 1. www.epa.gov/osw/conserve/materials/paper/basics.

———. 2011f. "Recycling." Last modified December 9. www.epa.gov/wastes/conserve/rrr/recycle.htm.

———. 2011g. "Used Oil Management Program." Last modified September 28. www.epa.gov/wastes/conserve/materials/usedoil.

———. 2012a. "Children's Health Protection." Last modified February 15. http://yosemite.epa.gov/ochp/ochpweb.nsf/content/homepage.htm.

———. 2012b. "Computational Toxicology Research Program." Last modified February 3. www.epa.gov/ncct.

———. 2012c. "An Introduction to Indoor Air Quality: Volatile Organic Compounds (VOCs)." Accessed January 23. www.epa.gov/iaq/voc.html.

———. 2012d. "Pollutants: Carbon Monoxide." Last modified January 17. www.epa.gov/otaq/invntory/overview/pollutants/carbonmon.htm.

US FDA (United States Food and Drug Administration). 2008. *Triclosan: Supporting Information for Toxicological Evaluation by the National Toxicology Program*. Silver Spring, MD: US FDA. http://ntp.niehs.nih.gov/ntp/htdocs/Chem_Background/ExSumPdf/triclosan_508.pdf.

USGS (United States Geological Survey). 2012. "Water Resources of the United States: Hydrologic Unit Maps." Last modified January 3. http://water.usgs.gov/GIS/huc.html.

Wargo, John. 2002. *Children's Exposure to Diesel Exhaust on School Buses*. North Haven, CT: Environment and Human Health, Inc. www.ehhi.org/reports/diesel/dieselintro.pdf.

WCRF and AICR (World Cancer Research Fund and American Institute for Cancer Research). 2007. *Food, Nutrition, Physical Activity, and the Prevention of Cancer: A Global Perspective*. Washington, DC: AICR. http://eprints.ucl.ac.uk/4841/1/4841.pdf.

Wells, Nancy M., and Kristi S. Lekies. 2006. "Nature and the Life Course: Pathways from Childhood Nature Experiences to Adult Environmentalism." *Children, Youth, and Environments* 16 (1): 1–24.

WHO (World Health Organization). 2011. "Obesity and Overweight." Last modified March. www.who.int/mediacentre/factsheets/fs311/en.

WMO (World Meteorological Organization). 2011a. "Causes of Climate Change." Accessed November 21. www.wmo.int/pages/themes/climate/causes_of_climate_change.php.

———. 2011b. "Elements of Change." Accessed November 21. www.wmo.int/pages/themes/climate/elements_climate_change.php.

———. 2012. "Frequently Asked Questions: What Is Climate?" Accessed February 7. www.wmo.int/pages/prog/wcp/ccl/faqs.html.

Photography Credits

Photograph on page iii copyright iStockphoto.com/ZoneCreative

Photograph on page vi copyright iStockphoto.com/naumoid

Photograph on page x copyright iStockphoto.com/yaruta

Photograph on page xii copyright iStockphoto.com/fotostorm

Photographs on pages 2, 4, 11 (right), 16 (left), 55, 64, 65, 109, 121, 161, and 164 courtesy of Patty Born Selly

Photograph on page 11 (left) courtesy of Emily Hoffman Hedges

Photographs on pages 13 and 16 (right) courtesy of Dani Porter Born

Photograph on page 14 copyright iStockphoto.com/ParkerDeen

Photograph on page 15 courtesy of Dominic Selly

Photographs on pages 17, 19, 70, 102, and 218 courtesy of Sara Martin

Photographs on pages 44 and 210 copyright iStockphoto.com/kirin_photo

Photographs on pages 75, 77, and 233 courtesy of Rena Wiltfang-Roepke

Photographs on pages 104, 149, 159, and 206 courtesy of Tiffany A. Teske

Photograph on page 136 copyright iStockphoto.com/jrsower

Photograph on page 163 courtesy of Jim Handrigan

Photograph on page 184 copyright iStockphoto.com/sefaoncul

Photograph on page 188 copyright iStockphoto.com/kate_sept2004

Photograph on page 223 copyright iStockphoto.com/Squaredpixels

Index